THE ARAB—ISRAELI CON....

CONTEMPORARY WORLDS explores the present and recent past. Books in the series take a distinctive theme, geo-political entity or cultural group and explore their developments over a period ranging usually over the last fifty years. The impact of current events and developments are accounted for by rapid but clear interpretation in order to unveil the cultural, political, religious and technological forces that are reshaping today's worlds.

SERIES EDITOR
Jeremy Black

In the same series

Britain since the Seventies
Jeremy Black

Sky Wars: A History of Military Aerospace Power
David Gates

War since 1945
Jeremy Black

The Global Economic System since 1945
Larry Allen

A Region in Turmoil: South Asian Conflicts since 1947
Rob Johnson

Altered States: America since the Sixties
Jeremy Black

The Contemporary Caribbean
Olwyn M. Blouet

Oil, Islam and Conflict: Central Asia since 1945
Rob Johnson

Uncertain Identity: International Migration since 1945
W. M. Spellman

The Road to Independence?: Scotland since the Sixties
Murray Pittock

The Nordic Model: Scandinavia since 1945
Mary Hilson

Cuba in Revolution: A History since the Fifties
Antoni Kapcia

Europe since the Seventies
Jeremy Black

THE
ARAB–ISRAELI
CONFLICT

A HISTORY

IAN J. BICKERTON

REAKTION BOOKS

To Jenny, who brings much joy

Published by Reaktion Books Ltd
33 Great Sutton Street
London EC1V 0DX, UK
www.reaktionbooks.co.uk

First published 2009, reprinted 2010

Printed and bound in Great Britain
by CPI Antony Rowe, Chippenham, Wiltshire

British Library Cataloguing in Publication Data
Bickerton, Ian J.
The Arab-Israeli conflict : a history. – (Contemporary worlds)
1. Arab-Israeli conflict – History.
I. Title II. Series
956'.04-DC22

ISBN 978 1 86189 527 1

Contents

Preface

We had fed the heart on fantasies,
the heart's grown brutal on the fare;
More substance in our enmities
Than in our love;

Meditations in time of Civil War
William B. Yeats

The Arab–Israeli conflict is a touchstone for the twentieth and twenty-first centuries. It spans World War I and World War II, the Cold War and the War on Terrorism, and many nations have been touched at least indirectly by some aspect of the dispute. It has seen, and participated directly or indirectly in, the rise and fall of Empires, the Ottoman and British. The conflict has been instrumental in shaping our view of Jews, Muslims, Christians, Arabs, the Middle East, oil and the role of superpowers, especially the United States, in world affairs. The events and people involved have demonstrated the tremendous power of nationalistic ideology, and religious and ethnic identification in the modern world. The ongoing destructive violence of the conflict leads us to reflect upon the horrors, the efficacy or futility, of war, and the reckless readiness of leaders – and followers – to embrace military force and brutality as a means to achieve what are perceived as essential goals. The seemingly insoluble conflict forces us to reconsider the meanings of tolerance and intolerance, forgiveness and vengeance, as we witness the ongoing violence.

Few areas of the contemporary world have attracted more attention in the past sixty years than the Middle East. The most obvious reason for this is that the region is the major source of petroleum, containing two-thirds of the world's known petroleum reserves. But there are other reasons as well. If one includes Islamic North Africa, the Middle East extends from the Indian Ocean in the East to the Atlantic Ocean in the West, encompassing 21 countries (if Palestine is included) in an area considerably larger than Europe. It is the birthplace of the world's three great monotheistic religions, Judaism, Christianity and Islam, and in 2007 was home to more than 430 million people (up from 104 million in 1950). Strategically located between Europe and Asia, it is geographically, culturally, linguistically and religiously diverse, and has fascinated adventurers for centuries. And for the past sixty years it has been the scene of one of the most intractable conflicts in living memory, the Arab—Israeli conflict.

The decision of the newly established United Nations following World War II to partition the small sliver of land between the Jordan River and the eastern shore of the Mediterranean Sea – since 1919 the British mandate of Palestine – which created the international legal framework for the estab-lishment of a Jewish state, Israel, against the wishes of the predominantly but far from exclusively Muslim local population, triggered a conflict that con-tinues to the present. For Jews around the world this created an entirely novel and unprecedented situation. For the first time in almost two thousand years a Jewish state existed, providing Jews an opportunity to return to an ancient homeland. For Arabs it was also an entirely new and unexpected develop-ment. For the first time since the founding of Islam, Jews lived in an inde-pendent state in their presence, claiming historic religious and national rights to ownership of one of Islam's holiest cities, Jerusalem. In their determina-tion to establish or maintain their rights and to reinforce or retrieve their physical circumstances by whatever means at hand, the two groups ignored the rights and needs of the other, and resorted to military force. The outcome has been an unrelenting and cruel conflict that has not resolved any of the issues dividing them.

The proclamation made of the existence of Israel on 14 May 1948 was an epochal event in the history of Jews, Muslims and Christians. For the majority of world Jewry, it was the answer to a two-thousand-year-old dream, signalling the birth of a Jewish state for the first time in 2,000 years. For some Jews, Israel was a miraculous event, the fulfilment of God's promise to Jews that they should inherit 'the promised land'. Those who had migrated to the land over the previous half century saw the achievement as the result of a hard-fought military victory. To Muslims worldwide, the presence of a Jewish state in their midst was incomprehensible. To those Arabs whose families had lived in the region for generations, it was a catastrophe. To many in Christian Europe, Israel was compensation for their failure to intervene to save Jews from the

Nazi-led Holocaust in which more than six million Jews were killed. Some Christians, mainly US evangelicals, saw it as the beginning of their apocalyptic vision heralding the Day of Judgement.

The event did not take place in a vacuum: 14 May 1948 for Jews was the culmination of three-quarters of a century of migration that had had as its goal the establishment of a Jewish state. For the local Arabs it was an acknowledgement that they had failed in their efforts to prevent the creation of 'a Zionist entity'. The momentous events of that day, in which the last British troops withdrew from Palestine and David Ben Gurion, head of the Jewish Agency in Palestine, declared the state of Israel, had been preceded for at least six months by relatively large-scale, if somewhat sporadic, military encounters between Jews and Arabs. And prior to that day, uneasy, frequently violent encounters had been occurring for the previous quarter-century.

Over the next sixty years the existence of Israel transformed the landscape of what was formerly known as Palestine. The newly formed government of Israel took over the existing infrastructure and transformed the former British Mandate into a Jewish state as thousands of refugees from displaced persons camps in Europe and those expelled from nearby Arab states poured into the fledgling nation. Chaos and improvisation were the order of the day for the first few years. New towns, roads, schools, hospitals and infrastructure were built as Israelis set about consolidating their newly acquired country. Hundreds of Arab villages were either destroyed or given Hebrew names. Hundreds of thousands of local Arab inhabitants fled with little more than what they could carry to Jordan, Syria, Lebanon or Egypt. Refugee camps appeared overnight to house the displaced Palestinian Arabs and (for a short period) the new Jewish arrivals. Palestinians sought to rebuild their shattered lives and to redress what they regarded as a national injustice.

Resistance and retaliation led to war. Over the sixty-year period from 1948 to 2008 several wars were fought as Jews and Arabs could not, or would not, reach acceptable agreements over the huge range of issues set in train in the Eastern Mediterranean in the years immediately following World War II. Geography was at the heart of the confrontation, but religion, ethnicity/race and history added to the ferocity of the fighting. Neighbouring Arab states as well as the Soviet Union, the United States and Europe were drawn into the increasingly complicated and bitter conflict. Israel framed the conflict as an existential one threatening the very survival of the state. Palestinians depicted it as a struggle for national recognition and natural justice. As the years wore on and casualties mounted, both sides became more intransigent, ramping up not only the rhetoric but the intensity of the hostilities. In the end, the violence has led only to more violence.

This book emphasizes that the use of armed force has not resolved the issues dividing the parties. In the struggle for sovereignty over historic Palestine that has been taking place since the end of World War I, violence has only strengthened the determination of all concerned not to give ground. Armed combat has only reinforced the already existing reluctance of the diplomats to settle peacefully. Leaders of each side have framed the issues in absolute terms, and they cannot accept any claims of the other as legitimate, or compromise on their own. Wars have not created a greater Israel or a greater Palestine, nor will they. Neither side has succeeded in achieving its goals, and the wars have increased the number of unresolved issues. If or when a Palestinian state is proclaimed, it will be considerably smaller than that drawn up by the General Assembly 62 years ago, and Israel will still be there. Much needless bloodshed would have been saved had peace opportunities not been missed. It might be argued that such cessations of violence would have proved short-lived. But the treaties reached between Israel and Jordan and Egypt have lasted, and suggest that compromise is possible. Certainly any peace is preferable to the alternative.

It is not easy to make the case pointing out the futility of force to a generation of Israelis who experienced and remember the terrible Nazi Holocaust directed against the Jewish population of Europe, especially when it appears to many that an earlier armed intervention against Hitler's regime would have saved thousands, perhaps millions, of lives. The Holocaust is an inescapable, overwhelming presence as far as Israel is concerned. 'Never Again' has become the central metaphor for Israelis, who are determined to use all the means at their disposal to preserve the Jewish state against what they see as the determined and implacable enemy surrounding them. The frightening rocket attacks on Israeli towns launched by Palestinian and Hezbollah militants simply confirm their fears.

It is equally difficult to a generation of Arabs to accept that the use of military force is counterproductive, especially those in refugee camps in the West Bank and the Gaza Strip who have known nothing but dispossession, dislocation and brutal collective punishment at the point of a gun. They have seen their homes and lands expropriated, their orchards and towns destroyed by tanks and airborne missiles.

The majority of Israelis and (especially Palestinian) Arabs believe they cannot afford the risks they associate with non-violent approaches to the resolution of their seemingly never-ending conflict. However, it is essential to bear in mind that the searing tragedies they have experienced and witnessed have been the result of decisions made by political and military leaders. They were not, and are not, inevitable.

Perhaps more than any war of the twentieth or twenty-first centuries, the Arab–Israeli conflict reveals the futility of armed force as a means of solving international problems. The conflict, a series of short brutal wars followed by periods of so-called 'low intensity' violence, has been going on for 61 years and shows little sign of ending. The summer of 2006 provided a striking demonstration of the impotence of military power. In Lebanon, the Shia militia, Hezbollah, held off the vastly superior military might of Israel, forcing a withdrawal after an unsuccessful month-long aerial and artillery bombardment aimed at destroying them. The fight over land that could have been peaceably shared has lasted more than half a century and is still the defining issue for the Arab world, and for Israel.

The conflict itself is, in large part, an unintended consequence of the twentieth century's wars. Great Britain set the stage for the conflict following World War I, making contradictory promises before assuming a mandate over Palestine from 1920 to 1948. After World War II the United States added fuel to an already volatile situation when President Harry S. Truman urged the relocation to Palestine of 100,000 Jewish survivors of the Holocaust. There were, of course, localized developments that stimulated and maintained the conflict, and since 1948 the dispute has followed its particular path in response to immediate and provocative actions by all parties concerned.

The Arab–Israeli conflict exposes what happens when extremists advocating violence take control of peoples' destinies, either with the overt or inadvertent support of a population. In 2002 Israeli writer Amos Elon noted that, on both sides, the extremists were dominant.[1] The situation is even worse in 2009. In Israel and Palestine militant extremists veto all progress toward peace. Disasters follow one after another daily, and the end is not in sight. Hamas has usurped the Palestinian national movement, while hardline religious groups seem to be usurping the Jewish national cause.

In both cases these shifts are the result of popular choice. As Elon points out, Israelis enthusiastically chose to become a colonialist society, ignored international treaties, expropriated lands, transferred settlers from Israel to the occupied territories, engaged in theft and found justifications for all these actions. The settlers were praised by every Israeli government as patriots, good citizens, good Zionists. In the West Bank, the settlement project became a cornerstone of Zionist and Israeli national identity. By now there is a second generation of settlers who see no difference between themselves and other Israelis who live in Tel Aviv or Tiberias. Palestinians, increasingly infuriated by the inevitable controls, curfews and violence caused by the settlers, disgusted by the venality of their leadership, and frustrated by their failures to end the occupation through diplomacy, turned to the intifada, Hamas and suicide bombers.

Although there seems no end of the conflict in sight, any search for a solution must be grounded in a thorough understanding of the history leading from 1948 to 2009, one that is sympathetic to both sides and one that hopefully can suggest avenues for future mutual conciliation and an ultimate resolution of those issues that most seriously undermine peace between the Palestinians and Israelis and among the Arab states and the West. Part of the process of historical investigation should be to uncover missed opportunities and to suggest that some of them warrant pursuit in the twenty-first century. It is, after all, the Israeli-Palestinian impasse that more than any other single factor disrupts the Middle East and the Arab search for reconciliation with the United States, a reconciliation that is the fundamental precondition for real peace in the region whose petroleum reserves make it the inevitable target of largely unwanted US attention.

Oddly enough, the events of 2007 in Ireland provide some hope that a resolution of the Arab—Israeli conflict that meets the aspirations and needs of all parties is possible. After almost a century of communal violence in Northern Ireland between Protestants and Catholics, fuelled by religious fanaticism and intolerance and divided ethnic loyalties, sworn enemies who vowed never to talk to each other put down their weapons, negotiated an agreement and now share the same Cabinet table. Long-standing British troops have withdrawn and relations between Northern Ireland, the Republic of Ireland and Great Britain have been normalized. These developments were unimaginable less than twenty years ago, and demonstrate what can be done when the shooting stops.

Introduction

Things and actions are what they are, and the consequence will be what they will be; why then should we desire to be deceived?[1]

In mid-2008, articles appeared in the international media celebrating Israel's sixty years as a nation. In one such piece, Herzliya University professor Barry Rubin wrote:

> Israel is a fully realised state with a mass of subcultures, an overarching national ethos and sense of unity, a distinctive language, and a powerful set of cultural-psychological norms built on history, both 3,000-year history and 60-year history . . . Israel is a fully realised vision of what Jews as a people should be and be doing.[2]

Writer Jeffrey Goldberg, in a long analysis of Israel at sixty published in the May 2008 issue of *Atlantic Monthly* exploring the debate within Israel over the July 2006 invasion of Lebanon, observed that by almost any measure Israel is an astonishing success. Israel has, he wrote,

> a large, sophisticated, and growing economy (its gross domestic product last year was $150 billion); the finest universities and medical centers in the Middle East; and a main city, Tel Aviv, that is a center of art, fashion, cuisine, and high culture spread along a beautiful Mediterranean beach. Israel has shown itself, with notable exceptions, to be adept at self-defense, and capable (albeit imperfectly) of protecting civil liberties during wartime. It has become a worldwide

center of Jewish learning and self-expression; its strength has straightened the spines of Jews around the world; and, most consequentially, it has absorbed and enfranchised millions of previously impoverished and dispossessed Jews. Zionism may actually be the most successful national liberation movement of the 20th century.[3]

David Hazony, one of Israel's leading writers, in a thoughtful article in the *New Republic*, declared: 'For 60 years, the Jewish state has struggled to attain a "place among the nations", to quote Benjamin Netanyahu's book by the same name, in which Israelis would live harmoniously with their surroundings the way other, 'normal' countries do.' Hazony continued:

> Every country has a national narrative that seeks to explain itself as special in some way. (In the United States, it is the widely shared belief in American Exceptionalism.) Why should Israel insist on being any different? . . . Maybe it is time for Israelis to finally accept their country for what it is – extremely normal and perplexingly abnormal, both at the same time. This, after all, is exactly the sort of state that early Zionists had in mind: a homeland for an exiled people who would be allowed to defend themselves, as normal people do, while also showing the world what unique things they had to say.[4]

These introspective, congratulatory pieces were entirely understandable and predictable. But some commentators, Israeli and non-Israeli, focused their attention on another, darker, side of Israel's experience as a modern state; its occupation and rule over territories and people gained through war. Goldberg, for example, noted that 60 years of independence had not provided Israel with legitimacy in its own region and that the state faced severe internal threats. He believes this unsatisfactory situation exists because Israel's greatest military victory, in 1967, 'led to a squalid and seemingly endless occupation, and to the birth of a mystical, antidemocratic, and revanchist strain of Zionism, made manifest in the settlements of the West Bank.' In Goldberg's view, 'These settlements have undermined Israel's international legitimacy and demoralized moderate Palestinians. The settlers exist far outside the Israeli political consensus, and their presence will likely help incite a third intifada. Yet the country seems unable to confront the settlements.'[5]

Oxford Middle East historian Avi Shlaim also drew attention to the consequences of Israel's occupation of the West Bank:

Sixty years on, Israel is not fighting for its security or survival but to retain some of the territories it conquered in the course of the war of June 1967. Israel within the 'green line' is completely legitimate; the Zionist colonial project beyond that line is not. The war that Israel is currently waging against the Palestinian people on their land is a colonial war. Like all other colonial wars, it is savage, senseless, directed mainly against civilians, and doomed to failure in the long run.

Shlaim concluded his stinging critique of Israeli policy with the comment:

The longer Israel persists in denying the Palestinians their right to national self-determination, the more its own legitimacy would be called into question. Israel should negotiate withdrawal from the bulk of the West Bank, not as a favour to the Palestinians but as a huge favour to itself. For, as Karl Marx observed, a nation that oppresses another cannot itself remain free.[6]

That Israel's intellectual culture can accommodate and withstand such diverse opposing views is a reflection of the vitality and strength of its democracy. But these dissenting voices remind us that there is another narrative inextricably linked to that of the Israeli account, that of Palestinian Arabs. Not surprisingly, the Arab narrative detailing a story of dispossession, betrayal and struggle is completely at odds with the traditional dominant Israeli story. Focusing primarily on personal and collective tragedies, these accounts rarely contain the nuances that characterize the more recent narratives by Israeli scholars upon which many of them depend for their documentary evidence. It is a narrative that describes how an initially small group of Europeans with the assistance of the great powers, first the United Kingdom and France, and later the United States, set in motion a process that led to the displacement, dispossession and denial of statehood of the existing Arab population.

We still have a distance to go before we see Arab narratives critically assessing their side of the story. While passionately rejecting and contradicting the Israel narrative, Arab accounts of the conflict graphically describe

Palestinian suffering and sense of loss. For the most part they are reliant upon personal memories and collective memory with the inherent limitations of those literary forms; there is little attempt to ask why or to explore Arab responsibility for the course of events. When looking for supporting additional evidence of Israel's wickedness, Arab historians have largely relied upon the new Israeli historians, as the official archives of the Arab parties are not yet open, or at least only available to sympathetic authors. Arab accounts have yet to recognize the traditional Zionist story and the role of their own leaders in furthering the conflict.

For years Israeli spokesmen maintained there was a certain kind of inevitability about the way the Arab–Israeli conflict was unfolding. This view was best encapsulated by the eloquent Israeli foreign minister, Abba Eban, when he observed that the Arabs never miss an opportunity to miss an opportunity. This remark was, of course, pure sophistry. Israel has passed over its share of opportunities to achieve peace. There is no inevitability about the way history unfolds. Decisions are the result of choice. And decision-makers on both sides, not just one, make those choices. Furthermore the decisions of one side – even foolish or provocative ones – do not make the decisions of the other inevitable. They are still free to choose one course of action over another. Both sides have made numerous impetuous and unwise decisions. The new histories coming out of Israel go a long way in laying them out.

I have adopted a chronological rather than a thematic approach to the subject of this book. I have not done so simply because 'history is just one damn thing after another', but because, although it has the appeal of appearing to clarify issues, a thematic approach tends to diminish the complexity and confusion surrounding decisions and events as they occur. For all concerned, participants and observers alike, the Arab–Israeli conflict is, like all conflicts, immensely complicated. We may know how things turned out with the benefit of hindsight, but to those making decisions the present was confusing enough, and the future? – well, the future was unknown. Placing as many relevant events as is manageable in chronological order, within the space constraints available, enables me to provide something of the sense of uncertainty and randomness that characterizes the conflict. It is hoped the result will be a fair-minded synthesis that prods all parties to the conflict to a greater openness in their proclaimed search for resolution of what can be seen as the world's longest ongoing war.

I believe that using an historical approach enables us to explore which propositions, which actions, have a sound basis in the experiences and expectations of the participants, and which, therefore, by reflecting embedded values and common memories, might bring about a change in the direction and shape of the conflict. Even putting events into a simple chronology changes the perspective within which they can be viewed. The current crises have grown out of political, social and economic transformations that took place in Palestine almost a century ago and set these two groups against each other. These transformations led the two parties over time to redefine themselves in ways that led to conflict. An historical analysis assists us to see which way the parties might move to lessen that conflict.

Passions run high on this volatile subject, and readers expect some indication of an author's background and approach. My awareness of the Arab–Israeli conflict coincides with Israel's expansion into the West Bank. I was ten years old when Israel was established and I have no recollection of the nuns speaking of it at the small Australian country parochial primary school I was attending, although I no doubt heard it mentioned in the Australian Broadcasting Commission 'School of the Air' broadcasts of world events we listened to in class one day every week. As a teenager I recall thinking with pride, like most Australians, how important the Australian prime minister, Sir Robert Menzies, must have been as he sailed out of Australia in 1956 to 'sort out' the 'Suez crisis' although, again, I had little idea of Israel's role in that abortive Anglo-French-Israeli venture to force President Nasser to 'disgorge' the Suez Canal. As a graduate student in California, I do remember the 1967 war, however. Like most, I was amazed at Israel's quick and overwhelming success in that short war. Like most, I wondered what the future held for Israelis, Palestinians and neighbouring Arab states as I became conscious of the plight of the displaced Palestinian Arabs. At that time I had just finished researching President Harry S. Truman's recognition of Israel, and in 1968 the *American Jewish Historical Society Journal* published the results of that study in what was probably the first major scholarly article on the topic to appear in the us.[7] Since then I have watched with dismay as the conflict between Israel and the Palestinians (and Lebanon) has unfolded with increasing brutality despite peace treaties between Israel and its two neighbours, Jordan and Egypt.

I first visited the region in 1978 on the occasion of Israel's thirtieth birthday. Whenever I returned in the 1980s and '90s I found among the majority of Israelis I met a total disinterest and ignorance of Palestinian life in the West Bank and Gaza Strip. Israelis were afraid to accompany me to refugee camps in the Gaza Strip and regarded my going there almost as an act of betrayal. Despite the crowded and elementary 'temporary' camp housing, the residents walked the dusty unpaved streets proudly, even defiantly, in the face of Israeli armed patrols, and the traditional clothing worn was spotlessly clean. Israeli soldiers were stationed in the centre of the camps within armed fenced-off compounds. On one occasion, a young soldier, in an attempt to intimidate and no doubt to demonstrate his discretionary power to do so, pointed his automatic rifle at me as I entered an UNRWA-run maternity hospital.

The whole scene had a surreal feel about it. Young Palestinian camp residents and Israeli soldiers were engaged in a constant game of provocation – but it was a game that could become deadly at a moment's notice and without warning. A few days later I read that Israeli soldiers had tear-gassed the hospital when young Palestinian stone-throwers ran into it seeking refuge. In West Bank towns I met with families whose small overcrowded cement-brick houses had been boarded up because of the alleged activities of their sons or daughters, to find that this practice had made heroes of the sons or daughters and had only increased the determination of family members to resist, fuelling their sense of resentment. Taxi drivers were subjected to random, frequent and lengthy searches of their vehicles, and their identity cards and licences were closely scrutinized by Israeli soldiers. Despite all the daily frustrations and inconveniences, it appeared to me that people on both sides were trying to get on with their lives and there was a sense of cautious optimism in the air. I had the sense of movement toward reconciliation.

In 2000 the situation was quite different. The separation between Israelis and Palestinian Arabs was even more pronounced. Israelis travelled on divided highways from Jewish town to Jewish town in the West Bank with no Palestinians to be seen, but there was an increased awareness among Israelis of the Palestinian presence. Settlement building by Israelis was far more evident, especially around Jerusalem and between Jerusalem and Bethlehem. The gap between the standards of living of the two groups was more apparent, and the hostility between the two was palpable. There was greater uncertainty and anxiety among Israelis in Tel Aviv and Jerusalem, security was far tighter. People were understandably wary of strangers on the buses. Positions on both sides had hardened, the list of grievances was longer and the resentments deeper. Optimism had evaporated and had been replaced by fear and loathing. It did not feel good. And from all accounts it has gotten worse.

I come to the subject with a background in Irish Catholicism about which I have serious reservations. As a graduate student I became interested in the question of ethnicity and its role in US foreign relations, and explored US–Israeli relations in this context. I am still puzzled as to why, after seeking to distance myself from being identified as a member of a minority religious and ethnic group until recently persecuted and discriminated against, I find myself involved in the enterprise of seeking to unravel the intricacies of two other ethno-religious groups locked in combat, discriminating against and persecuting each other – and indeed being discriminated against and persecuted worldwide. I do not pretend to add any 'insider' insights in this book, any 'new' details revealed to me by one party or the other. What I bring, I hope, is a sense of detachment – the detachment of an historically informed secular humanist with a conviction that resort to the force of arms is not the way to solve problems.[8]

The disinterested scholar/analyst/historian hoping to create a balanced history of the Arab–Palestinian–Israeli conflict is faced with the daunting task of balancing three disparate viewpoints: traditional Israeli, new or 'revisionist' Israeli, and Arab interpretations. I have found the narratives and evidence presented by the new Israeli historians compelling. In 1990, when I visited the Israeli National archives to conduct research into the US–Israel relationship during the administration of President Dwight D. Eisenhower, I became aware of the huge gap between the public and private voices of Israeli leaders. What I found was an Israeli leadership full of deep-seated hostility toward, and suspicion of, Arabs. The majority of Israel's leaders disregarded Palestinian aspirations and were unwilling to compromise on any issue. They pressed relentlessly and persistently to protect and extend their borders and to obtain economic and military assistance from the United States, and in this they were highly successful. At the same time they devoted considerable efforts at home and in the United States to project themselves as reasonable men surrounded by implacable foes devoted to Israel's destruction. I was not surprised by any of this.

Reading documents in the Eisenhower Presidential Library in Abilene, Kansas – and those in other US presidential libraries – I had found a similar gap between rhetoric and reality in US policy formulation. It is the almost inevitable nature of diplomacy that public statements do not reveal the reality or complexity of government deliberations and decisions. Israel is no exception to this rule. But because my research was so narrow and focused, I hesitated to extend my findings into the broader narrative of the Arab–Israeli conflict. The revisionist Israeli historians, however, with far more extensive research into the Israeli records, have done just that. Their findings are not only at shocking odds with the traditional heroic, triumphalist narrative formerly widely accepted in Israel and the West, they are utterly convincing.[11] They have recognized that Israel's enemies, too, have a story to tell, and have acknowledged that Israel has played its part in perpetuating the conflict.

It is important that I state clearly my perspective on the conflict. I start with the simple observation that Israel is now, and has been for most of its short history, the major military power in the region. It is also the case that Israel stands alone; no other nation speaks its language or shares its religion or culture, and this obvious reality has had a tremendously sobering impact upon the psyche of Israelis. Israel is, nevertheless, a success story. This is hard to accept by those (mainly Jews) used to thinking of Jewish history as a story of unremitting persecution and discrimination against Jews.

Paradoxically, the Palestinian story is also one of success, and the establishment of a Palestinian state appears only a matter of time. Against all odds, Palestinians have overcome years of displacement, political rejection and military humiliation to emerge as a nation in all but name. Some have difficulty recognizing that the establishment of the state of Palestine is not solely dependent upon the attitudes or actions of Israel. A Palestinian state is a matter for the Palestine Authority (PA) to work out with Israel – and with Hamas, which since June 2007 has controlled the Gaza Strip. The Palestine Authority has all the attributes of a government. When it declares Palestine a state, it will receive overwhelming international recognition and thereby become a reality – as did Israel in not dissimilar circumstances in 1948. The PA has not done so because it fears such unilateral action would preclude negotiations with Israel on outstanding issues.

As peace and stability are accepted as the norm, all parties in the vicinity will benefit as the area is incorporated into the world economy. I see few reasons why Israel should oppose or fear the establishment of a Palestinian state. The disparities in economic and military strength are such that Israel has little to worry about from a newly formed Palestine. The state of Palestine would possess no fighter aircraft, tanks or missiles with which to challenge the military might of Israel. Furthermore, the acts of terrorism perpetrated by both sides against each other will not significantly weaken the resolve of those committed to peace. Rather than dwell on the advocates of violence, this book highlights the actions of those who have sought peace rather than war to resolve outstanding issues.

Participants in the Arab–Israeli conflict, and partisan observers, believe that the more facts you know the greater your understanding of the conflict. This is a mistaken notion. Many participants in any conflict seek always to justify their position. One of the ways they do this is by accumulating so-called facts, the more the better, they think. There is no end to the number of facts that can be educed in relation to the Arab–Israeli conflict – or any other conflict for that matter. It is ridiculous to think you can add up all the facts. Facts are no more than carefully selected events that are woven together to form a narrative that supports a particular viewpoint. Participants all too frequently find facts to confirm their predisposition. They seek the moral high ground because they want their side to be engaged in a just war. They seek to find who fired the first shot – if you like, the shot heard around the world. The point is not who fired the first shot, the point is that a shot was fired at all. And that a second shot was fired in return. Once the parties take up a gun, that is, once they resort to military force, there is no moral high ground, it is just a question of who wins, if in fact there is such a thing as winning a war.

After seven wars and sixty years of intermittent warfare, no one has won the Arab–Israeli conflict. It continues unresolved, and there are no winners. That is because shooting does not solve problems, it just create new ones. The only way to resolve disputes is through dialogue and consultation, recognizing and reconciling differences. If differences are not recognized there is little chance of reconciliation, and if there is no reconciliation then the shooting will continue. The cost is human lives. Tens of millions were killed in the name of nationalism in the nineteenth and twentieth centuries, and thousands have been needlessly lost in this encounter. Once we place ideology over the value of human life and dignity, in the words of Robert Frost, we are lost piecemeal to the animals.[9] All this may sound rather simplistic or naïve, but the real simpletons are the ones who think that when they win the battles they have won the war. As Shelley once wrote of one such dreamer:

'My name is Ozymandias, King of Kings:
Look on my works, ye Mighty, and despair!'
Nothing beside remains. Round the decay
Of that colossal wreck, boundless and bare,
The lone and level sands stretch far away.[10]

The Arab–Israeli conflict is an unusual conflict in many ways. This book can do little more than give the reader something to talk about in the inescapable debate about the subject. The struggle is far larger than anything that can be written in a single volume and is full of inconsistencies and contradictions. On the one hand it is a series of extremely short wars and skirmishes conducted between two relatively small groups over a specific, very small, space scarce in natural resources and water-poor – which adds to the intensity of the conflict. On the other hand, it has been broadened into a universal ideological conflict between Jews and Arabs, Judaism and Islam, West and East. At times, Israelis have been supported by Arab regimes, and at times Israel has supported Arab regimes. Christians have supported both Jews and Muslims at various points in the dispute. While many Arab regimes refuse diplomatic or economic relations with Israel, others have signed peace treaties, and even more have opened economic links.

Currently, Israel sees its greatest threat coming from Iran, not an Arab country at all, although an Islamic one, while an avowedly secular Islamic state, Turkey, is one of its closest allies in the region and one of its largest trading partners. To add to the irony, for the first half of Israel's existence, Iran supplied Israel with oil despite an Arab economic boycott. Perhaps the greatest irony of all is that Angela Merkel, the Chancellor of Germany, the country that sought to destroy European Jewry, in a speech to the Israeli Knesset in May 2008, pledged that Germany would stand by Israel's side against any threat.

Not only has the Arab–Israeli conflict been one of the longest and most bitter in living memory, its implications go far beyond the small area of the globe in which it has taken place. To Jews, the establishment of Israel is the pivotal event of the past two thousand years. To Muslims, the existence of Israel is one of Islam's greatest challenges. Christians also feel involved because the fight is centred in the area they identify as 'The Holy Land'. The land, its names and places, are familiar to most Christians through their reading of the Old and New Testaments, and the fate of the Holy Land is important to them. Christians have had, and retain, a love–hate relationship with Jews. For centuries they have persecuted Jews and discriminated against them, and, following the Holocaust, they watch closely as Jews work out their own destiny in a Jewish state. Christian attitudes toward Arabs/Muslims have traditionally been, and remain, based largely on ignorance and fear.

If we add to these considerations the fact that the Middle East is the location of much of the world's oil supplies and reserves, and further that the region became caught up in the great-power rivalries of the Cold War, it is easy to see why the Arab–Israeli conflict has absorbed so much of the world's attention in the past half century. Echoes of the dispute resonate in the lives of Americans as well as those directly involved in the region. Increasingly, the politically active Jewish and Muslim communities in the United States will ensure more and more Americans have an immediate involvement in the issues and outcome of the confrontation.

The Arab–Israeli conflict is mystifying in other ways. The very use of the term 'Arab–Israeli conflict' presents problems. While Israel describes itself as engaged in a clash with the Arab world, Palestinians reject this notion, seeing the quarrel as a struggle between Israelis and Palestinians. The term suggests that Israel is somehow involved in the broader, much larger, regional wars that have taken place in the Persian Gulf area since 1945. This is not so. Those wars relate only tangentially to the issues between Israel and its neighbours. The antagonism we are dealing with consists of a series of seven short military campaigns fought between Israel and contiguous Arab states over a period of sixty years followed by periods of uneasy, asymmetrical hostilities between Israel and Palestinian Arabs, all fought over the sovereignty of what was formerly known as Palestine. The major military campaigns themselves have been very short when measured against the wars of the twentieth and twenty-first centuries. With the exceptions of the 1948 and 1973 wars, the wars have been fought outside Israel, and many of the current military operations by both sides are carried out in what remains occupied or disputed territory.

The argument started out as what appeared to be a local affair between two, by and large, poorly armed groups in the decade or so before World War II. But the dispute had never been a merely local issue. Zionism, the political movement which led to and sustained a Jewish state in Palestine, had been international from its rebirth in the nineteenth century, and the Palestinian

Arabs had been under the rule of the Ottoman Empire for centuries. The founding father of modern Zionism, Austrian journalist and playwright Theodor Herzl, wrote in his 1895 colonial manifesto *The Jewish State*, 'Let sovereignty be granted us over a portion of the globe adequate to meet our rightful national requirements, we will attend to the rest.'[11] 'Attending to the rest' has been at the heart of the Arab–Israeli conflict. So there were international implications from the beginning, but, nevertheless, the fight between the Jews and Arabs in Palestine was essentially local.

The dispute did not remain local for long, however. The Christian, Muslim and Jewish worlds could not stand by; for one thing, the future of the city of Jerusalem and vicinity was intrinsic to the outcome. Also, both sides described the outcome of the conflict as central to their existence as a people and culture. In addition, World War II and its aftermath drew in the world powers once again. In the post-war years Palestine was a strategically important gateway to the Middle East and its increasingly valuable oil reserves.

The Arab–Israeli conflict was not the first, or the last, local dispute to develop into an international one. The outbreak of World War I was caused by a local disagreement, as were the Korean and Vietnam Wars. Equally, many wars do remain localized; we only have to think of Sudan and Eritrea to see how long, destructive, essentially civil, wars do not attract the worldwide interest or involvement the way the Arab–Israeli confrontation has. So how did this friction develop into an international issue that is out of control for so many years?

Palestine was the scene of critical battles in World War I. The Balfour Declaration and the (British) mandate created by the League of Nations in 1922 ensured that a major world power would have a controlling interest in the future of Palestine for the next quarter century. World War II and its aftermath drew in the world powers once again. Palestine in the post-war years was a strategically important gateway to the Middle East and its oil reserves. More importantly, control of Jerusalem and its sacred sites was, and remains, a core issue in the conflict. Both sides regard the future status of Jerusalem as central to their existence as a people and as a religious culture or community. The Muslim, Jewish and Christian worlds were not about to stand by and leave the fate of Jerusalem to the vagaries of decisions made to suit the local convenience of one side or the other. They were going to have their say.

When, in 1948, the first military action involving recognized armies took place, the Jews and Arabs of Palestine were not much better armed than they had been for the previous decades of intermittent fighting. At that time, both sought and received international military and economic assistance, although the major protagonists in the conflict were limited to Israel and its contiguous Arab states, Egypt, Jordan, Syria, Lebanon, as well as Iraq. The Israelis were far more successful than the Palestinian Arabs in their endeavours to gain international support during the Cold War. Twenty-five years later, during the 1973 war, Israel received the unqualified support of the United States against its enemies, and the relationship between Israel and the United States strengthened to the point of a virtual alliance. In the first decade of the twenty-first century Washington regards Israel as a front-line ally in its war against terrorism, and Israel can rely on United States economic and military assistance in its struggle against those it identifies as enemies.

As the first decade of the twenty-first century comes to a close, Israel possesses by far the most powerful military forces in the region, including nuclear weapons. Although they received limited support from Iraq and Iran, the Palestinians languished until the 1990s, relatively powerless as they sought to consolidate their identity as a people in their own right. While now recognized as a people having a legitimate cause, Palestinians are not only still without a state, they are bitterly divided and their leaders are regarded by much of the world as terrorist pariahs. There are several reasons for this transformation in the fortunes of the two parties to the conflict; hostility to Islam is one of them.

If European anti-Semitism was a key factor in creating the need for a Jewish homeland and subsequent state, there can be little doubt that suspicion and fear of Islam was, and is still, a major factor in the failure of the West to substantially assist the Palestinians in their struggle for a state – especially since 9/11, 2001. American evangelical Christians, encouraged by us Zionists, have worked tirelessly and effectively to make support for Israel an essential plank of us Middle Eastern policy. At the same time, Americans have failed to appreciate the virtues or past contributions of Islam and Arabs to Western civilization. The negative view of Arabs also partly stems from American resentment that the tiny Arab states are enriching themselves at the expense of us motorists and industry through their ownership and control of oil and ever-increasing oil prices. Furthermore, for more than forty years, Israelis and the Arabs became caught up in the great power rivalry known as the Cold War. Despite the initial, vain, best efforts of some Arab states to be accepted as allies by the Western powers, the majority were perceived by Americans as preferring to align themselves with the Soviet Union in the Cold War, thereby alienating Washington.

Finally, the Palestinian tragedy was that in 1948 and in 1967 those displaced fled to relatively impoverished surrounding Arab states. Israel and most of the world thought the Arab countries would, and should, take responsibility for the Palestinians as refugees because they were Arabs and mostly Muslim, but they did not do so. The Arab regimes, many still in their infancy themselves, had their own nation-building agendas, which did not include incorporating a massive influx of foreigners, or engaging in military campaigns against Israel over a future Palestinian state. Thus the struggle became an asymmetrical one. A strong Israel used its military and economic strength to intimidate neighbouring states that it regarded as hostile and determined to destroy it. Israel extended its control over territories occupied in war, ostensibly to ensure the state's security. The Palestinians, in desperation, turned to acts of terror, believing they had neither the economic nor military means for any alternative.

The Arab–Israeli conflict is taking the shape of twenty-first century warfare. No longer do large national armies face each other in set-piece land, sea and air battles. Insurgency operations are conducted by small nationalistically or ideologically (often religious) driven groups against states who use the sophisticated, overwhelming military apparatus of the nation state to repress them. Thus relatively low-level but nonetheless destructive war continues pointlessly in what was once called Palestine.

It is easy to get lost or caught up in exploring the detail of the conflict, screened and commented upon worldwide as it is on an almost daily basis. To do this is to lose sight of the big picture. Most of the reports depict the deaths or funerals of participants lamenting their own loss while vowing revenge, dismissing the suffering their actions will cause the other side. While in statistical terms the Arab–Israeli conflict has caused relatively few casualties when measured against those of other wars, it is a cruel, savage, unrelenting, unforgiving confrontation. Both sides make and break promises to each other and outside parties who try to mediate, all the while publicly blaming the other for the ongoing violence. Now insisting that Palestinians recognize Israel as a 'Jewish' state, rather than merely acknowledge its existence, Israel denies the rights of Palestinians to their land, and refuses to recognize the Palestinian

Authority's democratically elected Legislative Council, which acts as a de facto government because it regards the dominant electorally victorious party, Hamas, as a terrorist organization. On top of all this, although and because the conflict is contemporary and conducted in the glare of television, radio and the printed press, detailed documentary evidence on any issue is hard to obtain. In the end, observers trying to make sense of it all are reduced to relying upon what resides in their own hearts and minds. And what is in their hearts and minds is shaped in large part by their personal history.

Someone once said that the world is made up of two kinds of people: those who look to the past and those who look to the future. It is not, of course, whether or not one looks to the past, it is what one sees there. It is what one chooses to remember or to forget in the past that matters. The past enables us to locate ourselves in relation to where we are and where we are going. The past can be a liberating or a repressive experience; it can radicalize and revolutionize, or it can be a weapon of conservatism. In their always uneasy, suspicious, often hostile, ongoing negotiations, leaders of both sides have been and remain trapped by their history and culture. One has only to think of William Faulkner's observation: 'The past is never dead. It's not even past.' They are locked into the dreams and grand narratives they have created for themselves. They see through a kind of tunnel vision only what they, and their followers, remember, and what they forget. Or, rather, what they choose to remember and what they choose to forget.

Israel's leaders are trapped by the collective Zionist memory of persecution and discrimination. Palestinian leaders cannot free themselves from the diet of grievances against the invading Zionist enemy recounted to them since childhood by family members. Constructing and controlling 'the truth' about the past in order to legitimize and justify one's actions in the present is an important function in all international conflicts. However, there is a reality that exists outside the mind. Leaders on both sides have forgotten, or overlook, the countless acts of cooperation, heroism and generosity shown by individual Palestinians and Israelis toward each other over the past sixty years. Even if they wanted to, it may be that their people would not permit either leader to throw off the shackles of their respective agreed to and approved histories. Until both sides shift the central focus of their historical paradigm and choose to forget the violence perpetrated against each other and their real and imaged grievances, and remember the values and cultural patterns they share, focusing on past examples of cooperation and generosity, and empha-size the potential to shape future common goals, there will be no peace.

It is a truism to note that every generation writes its own history, creates for itself a vision of the past that makes sense of the present and points a way to the future. For this reason, if no other, it is important that we look afresh at the past sixty years of the relationship between Israel and its neighbours. Israeli historians, participants and commentators in the 1950s and '60s, blinded by the immediacy of they and the uncertainty of the state's future, wrote of the triumph of Zionism. In the 1970s and '80s, in the heady after-math of the victory of the 1967 war, they saw a glorious future for greater Is-rael and overlooked the Palestinians altogether, other than as terrorists. By the early 1990s reality was slowly beginning to set in, and now at the end of the first decade of the twenty-first century the majority of Israeli commenta-tors acknowledge that the future involves finding a way to live in harmony with the Palestinians, and Israel's neighbours.

For their part, in the 1950s and '60s Palestinian and Arab spokesmen refused to recognize Israel as a state other than to declare their total hostility and opposition to the foreign intruder in their region. As the realization that their military efforts were futile and that the Jewish state was here to stay, in the 1980s and '90s mainstream Palestinian leadership focused on rebuilding their own national consciousness and institutions. In the past decade, despite internal divisions, Palestinian commentators have described their attempts to accommodate and to negotiate a settlement with Israel.

Observing the Arab–Israeli conflict is rather like looking at a magician: it is all smoke and mirrors. We are left most often with the task of discussing and analysing press perceptions – the spin – put on events by publicists and correspondents. We rarely get beyond the public events. The conflict is really two conflicts: an inter-state conflict between Israel and neighbouring Arab states, and an inter-communal conflict between Israel and Palestinian Arabs. While the two struggles are linked they should not be confused. In relation to the first conflict the Israelis have taken the view that the danger they faced and the primacy of their national claim obliged them to react with force. They believe to have done otherwise would have risked being driven into the sea by their Arab enemies.

In relation to the second – the inter-communal conflict – Israel and Palestinian Arabs have been locked into what they have both regarded as –

at least until very recently – an existential conflict. Meron Benvenisti described this relationship as a fatal embrace, a dance of death. The Jewish community, far stronger militarily, sought to subdue the Arab Palestinians in order to achieve peace and tranquillity. The Palestinians in the face of all logic refused to acknowledge their defeat and continued to pursue a campaign of violence that in turn denied the Israelis the victory they seek. The Palestinians, deprived of any legitimate means of struggle, turned to violent insurrection. This led the Israelis to respond in the same way.

At one level the conflict takes place within a clearly recognized international system where assumptions are utilitarian and pragmatic, and resolutions can be worked out through diplomacy. At another, deeper, level, the conflict has assumed a different dimension. The inter-communal conflict centres on fundamental questions like identity, religion, self-expression, fear, symbolic entities. The rhetoric of rational discourse hides the real agenda of absolute values.

To a large extent, the tragedy of the Arab–Israeli conflict is that the participants adopted an ideology in which Destiny and God shape events rather than individual human beings. The ideology of nationalism driven by a sense of divine destiny has shaped much of the behaviour of both parties, justifying the most brutal and puerile of acts. This extreme view has provided both sides with a sense of inevitability, a sense of power and the superiority of their claim over that of the other. It has led both sides to overlook the realities and limitations within which they must act. This in turn has subverted individual responsibility and the ability to reach a more complete assessment of the values of the culture to which he or she belongs.

Acquiring a mature and balanced understanding of the cultural, political and military conflict that divides Israelis and Palestinians, and Israel and the Arab states, must rest first on a detailed grasp of the current situation, and next on a comprehension of how the contemporary conditions evolved over time from what many saw as the hopeful beginning of 1948. This book develops its case for understanding the Arab–Israeli conflict in that manner.

CHAPTER 1

The Unfolding Situation, 2008–9

In late August 2008 United States secretary of state Condoleezza Rice visited Israel and the Palestinian Territories to advance Israeli-Palestinian negotiations that had been taking place for some months without much visible progress. It was her eighteenth visit in two years. In November 2007, after a seven-year hiatus, Israeli and Palestinian leaders, together with representatives of a number of Middle Eastern and European countries, including Russia, had met at a US-sponsored peace conference in Annapolis, Maryland, and pledged to make every effort to conclude an agreement on the establishment of a Palestinian state alongside Israel before US president George W. Bush ended his term in January 2009. All the 'core issues' were discussed at the one-day meeting, the most important of which were borders and Israeli settlements, the status of Jerusalem, and the fate of the 4.5 million United Nations-registered Palestinian refugees.

Mahmoud Abbas, president of the Palestine National Authority (hereafter referred to as Palestinian Authority), and Israeli prime minister Ehud Olmert had been meeting frequently since June 2007 to try to agree on some basic issues ahead of the gathering. Immediately before the summit, Bush met with the Israeli and Palestinian leaders in the White House, and read from a joint statement supporting a two-state solution: 'We agreed to immediately launch good faith, bilateral negotiations in order to conclude a peace treaty resolving all outstanding issues, including core issues, without exception . . . The final peace settlement will establish Palestine as a homeland for the Palestinian people just as Israel is the homeland for the Jewish people.'[1] Significantly the word state was not used to describe either homeland.

Several meetings had taken place in the first half of 2008 between the then Israel foreign minister Tzipi Livni and former Palestinian prime minister Ahmed Qurei, and although there had been some progress, the two parties were still a long way from a comprehensive peace agreement. Rice hoped to act as an arbiter to facilitate progress. Foreign minister Livni cautioned the US secretary of state against expectations of an early peace deal. She warned that applying too much international pressure could prove harmful. The circumstances, she stated, were rather similar to the year 2000 when misunderstandings led to the second Palestinian intifada following the breakdown of negotiations between Israel and the Palestinians toward the end of the Clinton Administration. Her Palestinian counterpart, Saeb Erekat, agreed with Livni, stating that he opposed any attempts by outsiders to impose proposals or to force acceptance of a partial agreement.

The situation was complicated, as always, by Israeli and Palestinian domestic politics. The leaders of both sides faced internal constraints. Olmert headed a fragile coalition, many of whose members opposed any Israeli concessions, and Abbas controlled only the West Bank. Neither could carry out their commitments without fear of being ousted. Olmert, who had been holding private talks with Abbas, was embroiled in a corruption inquiry, and on 30 July 2008 he announced that he would resign when the Kadima party, which he led, chose a new leader in September. Livni hoped to be that person, and she believed her shift to a more moderate position strengthened her chances. She is reported to have stated on 21 August, 'Now most Israelis understand that having two states in the lands comprising historic Palestine is an Israeli interest.'[2] Livni was, in fact, elected head of the party in late September but could not form a government and Olmert stayed on as interim prime minister.

Abbas, although president of the Palestinian Authority (PA), had been forcibly expelled from the Gaza Strip in fierce fighting between the two major factions of the Palestine liberation movement, Hamas and Fatah. Abbas was head of Fatah, and as a result of his expulsion from Gaza had set up headquarters in the West Bank city of Ramallah in June 2007. The Islamist party, Hamas, regarded by Israel and the US as a terrorist organization, had won a majority of seats in elections for the Palestinian Legislative Council in January 2006. Neither Israel nor the United States recognized the legitimacy of the

Hamas-controlled government, and when, following a brief interlude of a National Unity Government brokered by the Saudis, Fatah challenged the outcome, Hamas took over control of the Gaza Strip. Abbas hoped an agreement with Israel would bear fruit and strengthen his position.

The Gaza Strip had been in turmoil since the victory of Hamas. In June 2006 Hamas captured an Israeli soldier, Gilad Shalit, from the Israeli side of Israel's 'security barrier' and took him hostage in Gaza. Israel responded by 'arresting' 60 members of Hamas, 30 of whom were members of the Palestinian parliament, eight of whom were ministers of the government. The mayors of Bethlehem, Jenin and Qalqilya were also 'detained'. In addition, Israel sealed all eight commercial and pedestrian crossings into Israel, effectively creating a 26 mile-long and eight-mile wide prison for the population of 1.5 million Palestinians. Rafah in the south, which crosses into Egypt, was also closed. When Hamas took full control of the strip in June 2007 Israel tightened its siege by imposing an economic blockade restricting imports and exports of food stuffs, fuel and medical supplies, and the movement of people. They did so, they claimed, to prevent the firing of home-made rockets into Israel, which was occurring on an almost daily basis. The assumption that the siege would force the militia to stop launching rockets, or that the population would rise up and overthrow Hamas, proved false. If anything, Israel's siege and frequent military air strikes and incursions aimed at 'terrorist operatives' enabled Hamas to consolidate its position. Israel's policy of targeted assassination also had the troubling effect of strengthening far more radical militant groups within Gaza, Islamic Jihad and a small al-Qaeda related group, the Army of Islam.

The people of Gaza believed they had been abandoned by Abbas and the Palestinian Authority. Their situation remained dire. They suffered from the collective punishment imposed by Israel on the one hand, and inept leadership on their side. And the rockets and mortar fire into Israel continued, although the fatalities from the military exchanges were far higher on the Palestinian side. Between January and June 2008, four Israelis were killed by rocket fire from Gaza while 333 Palestinians in Gaza were killed by Israeli artillery and airstrikes, including 56 children and around 130 adult civilians. Egypt brokered a fragile six-month ceasefire between Israel and Hamas on 19 June 2008, in which both sides agreed that the violence between Palestinian militants and Israel would end and Israel would lift its blockade. Separate negotiations were to continue about a prisoner exchange, which would include the return of Corporal Gilad Shalit. Within a couple of weeks both sides were accusing each other of failing to abide by the terms of the agreement.

In the meantime, after eight years, in June 2008, Israel and Syria had resumed parallel – indirect – peace talks. They did so through Turkish mediators in Istanbul. The talks were held on the basis of the framework established at an October 1991 peace conference held in Madrid, Spain. To the Syrians there was only one issue to discuss – restoring the Golan Heights to their control. Israel, however, had a broader agenda. It included weakening Syria's support for Hezbollah and Hamas, removing the presence of radical Palestinian organizations in Syria's capital, diminishing its status in Lebanon and, finally, breaking down Syria's relationship with Iran. Olmert had indicated that the return to Syria of the Golan Heights, seized by Israel in the 1967 Six Day War, was on the agenda, but he demanded that Syria cease to support and transfer weapons to the Iranian-backed Shia militia, Hezbollah, in Lebanon. Israel, and the United States, regarded Hezbollah as a terrorist group. Because of Syria's support of Hezbollah and its military presence in Lebanon, to Israel the two countries were inseparable.

In the summer of 2006 Israel had sought to destroy the radical militia's influence in Lebanon with a series of devastating aerial attacks on its locations in southern Lebanon and Beirut but had been forced into a humiliating retreat when it failed to defeat the highly elusive and well-prepared group.

In May 2008, after two weeks of very fierce fighting in which Hezbollah gunmen took over parts of Beirut, an Arab-mediated agreement was reached to stabilize the feuding factions in Lebanon. To the chagrin of Israel, and the us, Hezbollah was allowed eleven seats in the thirty-seat cabinet, effectively enabling it to veto any government decision. Referring to Hezbollah and Hamas, Syria indicated that if there was a peace agreement there would no longer be the need to support the presence of such organizations. In mid-August 2008 a unity government was formed in Beirut that gave Damascus's ally a strong say in decision-making. Syria and Lebanon immediately agreed to establish full diplomatic ties for the first time in a step toward easing the tensions between the two countries that have fuelled Lebanon's turmoil.

The indirect negotiations between Israel and Syria were further complicated in August 2008 when hostilities broke out between Russia and Georgia, a former Soviet republic. The United States and Israel – among others – condemned the Russian invasion of Georgia that had taken place in response to Georgia's attack on Ossetia, a province on its border with Russia. Russian generals complained that Georgia's military had received training and arms from Israel, while Syria, a friend and ally of Moscow, supported Russia's actions. President Basher al-Assad travelled to Russia in late August in a visit widely regarded as an arms-buying mission for long range anti-aircraft missiles. Olmert planned his own visit to Russia later in the year to strengthen ties and if possible prevent any sales of advanced anti-aircraft missile systems to Syria. He told the Russian president, Dmitry Medvedev, that Israel would eventually have to destroy any missile system that threatened Israeli airforce planes in Israeli airspace. In November 2007 Israel had bombed what it called a nuclear reactor facility in Syria. Whether or not the us had given Israel the 'green light' at the time was unclear, although Israel informed Washington of the impending attack. Israel continued military overflights of Lebanon that the military described as defensive. The Russians denied that they would sell any weapons to Syria that would violate the regional balance of power, and would sell only defensive weapons.

These two sets of talks – Israel–Palestine and Israel–Syria – reflect the multilayered nature of the Arab–Israeli conflict and the interconnectedness of the issues. The Israeli daily *Ha'aretz* reported that Israel informed Egypt and the Palestinian Authority of the indirect talks with Syria before they were officially announced. Israel sought to assure the Palestinians that it was in no way opting for the Syrian track at the expense of negotiations with the Palestinian Authority.[3] Palestinian prime minister Salam Fayyad, speaking in the West Bank, said he was not worried Israel would pursue peace with Syria at the expense of progress in the us-brokered negotiations with the Palestinians.

Every aspect of the developments mentioned above was highly calculated and subjected to the most minute analysis by participants and commentators alike. To take just one comment as an example, in her attempt to maintain Israeli control of negotiations with the PA, Livni warned that international pressure could lead to violence as did the breakdown of the Camp David talks of 2000. That was a highly political and contentious remark and reflected a particular, narrow, Israeli interpretation. Most observers, including many Israelis, recognize that the second intifada was caused not by the breakdown of the Camp David talks, which imputes blame directly to the Palestinians, but by the provocative, and political, gesture made by Ariel Sharon in visiting the Temple Mount in Jerusalem on 28 September 2000 – a view which at least shares responsibility for the violence. Livni's remark was calculated to delay and lessen US – and Palestinian Authority – pressure on Israel to make concessions.

Some indication of the distance between the two parties in negotiations on the core issues was revealed in mid-August 2008 when *Ha'aretz* published a secret two-state proposal Olmert had presented to Abbas. The Israeli prime minister had been working on the plan for some months.[4] According to the newspaper, Olmert also passed it on to the Americans in an effort to obtain their support for Israel's position. Neither side wanted the proposal released, the prime minister's office would not confirm or deny the report and the Palestinian Authority denied receiving it, but spokesmen from both commented upon it.

Under Olmert's reported proposal, Israel would return to the Palestinians 93 per cent of the West Bank, as well as the Gaza Strip. In exchange for West Bank land that Israel would keep, Olmert proposed a 5.5 per cent land swap giving the Palestinians a desert territory adjacent to the Gaza Strip. The Palestinians would be given free passage between Gaza and the West Bank without any security checks. Israel would keep 7 per cent of the West Bank, while the Palestinians would receive territory equivalent to 5.5 per cent. Israel viewed the passage between Gaza and the West Bank as compensating for this difference, although it would officially remain in Israeli hands. The land to be annexed to Israel would include the large settlement blocs and, as widely expected and predicted, the border would follow the current separation barrier. Israel would keep Ma'ale Adumim, Gush Etzion, the settlements surrounding Jerusalem and some land in the northern West Bank adjacent to Israel as well as the two settlements of Efrat and Ariel.

Olmert's proposal stated that once a border was agreed upon, Israel would be able to build freely in the settlement blocs to be annexed. The settlements outside the new border would be evacuated in two stages. First, after the agreement in principle was signed, the cabinet would initiate legislation to compensate settlers who voluntarily relocated, and in the second stage, once the Palestinians completed a series of internal reforms and were capable of carrying out the entire agreement, Israel would remove any settlers remaining east of the new border.

Regarding the future of Palestinian refugees, the proposal rejected a Palestinian 'right of return' and stated that the refugees could only return to the Palestinian state, other than exceptional cases in which refugees would be allowed into Israel for family reunification. There is a certain amount of

The 'Olmert' Parameters, September 2007.

agreement between the two parties on the future of the refugees. The peace initiative put forward by the Arab League in 2002 leaves no doubt that Arab countries will accept a nominal and symbolic return of refugees into Israel in numbers approved by Israel, with the overwhelming majority being repatriated into the new Palestinian state, their countries of residence, or into other countries prepared to receive them.

Abbas immediately rejected the proposal as reported. It did not even go as far as the offer made by then prime minister Ehud Barak to Palestinian Authority president Yasser Arafat at Taba in January 2001. There were a number of unacceptable features in Olmert's proposition. In the first place it did not provide for a Palestinian state that was contiguous, or with Jerusalem as its capital. And while Israel believed the passage connecting the two halves of the Palestinian state was one the Palestinians did not enjoy before 1967, when the Gaza Strip was under Egyptian control and the West Bank was part of Jordan, it was not satisfactory that Israel retained sovereignty over the passage. Abbas had been proposing that Israel retain only 2 per cent of the West Bank, not the 7 per cent envisaged by Olmert.

Furthermore, Israel received immediate benefits from the plan while the Palestinian Authority's benefits were conditional, gratuitously and insultingly so – and Israel, presumably, would be the referee to the implementation of the agreement. The land to be transferred to the PA would only be delivered after Abbas had regained control of the Gaza Strip. Olmert and Livni's position was that nobody in the region could afford a terror state, or a failed state, or an extreme Islamic state between the Jordan River and the Mediterranean Sea. Few attitudes could be more calculated to enrage Palestinians than a demand that their government control extremist elements coming from a government that had elected at least three former terrorist leaders to the office of prime minister and whose policies were held hostage by the most extreme religious and nationalist elements in the Knesset.

The concept Abbas had in mind did not differ significantly from those put forward eight years earlier at Camp David by former PA president Yasser Arafat, which would have allowed Israel to annex only a few settlements, along with their access roads, and ruled out allowing Israel to retain the settlement blocs. Israel argued that since then the separation fence had been built in the West Bank, and a new physical reality had been created in the areas where the fence had been completed. There were also difficulties with security arrangements. The Israeli prime minister's scheme included a demand that the Palestinian state be demilitarized and without an army. The Palestinians, in contrast, insisted that their security forces be capable of defending against 'outside threats'.

Jerusalem was not dealt with in the plan. The Israeli prime minister had given way to threats from the ultra-Orthodox Shas Party that it would leave his coalition government if Jerusalem were put on the negotiating agenda. Israel knew Abbas could not agree to any proposition that did not include the question of sovereignty and control over Jerusalem and its holy sites. Arafat had refused a division on Jerusalem when it was suggested by Ehud Barak in 2000, so Olmert suggested that negotiations be held under international auspices with a five-year timetable to reach agreement. According to *Ha'aretz* journalists, Olmert was probably planning to include in the negotiations members of the international Quartet (the UN, US, EU and Russia), as well as Jordan, Egypt, the Vatican and possibly the king of Morocco. From Israel's point of view, broadening the international, inter-faith element increased the chances of finding an acceptable agreement, even though it risked involving parties opposed to Israel's sovereign control over the city's holy sites.[5]

Olmert hoped any agreement with the Palestinians would entrench the two-state solution in the international community's consciousness. In his opinion, this was the only way Israel could rebuff challenges to its legitimacy and avoid calls for a 'one-state solution'. His position had received strong support from the US administration. However, Nabil Abu Rdainah, Abbas's spokesman, accused Olmert of a 'lack of seriousness'. Senior Palestinian negotiator Ahmed Qurei stated that the Palestinians might demand to become part of a bi-national state if Israel continued to reject the borders the Palestinians proposed for a separate country. Qurei told Fatah party loyalists that a two-state solution could be achieved only if Israel withdrew from all Palestinian territory it had captured in the 1967 Six Day War.[6]

One great advantage of his scheme as far as Olmert was concerned was how it could be 'spun'. He would try to sell the deal to the Israeli public based on a staged programme of implementation. He could tell the Israeli public that Israel was receiving 7 per cent of the West Bank and an agreed-upon border, while the Israeli concessions would be postponed until Hamas rule in Gaza ended. And there were benefits for Abbas, Olmert's public relations persons argued. They patronizingly said that Abbas could tell the Palestinians that he had succeeded in obtaining the equivalent of 98 per cent of the West Bank from Israel, along with a promise to remove all Israeli settlers across the border into Israel. Despite the negative response by Abbas, Olmert's spokesman Mark Regev said the prime minister was serious about continuing the peace talks. But another Israeli official said Olmert was merely trying to establish his legacy. 'There is going to be no agreement, period', the unidentified voice said on condition of anonymity.[7]

Abbas was attacked by Israeli commentators for his rejection of what was described as a generous offer, which, it was claimed, promised a Palestinian state in 93 per cent of the West Bank. The realities on the ground reveal a somewhat different picture. The clearest indication of Israel's intention can be seen in the location of the 450-mile security barrier being built to separate Israelis and Palestinians. The area to be included between the Green Line (the armistice lines of the June 1967 War) and the barrier is just under 10 per cent of the West Bank. However, in a report published in July 2007, the United Nations Office of Coordination of Humanitarian Affairs (UNOCHA) reported that almost 40 per cent (38 per cent) of the West Bank was under Israeli control, to the total or virtual exclusion of Palestinians.[8]

The area controlled by Israel included settlements, outposts, military bases and closed military areas, nature reserves and road networks. More than 450,000 Jewish settlers lived in 149 settlements, including East Jerusalem. A total of 57 per cent of the settlers lived within six miles of Jerusalem and 80 per cent within fifteen miles of Jerusalem in locations close to Bethlehem and Ramallah. Between 1987 and 2004 the population of the settlements had increased by 160 per cent, at a rate of 5.5 per cent a year. Since 1993, when it was agreed in the Oslo Accords that settlements would be a 'final status' issue to be negotiated later, 163,000 settlers had moved into the West Bank, an increase of 63 per cent. The rate of population increase in the settlements had been more than double that of the rate within Israel (4.5 per cent compared to less than 2 per cent). The rest of the West Bank, including major population centres such as Nablus and Jericho, was split into enclaves; movement of Palestinians between them was restricted by 450 roadblocks and 70 manned checkpoints. The UN report found that the remaining area was very similar to that set aside for the Palestinian population in Israeli security proposals in the aftermath of the 1967 war.

Israel claims that UN Security Council resolutions 242 and 338, which all parties agree constitute the basis for negotiations to settle the boundaries between Israel and a Palestinian state, refer to a return to the borders of 'countries' before the 1967 war. However, Israel contends that, as there was no Palestinian state/country prior to the 1967 war, it is free to alter the armistice line to guarantee its security needs. The Palestinians insist, on the other hand, that the borders that should have precedence are the partition boundaries set by UN General Assembly Resolution 181 of 1947, which Israel claims gave international legitimacy to the Jewish state, and which Palestinians argue recognized the equally legitimate patrimony and right to national self-determination of the Palestinian Arab population.

Israel enlarged its territory by 50 per cent in the war launched by the Arab countries to prevent the implementation of the UN partition resolution. If one were to apply the principle stated in the Security Council's Resolution 242 that it is illegal to acquire territory as a result of war, the question would then become how much of the additional land Israel acquired in the 1948–9 war it should be permitted to retain, not how much of the post-1967 war acquired territory it should be allowed to keep! If one follows the legalistic arguments a little further, according to UNOCHA, all Israel's settlements are illegal under various Geneva conventions.

Realities have overtaken these arguments, however, and there is no likelihood whatsoever of any such eventualities. The current facts on the ground were reinforced by US president George W. Bush when he wrote to Israeli prime minister Ariel Sharon following Israel's withdrawal from the Gaza Strip in 2004 that it was unreasonable to expect that Israel would surrender the settlements immediately surrounding Jerusalem. Sharon's intention in unilaterally withdrawing from Gaza in 2004, and dismantling several isolated settlements in the West Bank, was to gain US acceptance of Israel's unilateralism, not to set a precedent for an eventual withdrawal, and, as Bush's letter shows, he succeeded. Israel's human rights watchdog *Peace Now* reported in late August 2008 that settlement activity had more than doubled in the previous year, much of it over the Green Line within Jerusalem's municipal boundaries, an area in which 200,000 Jews now live. More than 2,600 housing units are under construction in West Bank settlements, including units in more than 1,000 new buildings. The organization states that slightly more than half of the new structures are going up east of the separation fence, and in several places construction is encroaching on the boundaries of Palestinian towns, such as Ramallah and Bethlehem.[9]

The rhetoric used by both sides to justify their actions hides the reality behind the claims they make. One of the first tasks in understanding the contemporary Arab–Israeli conflict is to unravel the language used by both sides. In all military confrontations there is a huge gap between the rhetoric used by the parties involved and the realities of the situation. In today's world it is called 'spin'. In an earlier age it would have been called propaganda. The Arab–Israeli conflict is no exception to this phenomenon; fought as it is in the spotlight of the modern international media, it provides an outstanding example of the effective use of spin and propaganda.[10] In this encounter rhetorical devices have taken on a life of their own, they have become the reality. Military terminology and discourse have become the dominant language. To give some typical examples used by Israel: the Israeli Defence Force states that it 'responds' or 'acts', it never 'initiates'; the Palestinians 'kidnap', the IDF 'arrests'; the IDF 'confirms', Palestinians 'claim'. Palestinians, for their part, state that they 'resist' rather than 'initiate', and 'defend' rather than 'attack'. Israelis rarely use the term 'occupied territories', preferring 'administered territories', or 'Judea and Samaria', or simply 'the territories'. Euphemisms such as 'peace process', 'terrorist operative' and 'targeted assassination' are widely used to conceal rather than describe reality.[11] The Arab states and Palestinians engage in similar deceptions. In addition to creating a new language to misrepresent the daily events of the conflict, both sides use spin to frame the contested issues.

Israelis claim they need to do so as they are surrounded by adversaries determined to destroy their state. They emphasize that the key issue is Israel's security. They claim that the Palestinians and neighbouring Arab states – with the exception of Egypt and Jordan, which have signed peace treaties – declare that Israel is an unacceptable occupying power, using cruel and oppressive methods to support religious and nationalist extremists in the West Bank at the expense of the local Arab population. Israel maintains that the Palestinians have missed opportunities for peace and point especially to Yasser Arafat's refusal to accept the offer of Ehud Barak at Camp David in 2000. They argue that the PA does not accept Israel's right to exist as a Jewish state, and that Hamas is a terrorist organization dedicated to the destruction of Israel and is supported by Iran and Hezbollah in Lebanon.

Palestinians contend that Israel is simply employing delaying tactics. They believe the Oslo process failed because Israel put off discussions of core issues, insisting instead on a 'gradualist' approach using 'confidence building measures', all the while continuing to build settlements and create further 'facts on the ground'. In August 2008 Palestinian negotiator Saeb Bamya asserted, 'I simply do not believe there is political will at the highest levels, on the Israeli side, to agree to a package that will lead to a viable Palestinian state.'[12] Many Israeli commentators support this view. They believe Israeli policies have contributed to the hostility against it, and to Israel's insecurity. They point to Barak walking away from serious talks with Syria over the Golan Heights in 2000, Israel's support of Islamists while deporting PLO moderates and jailing Fatah activists, the failure to respond to the 2002 Arab peace initiative, Olmert's rejection of the Fatah-Hamas national unity government in 2007, and the continuation and expansion of settlement building. The settlements, they argue, have not brought security from terrorist and rocket attacks against Israel; they have increased the number of attacks. Not only are the Palestinians determined that they be removed, the sympathy and support of western public opinion that Israel enjoyed in its struggle for survival has turned against the Jewish state on this issue. Israel's critics now believe that the continuation of settlement building, as well as inhuman practices such as arbitrary arrests, torture, unnecessary searches, curfews and checkpoints, land confiscations, uprooting of (mainly olive) trees and crops have caused Israel's legitimacy to be questionable.[13]

Secretary Rice found no outward sign of progress on her arrival in Israel and Palestine on 25 August 2008, although Israel had removed a few army checkpoints in the West Bank. The evident lack of progress demonstrated that there was little likelihood of reaching agreement, and each side blamed the other for the failure to do so. Olmert wanted to reach a 'shelf agreement' now – a deal whose implementation would be spread over a decade – because he wanted to end his career with a diplomatic achievement. He believed that Abbas also wished to reach some kind of agreement to keep his position viable, and the Bush administration certainly wanted one. Olmert faced opposition from the religious and nationalist parties on the right, and from within his own Kadima party. Defence minister Ehud Barak and foreign minister Tzipi Livni wanted to delay any concessions even longer than the prime minister. They were soon to face voters in elections, and preferred to wait for him to go. These were classic delaying tactics used effectively by Israeli leaders in the past. Abbas, who was in a weak negotiating position, faced opposition from Hamas, who believed the Palestinians get nothing from negotiating with Israel, and from many Palestinians who believed the leadership of the Palestinian Authority was inept and corrupt.

The failure to reach the agreement promised at Annapolis, of course, strengthened the radicals on both sides. On the Palestinian side it consolidated Hamas and increased the likelihood of the collapse of the Palestinian Authority, which could, in turn, lead to the resumption of full Israeli military administrative and political control of the Palestinian population – something some Israelis would no doubt welcome as a step toward the eventual removal of the Palestinians. On the Israeli side it confirmed the view held by hard liners that there is little point in trying to negotiate with intransigent enemies.[14]

The year 2008 ended with the outbreak of what was quickly dubbed the Gaza War. Both sides had used the uneasy six-month truce negotiated through Egyptian intermediaries in June to prepare for a further round of violence. Israel and Hamas accused each other of violating the truce. The Israeli government blamed Hamas for not stopping attacks often carried out by smaller Palestinian factions, while the Islamists argued that not only Israel's raids, but also its continued blockade of the impoverished territory were in violation of the truce agreement.

On 4 November, the day of the US presidential elections, the Israeli army broke the truce, killing more than six Palestinians when it destroyed a tunnel on the southern border of Gaza that it claimed was built by militants to smuggle arms from Egypt. Hamas retaliated with rocket fire into Israel. Israel in turn tightened its blockade and refused to allow fuel and essential medical and humanitarian supplies to enter the Strip, creating widespread hardship and, no doubt, causing many otherwise preventable deaths among the elderly and sick. During November and December tension mounted and, as the ceasefire ended on 19 December, Hamas militants resumed almost daily rocket attacks into Israel.

Despite explicit warnings from Prime Minister Olmert in late December that Israel was stronger than Hamas, and that military action would be taken if rocket strikes continued, the rockets raining into towns bordering Gaza continued. Although no Israelis were killed by the more than 250 Qassam rockets fired in the next week or so, at 11.30 am on Saturday 27 December 2008 Israel launched a long-planned, massive surprise air attack on the densely populated streets of Gaza City and other towns and refugee camps, using US-supplied F-16 multi-role fighter aircraft, Apache helicopters and unmanned drones armed with guided missiles. In less than two days Israel struck at least 230 targets it claimed were security compounds, rocket launching bases, police stations (located, like police stations everywhere, in civilian areas), command centres, training bases, illicit manufacturing warehouses and smugglers' tunnels in an effort to shut down Hamas's main conduit for arms and disable what Israel described as Hamas's 'infrastructure of terror'. Tanks were massed on the border and 9,000 reserves were called up in apparent preparation for a ground offensive. More than 280 Palestinians were killed and an estimated 800 wounded. Most of those killed were security men and police – officers responsible for maintaining order on the streets – but an unknown number of civilians, including several children returning home from school, were among the dead. Exact numbers were impossible to verify. Israel barred foreign journalists from entering Gaza after the operation began. The effect of the ferocious surprise attack was to a create a sense of 'shock and awe', similar to that following the American onslaught on Iraq in 2003. The IDF asserted that the strike on the Hamas chain of command would make it difficult for the organization to operate. It no doubt hoped for the dissolution of Hamas under the pressure of overwhelming air strikes, but Israel resolutely denied any desire for 'regime change'.

The bombardment caused the largest number of Palestinian casualties since Israel seized the territory from Egypt in the 1967 war, and as many as were killed by Israeli security forces in the first two years of the first intifada of 1988–9 when, according to the Israeli human rights group B'tselem, 289 and 285 Palestinians, respectively, died. The 2008 strikes caused panic and confusion among the 1.5 million Gazan residents. Hamas leaders vowed retaliation, and in Damascus exiled Hamas leader Khaled Meshal, taking a swipe at Mahmoud Abbas and his pro-Western Fatah administration, called upon Palestinians from both territories to unite under Hamas for a third intifada. As longer-range Katusha rockets began falling into Israel from Gaza, killing one Israeli near Netiyot, Israeli military sources estimated that Hamas militants were capable of firing as many as 200 rockets a day.

Television and internet footage of the carnage and destruction in Gaza flashed around a world shocked by Israel's extraordinarily disproportionate response. The reaction of many international leaders was somewhat muted at first, however, as Israel's leaders, especially foreign minister Tzipi Livni, immediately embarked upon an aggressive diplomatic public relations campaign to garner international support for Israel's actions. The purpose of the carefully crafted campaign, prepared months earlier, was to persuade the rest of the world of the justice of Israel's cause; that it was a victim with no choice but to defend itself in response to the ongoing barrage of Hamas rockets. The message was that Hamas had broken the ceasefire agreements, that Israel's objective was the defence of its population, and that Israel's forces were taking the utmost care not to hurt innocent civilians. The victims were blamed for their own misfortune. Civilians would die but Hamas was to blame for their deaths, not Israel. Hamas was portrayed as part of the axis of fundamentalist evil alongside Iran and Hezbollah. There was no suggestion of an Israeli reoccupation of the Gaza Strip.

The propaganda campaign was highly successful. The Bush administration was quick to support Israel. It blamed Hamas for Israel's response, describing the organization as a 'bunch of thugs' while half-heartedly calling for Israel to halt the attacks. Conservative Arab governments also condemned Hamas. Reassured by the favourable international reaction, Defence Minister Ehud Barak rejected calls for a ceasefire coming from Russia, Egypt, the European Union and the US. The majority of Israelis, who saw little of Palestinian death and destruction on their TV screens, supported the government's decision. A few, like *Ha'aretz* correspondent Gideon Levy, were horrified. 'Israel's violent responses', he wrote, 'even if there is justification for them, exceed all proportion and cross every red line of humaneness, morality, international law and wisdom. What began yesterday in Gaza is a war crime and the foolishness of a country.' Levy called Israel's actions unnecessary and ill-fated. Israel, he asserted, had not exhausted the diplomatic processes before embarking on another dreadful campaign of killing and ruin. Levy continued: 'Blood will now flow like water. Besieged and impoverished Gaza, the city of refugees, will pay the main price. But blood will also be unnecessarily spilled on our side. In its foolishness, Hamas brought this on itself and on its people, but this does not excuse Israel's overreaction.' He rightly concluded that the idea that a military operation would see an entrenched regime overthrown to be replaced by another one friendlier to Israel was no more than lunacy.[15] Distraught Palestinian parents asked if their dead and dying children were the Hamas leaders Olmert had asked them to disobey. One Palestinian told *Ha'aretz* reporter Amira Hass: 'This assault is not against Hamas. It's against all of us, the entire nation. And no Palestinian will consent to having his people and his homeland destroyed in this way.'[16]

Arab and Muslim public opinion was inflamed by the deadly assaults, and street protests took place in Arab communities in Israel and the West Bank – especially Hebron – across the Arab world, in some European cities and in San Francisco, California. Many in the Middle East regarded Israel's attacks as a joint operation by the United States and Israel as part of a wider generalized war against Islam. They noted that US–Israel military cooperation had increased in the past five years. During that period, the US had provided Israel with weapons and training facilities while utilizing Israeli tactics as a proving ground for fighting insurgencies in its own war on terror in Iraq and in Afghanistan. Arab leaders, however, were not so quick to condemn Israel. Palestinian President Mahmoud Abbas straddled the fence. He blamed Hamas for Israel's attack, although he did condemn Israel's 'aggression'. Many Palestinians believed that Egypt's President Hosni Mubarak and Abbas supported Israel's attack on Hamas, whose radicalism the two conservative leaders regarded as a threat to their regimes. As the ferocity of the attack became more apparent, Syria broke off indirect talks with Israel, and the prime minister of Turkey called the attack a crime against humanity.

The timing of the attack led many inside and outside of Israel to speculate that the war was more about political strategy than Israel's security. A general election was scheduled for 10 February 2009, and the war was certainly beneficial to ruling coalition members at a time of political uncertainty. It provided an opportunity for Israel's disgraced outgoing Olmert to use the last days of the compliant Bush administration to attempt to impose his will on Gaza before the possibly less supportive president-elect Barack Obama took office. The vicious assault also provided a boost to the electoral chances of Foreign Minister Tzipi Livni, a member of the Kadima party, and Defence Minister Ehud Barak, who headed Labor, both of whom had vowed to destroy Hamas. However, both politicians lagged behind the hard-line Likud leader Benjamin Netanyahu in the polls. Netanyahu welcomed the Israeli attempt to overthrow Hamas, and Livni hoped the war would make her look tough. Barak hoped that military success would lead him to electoral victory. Polls indicated that Barak and Labor were the main beneficiaries of the war.

It should also be noted that Hamas leaders had much to gain politically from the resumption of fighting. The mandate of Palestinian Authority president Abbas was to end on 9 January 2009. By forcing Israel into a military confrontation, thereby setting itself up as a victim, Hamas anticipated gaining increased support among the Palestinian population, not only in the Gaza Strip but also in the West Bank and the diaspora. This expectation was realized. Abbas was virtually sidelined as a spokesman for the Palestinians.

Air and naval bombardments continued throughout the following week. By 4 January 2009 Israel had destroyed government buildings, vehicles, a university building, a large mosque in Gaza City and more than 40 tunnels believed to be command centres and weapons and fuel depots. The number of Palestinian fatalities reached 460, one-quarter of them civilian, with close to 2,000 wounded. It was one of the bloodiest periods in the sixty-year conflict between Israel and the Palestinians. Despite the attacks, it appeared the Hamas leadership was still intact and so too were many of the estimated 15,000 Hamas fighting men. During the week Hamas fired more than 400 rockets into Israel, killing three Israelis. One long-range Katusha caused extensive damage to an empty high school in the desert city of Be'er Sheva, some 25 miles (40 km) from the border.

Four days into the assault the Israeli security cabinet rejected a French proposal for a 48-hour truce to permit humanitarian assistance to Gaza's population. Seemingly oblivious to the historical irony of his statement, an Olmert aide stated: 'There's no such thing as a humanitarian ceasefire. Gaza is not undergoing a humanitarian crisis. We're constantly supplying it with food and medications, and there's no need for a humanitarian ceasefire.' As Daniel Barenboim in his role as UN messenger for peace sadly asked: 'Is the entire population of Gaza to be held responsible for the sins of a terrorist organisation? We, the Jewish people, should know and feel even more acutely than other populations that the murder of innocent civilians is inhumane and unacceptable.'[17] On a visit to France, Livni told President Nicolas Sarkozy that 'Israel is part of the free world and fights extremism and terrorism. Hamas is not.'[18] At a time when between 600,000 and 700,000 Gazans had no water, raw sewage was running in the streets in some localities, and the homes of about one million Gazans had been without electricity for between five and seven days straight, foreign minister Livni declared that there was no humanitarian crisis in Gaza.

In the evening of 3 January 2009, after the week-long offensive had failed to halt Hamas rockets, Israel sent ground troops and tanks, backed by intense air, naval and artillery bombardments, across the border to reoccupy parts of northern Gaza. Fierce fighting ensued in the next week. On 6 January Israeli troops shelled a UNRWA school in the crowded Jabalya refugee camp, killing more than 40 civilians. The attack, and the claim by the UN that 30 Palestinian civilians in a family compound in the Zeitoun area of Gaza City had been killed by Israeli shelling, brought international condemnation of Israel. Israeli politicians claimed that Hamas had fired rockets from the school location, but three days later the IDF admitted that a mistake had been made in firing on the school. Defiant Hamas militants fired more than twenty rockets into southern Israeli towns. On 15 January the headquarters of the United Nations Relief and Works Agency (UNRWA) was also shelled, destroying tons of food and fuel intended for Palestinian refugees. It was becoming apparent to all, including the Israeli cabinet, that the more Israeli forces advanced the more complicated and dangerous the situation would become. Frantic efforts brought about a binding UN Security Council Resolution calling for an immediate ceasefire. The US, which usually votes against any resolution critical of Israel, did not use its veto; rather, it abstained. However, both Israel and Hamas rejected the UN resolution, stating it did not address their issues. Nonetheless, on 17 January, after 22 days of bombardment, Israel announced a unilateral ceasefire and withdrew its forces, just three days before the inauguration of US president Barack Obama.

It was estimated that between 1,300 and 1,400 people were killed in Israel's attack on Gaza, many of them women and children. The Palestinian Centre for Human Rights reported that of those killed, 926 were civilians, 236 were combatants and 255 were members of the Palestinian security forces. 100,000 Gazans were left homeless. These figures are disputed by Israel. 40 per cent of Gaza homes and 80 per cent of crops were destroyed and the population deprived of food, water and medicine. The damage caused was calculated at around US$1.9 billion. Thirteen Israelis were killed during the 22-day Gaza operation, including three civilians and four soldiers killed by 'friendly fire'.

Israel's plans to end the fighting had not been announced at the start of the military operation; perhaps it had not been known. The assault appeared to achieve achieved little, beyond, perhaps, some marginal impact on its own election results. It did not result in the hoped-for return of corporal Shalit. Israel was condemned in the eyes of world for its 'disproportionate' use of force, and, following the war, faced its worst diplomatic crisis in two decades. Neither side came out unscathed in world opinion. Questions were raised by international, and Israeli, human rights groups as to whether the conduct of the IDF toward civilians during the offensive constituted war crimes and Hamas was accused of war crimes for its use of civilians as human shields.

Olmert declared that Israel sought 'a normal life for the [Israeli] citizens of the south', and wished to create a 'new security reality in the region'. However, the targets selected in the Gaza suggested that the goal of the Israeli operation was to destroy the administrative and security infrastructure of Hamas in order to prevent it operating as a government. But what was to happen then? Just as Hezbollah was not weakened by the Second Lebanon War in 2006, Hamas did not appear weakened by the Gaza War.

Past experience has demonstrated that the assumption that Palestinian civilians will blame Hamas for their suffering and overthrow its leaders is a chimera. The majority of Gaza residents do not accept the proposition that Hamas is a terrorist organization; they believe it is a genuine religious-nationalist movement. Resorting to military operations and refusing to negotiate with Hamas will not advance peace. Hamas's conditions for a ceasefire are that Israel must open the border crossings into Gaza and allow freedom of movement of people and goods between Gaza and the West Bank, and it must cease IDF attacks into Gaza. Israel is demanding a real calm with no rocket attacks by any group. The question remains, if Israel was, in fact, willing to recognize Hamas's control of the Gaza on the condition that it assumes responsibility for the security of the territory, as it has with Hezbollah in southern Lebanon, why did the government not agree to these conditions, lift its blockade, and forgo the war?

In some respects, Israel's actions resembled the campaign it launched against Lebanon in 1982, which killed 17,500 Lebanese, mostly civilians, and destroyed much of Lebanon's infrastructure, ostensibly to prevent Palestinian militias from launching rockets into northern Israel. But Israel's military superiority and apparent victory did not prevent Hezbollah launching rocket attacks in 2006. Nor will military force provide Israel security from rockets launched in Gaza. Only negotiations in which Hamas is a party will do that. At the time of writing the wider implications of the war are unknown. One thing is certain: the Gaza war of 2008–9 will resonate across the region for many years to come.

In the Israeli general elections held in February 2009, foreign minister Tsipi Livni's Kadima party won 28 seats, gaining a narrow victory over Likud led by Benjamin Netanyahu with 27. Livni was unable to form a majority coalition, however, and President Shimon Peres asked Netanyahu to form a government. Netanyahu, who refuses to endorse a two-state solution, forged a right-wing coalition with the ultra-nationalist Yisrael Beitenu party led by Avigdor Lieberman and the Labor party, and took office in early April promising only that he would negotiate with the PA. However, on his first overseas trip, to Europe also in early April, US president Barack Obama firmly asserted that the United States was committed to a two-state solution and he believed Israel had made agreements to seek that outcome.

The developments of the two years prior to 2009 described above show the extent to which Israel shapes the agenda of the conflict and the pace and content of negotiations, especially with the Palestinians. They reflect the overwhelming military and economic superiority Israel possesses in relation to the Palestinians and Israel's other neighbours. They demonstrate the confidence Israel has in its support from the United States and in its international standing. Israel's behaviour also reveals the disregard and contempt, bordering on racism, with which Israeli leaders hold the Palestinian leadership and population. The current situation also reveals the converse determination of the Palestinian population to resist Israeli policies. Forty-one years of military occupation have not diminished their determination to assert their rights.

To understand how this situation has developed it is necessary to trace the history of Palestine/Israel, and adjacent countries, over the past three-quarters of a century. In 1918, at the conclusion of World War I, the Jewish population of Palestine was only 60,000. Jews represented less than 10 per cent of the population of Palestine and owned only around 2 per cent of the land. Zionism was an ideology in its infancy, very much a minority movement among Jews in the world. Yet in May 1948 a Jewish state was proclaimed in Palestine, and the area has been a battleground that has drawn in the world's major powers ever since. By 2008, with a population of 7.3 million (5.5 million [75 per cent] Jews and 1.5 million [20 per cent] Arabs), Israel has become by far the most powerful military force in the Middle East with a nuclear arsenal and a formidable fighting force. It is a prosperous, efficient, developed western country by virtually any measure – with all of the associated problems of inequality and corruption in high places. The Arab inhabitants of Palestine (estimated at 10.5 million worldwide, 3.7 million of whom live in the Palestinian territories) find themselves powerless, reduced to poverty, dispossessed and dispersed. The forces that shaped today's state of affairs and the conflict surrounding it had their origins during the 28 years, 1920 to 1948, in which Palestine was a British mandate. To that story we now turn our attention.

CHAPTER 2

Prelude: The British Mandate

The contemporary Arab–Israeli conflict has its origins in the 30 years from 1918 to 1948 when Palestine was under British rule. In 1918 Zionism was a small movement with few adherents in Palestine; by 1948 it had achieved the seemingly impossible task of establishing a state against the wishes of the majority Arab population. This chapter traces that transformation. Of all the events that took place in Palestine during the mandate period, the British administration's harsh military crackdown on leaders of an Arab general strike in 1936, called in protest against increased Jewish immigration, was probably the most highly instrumental in bringing about the establishment of a Jewish state. In 1937 the Arab strike degenerated into a fairly widespread armed revolt against the British and Jews. British authorities, determined to put an end to the violence, increased the number of troops in Palestine and, joined by Jewish militia, arrested, executed and deported Arab leaders and their followers. When the revolt came to an end in March 1939, more than 4,000 Arabs had been killed and at least 15,000 wounded. The destruction of the main Arab political leadership in the revolt, and the emergence of the Jewish defence force, the Haganah, as well as the Jewish terrorist group, the Irgun, as major players in the mandate, greatly hindered Palestinian efforts to counter the establishment of the Jewish state a decade later.

During the British mandate, Palestine was ruled by a Christian power for the first time in almost eight centuries. Palestine had been a source, if not the scene, of conflict for a century or more before the end of the mandate in 1948.

In the 1850s Russia and France went to war partly to determine which country the Sultan of the Ottoman Empire, at that time the ruler of Palestine, would allow to act as protector of the area's Christian holy sites. The matter of which European country would take precedence in Palestine was not resolved until the defeat of the Ottomans in World War I, when the Allied Supreme Council at a conference in San Remo, Italy, in April 1920 decided that Great Britain should be granted a League of Nations Mandate over Palestine as part of the post-war settlements previously reached in Paris and London.

World War I had devastated the remote, somewhat neglected and underdeveloped Palestine. The population at the end of World War I had declined from around 738,000 in 1914 to approximately 690,000 – 630,000 Arabs (12 per cent of whom were Christians) and 60,000 Jews – in 1918. The British governed Palestine as if it were a Crown colony. The result was an increase in population, prosperity and polarization, all three of which contributed to the creation of an atmosphere of suspicion and fear and, frequently, to conflict. Precise population figures for Palestine during the mandate are problematic and difficult to come by. Borders were imprecise and porous, many local Arabs nomadic and elusive, birth rate figures unreliable, Jewish movements for much of British rule were outgoing as well as incoming, and both sides contest the accuracy of any figures other than their own. What can be said, however, is that by the outbreak of World War II there had been a very significant demographic alteration in Palestine. In the space of thirty years, the total population more than doubled, life expectancy extended, and the percentage of Jews rose from around 11 to more than 30 per cent. British rule prompted a major transformation of the economy and infrastructure. Post and telegraphic services were upgraded, railways extended, roads, port facilities, schools and hospitals built, and the standard of living in towns and on the land rose substantially.

The area of mandated Palestine (excluding Transjordan) was about 10,162 square miles (26,320 square km), about the size of New Hampshire or one-third of the size of Scotland. In addition to Palestine, Great Britain also acquired Turkish Middle Eastern lands and German colonial territories as mandates. One of the most difficult questions facing the allied powers and the Arab and Zionist leaders was exactly where the boundaries of these mandates should be drawn. As finally drawn up at San Remo, the Palestine mandate borders included the area known as Transjordan. Both Arabs and Zionists were unhappy with these boundaries. The World Zionist Organization (WZO) had presented a proposal to the Peace Conference in Paris in late February 1919 indicating the area Zionists sought as a Jewish homeland, by which they meant a state. This proposal provides a revealing, if uncomfortable, insight into Zionist thinking at the beginning of the Mandate period, and perhaps even into Israeli goals since the declaration of the state in 1948. The area to be included extended south from a line just north of Sidon (Lebanon), extending eastward to the Hejaz railway and then south along that railway on the eastern side of the River Jordan to the Gulf of Aqaba. The southern boundary was a line drawn to include all the Sinai Peninsula to the western boundary of the Mediterranean Sea. Jerusalem was, of course, included as part of the Jewish state.

While the French rejected and the British ignored the boundaries proposed by the WZO, US president Woodrow Wilson urged their adoption. Achieving these boundaries has remained a seductive idea to most Zionists ever since 1919. In November 1947 the Jewish Agency accepted the partition lines suggested by the UN General Assembly, but the Declaration of Independence read by David Ben-Gurion in Tel Aviv on 14 May 1948 deliberately made no reference to the state's borders. As was the case with the Declaration of Independence of the thirteen colonies that were to become the United States, the reason for the omission was, if not the explicit desire to expand, to leave the option on the table. Ben-Gurion had long believed the natural northern boundary of Israel to be the Litani River in southern Lebanon.

Israeli policy-makers, regardless of party alignment, have remained remarkably consistent in seeking to establish or maintain Israeli control over much of the area proposed by the WZO in 1919, especially the northern head-waters region of the Golan and southern Lebanon. Only two, Moshe Sharett and Yitzhak Rabin (and possibly Shimon Peres), deviated significantly from the general pattern of securing a military presence in what Israeli leaders see as these vitally strategic areas ensuring Israel's water supply. Sharett was prime minister very briefly, replaced by Ben-Gurion for his 'soft' approach to Arabs, Rabin was assassinated, and Peres quickly retreated to the mainstream position. Israel's first achievement in this respect in the war of 1948–9 was to include within its territory an area in the north bounded on both sides by land designated by the UN General Assembly to be included in the Arab state. It also gained more of the Negev than the UN allocated, although only part of Jerusalem was obtained. In 1956 Israel sought to incorporate the Sinai

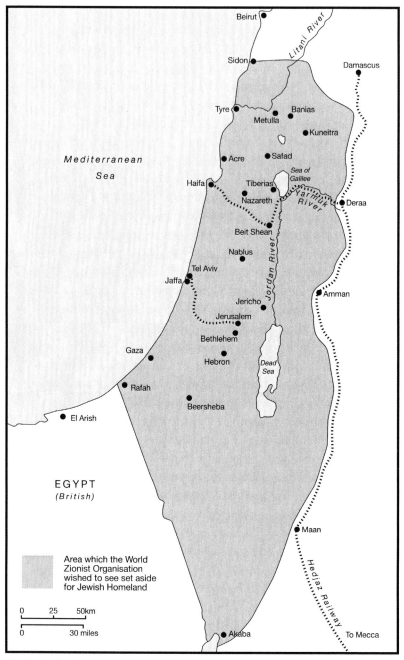

The Zionist plan for Palestine, 'Paris Peace Conference', February 1919.

and Gaza Strip but, following a successful military campaign, withdrew under pressure from the US and UK. In 1967 Israel was more successful. In addition to occupying the area west of the River Jordan, and the Gaza Strip, it gained valuable territory in the Golan Heights, which ensured the Israeli state virtually unchallenged control of the upper reaches of the River Jordan beyond Lake Kinneret (the Sea of Galilee or Lake Tiberias) and the strategic heights of Mount Herman. In 2005, in the face of continuing Palestinian harassment, Israel again withdrew from the Gaza Strip, but remains in the occupied territory (it calls it the contested territory) of the West Bank and the Golan Heights. Ironically, in some ways Lebanon has presented Israel with its greatest problems. Despite the fact that Lebanon is not Palestine and that none of the complications of contested sovereignty between Israel, Jordan and the Palestinians that surround the West Bank exist in the case of Lebanon, Israel has invaded Lebanon on three separate occasions and occupied the southern self-declared 'security zone' for more than 25 years, only to withdraw under fire in 2006.

The arrangements agreed upon at San Remo after World War I were officially recognized in the Treaty of Sèvres signed in August 1920. In March 1921, in part to clarify and hopefully resolve at least one of Britain's ambiguous promises to its Arab allies, British colonial secretary Winston Churchill authorized that the Palestine mandate east of the River Jordan be administered separately under the nominal control of the Hashemite Emir Abdullah, elder son of Arab ally Sharif al-Husayn of Mecca, answerable to the high commissioner. The League of Nations accepted this arrangement. Technically the two areas remained one mandate but most official documents referred to them as if they were two separate mandates.[1] This arrangement satisfied no one in Palestine west of the River Jordan. Abdullah's brother Feisal was threatening to attempt to reclaim Syria by force and, in August, the British installed Feisal as King of Iraq.

In June 1922 Churchill, in debates over the future of Palestine in the House of Commons, reaffirmed the Balfour Declaration while limiting Jewish immigration to meet the 'economic absorptive capacity' of Palestine. In early July 1922 the House approved accepting the Mandate and it was quickly ratified by the League of Nations. In September 1922 the British excluded Transjordan as an area in which Jews would be permitted to settle as part of a Jewish homeland. The British officially took control of the mandate in September 1923.

The decision to grant Great Britain the Mandate of Palestine was the culmination of secret negotiations that had been taking place since 1915 between France, Italy and Britain over the future partition of the Ottoman Empire after its defeat. The welter of secret agreements and public declarations both during and immediately following the hostilities resulted in misunderstanding, confusion and contradictions that have plagued the Middle East ever since. The British and French had reached an agreement on spheres of influence in the Sykes Picot Agreement of May 1916, which they revised in 1919. The British sphere of influence was to include Palestine and the vilayet (or province) of Mosul (in present-day Iraq), and in return Britain would support French influence in Syria and Lebanon. To compound what were intricate and complicated wartime negotiations, the British, through army officer Colonel T. E. Lawrence (Lawrence of Arabia), had promised the local Arabs of the Hejaz independence for a united Arab country covering most of the Arab Middle East in exchange for their support of the British against the Turks, and Egyptian high commissioner Sir Henry McMahon in correspondence with Sharif as-Sayyid Abdullah bin al-Husayn of Mecca had promised the Hashemite family lordship over most land in the region in return for their support.

The basic document setting out the responsibilities and powers of the mandatory power was the mandate instrument drawn up in London in July 1922. This document incorporated the Balfour Declaration, adding to the complexities facing Great Britain, and to the anxiety of the local and nearby Arab populations. The declaration had been issued by the British Cabinet during the war on 2 November 1917, in response to intercession by British Zionists headed by Chaim Weizmann. The mandate document opened with the statement:

Whereas the Principal Allied Powers have also agreed that the Mandatory should be responsible for putting into effect the declaration originally made on November 2nd, 1917, by the Government of His Britannic Majesty, and adopted by the said Powers, in favour of the establishment in Palestine of a national home for the Jewish people, it being clearly understood that nothing should be done which might prejudice the civil and religious rights of existing non-Jewish communities in Palestine, or the rights and political status enjoyed by Jews in any other country.[2]

Several articles of the mandate document made seemingly contradictory and incompatible demands of the British. These articles required the mandatory power to establish the political, administrative and economic conditions necessary to secure the establishment of the Jewish national home, and at the same time to develop self-governing institutions and encourage local autonomy for all the inhabitants of Palestine. Britain was to recognize the Zionist organization as the appropriate Jewish agency to bring about the establishment of the Jewish national home, and to facilitate Jewish immigration without prejudging the rights and position of the Arab population.

The issues that lay at the heart of the Arab–Israeli conflict today took shape during this period. All the parties involved in the conflict formulated positions that remain virtually unchanged almost a century later. At this early stage in the evolution of the conflict an international dimension played an ever present and important role in shaping events. The British were influenced by wider imperial concerns, the Jews by the world Zionist movement, and the Palestinian Arabs by events in the surrounding Arab world. The rise of Adolf Hitler in Europe, and restrictive US immigration laws, in particular, played a vital role in determining the rate of Jewish migration into Palestine. In their narratives of the period, both Arabs and Jews have sought to blame the British, or each other, for any events that were undesirable from their perspective, while refusing to accept any responsibility themselves. In reality, the majority on both sides viewed each other with fear, distrust, ignorance, arrogance and hostility.

Leaders recognized that two emerging national movements were fighting for supremacy over the future of Palestine. Zionist leaders, intent on transforming Palestine into a Jewish homeland (by which the majority meant a national state), had contempt for the local Arabs, and oscillated between arguing on one hand for their complete removal and on the other hand arguing that they could civilize and uplift the Arabs by introducing expertise and financial resources that would benefit all the inhabitants of Palestine. The Arabs of Palestine could not decide whether to accept those Jews content to practise their religion in traditional ways or to oppose all Jews on the grounds that if the majority Zionist immigrants achieved their goals the Arab way of life would be destroyed. Disagreements and tensions within each group were almost as profound as the divisions separating the two blocs. In the end, the triumph of those on both sides who advocated the use of force when confronted with opposition to the realization of their nationalist ambitions became so routine as to make long-term military confontation almost inevitable.

During British rule, relations between Arabs and Jews deteriorated dramatically. At first both Arabs and Jews had welcomed the British as liberators. Arabs believed they would be freed from the oppressive rule of the Ottomans and achieve independence. Zionist Jews, who had begun arriving in relatively significant numbers over the previous 30 years or so, believed that the British would facilitate the establishment of a 'national home' for the Jewish people in Palestine. In the next 28 years the ambitions of both groups were frustrated, although Britain did favour Jewish at the expense of Arab aspirations. The Arabs were particularly disillusioned. By 1948 the Jewish population had increased tenfold, from 60,000 to 650,000. Adhering to its 1917 promise, the British administrations had permitted Jewish purchases of land, the establishment of settlements, towns, industries, banks, schools and even an army.

The actions of the local Palestinian Arab population – Muslim and Christian – and the Arabs of the surrounding region toward the Jews migrating to Palestine prior to 1948 has to be understood in the context of British (and French) conduct in relation to the eastern Mediterranean following World War I. Britain and France had promised and encouraged them to think that if they supported the allies during the war they would be granted independence. Not only were the Arabs not granted independence, the very countries that had made the promises became their rulers as mandatory powers. Much of today's hypersensitivity of Palestinians stems from what they see is a Western, or Christian, failure to recognize their circumstances and their viewpoint. The West de-historicizes the Palestinian experience while, encouraged by Zionist historiography, it embraces the Jewish historical experience.

At the beginning of the mandate, the British were well aware of Arab hostility to the Zionist project. As early as the 1890s, leaders of Arab communities had expressed their opposition to Jewish land purchases. They recognized that land ownership was an essential first step in creating a political entity. The issues were not merely the increase in the number of Jews entering Palestine or even British acquiescence of the new arrivals in terms of land purchases and settlements. It was more British encouragement of Jewish participation in the governance of Palestine and the recognition of Jewish political autonomy. It is difficult to imagine the depth of disappointment, bitterness, frustration and anger Arab leaders and their followers in Palestine felt at the way things were going during the British mandate. The overwhelming sense gripping the population was one of betrayal. The post-war settlements were supposed to take account of the national aspirations of peoples like themselves who had previously been subjected to foreign rule. United States president Woodrow Wilson, however, had been unable to enforce the implementation of the provisions for independence contained in his Fourteen Points, and Palestinians, as did other Middle Eastern Arab populations, experienced a twentieth-century version of nineteenth-century colonialism.

The Arabs could accept increased Jewish migration but not statehood, especially when it had been denied to them. Although historically Jews living under Islamic rule were never free from discrimination, they were rarely subjected to persecution. Bernard Lewis has observed that:

The situation of Jews living under Islamic rule was never as bad as Christendom at its worst, nor ever as good as in Christendom at its best. There is nothing in Islamic history to parallel the Spanish expulsion and Inquisition, the Russian pogroms, or the Nazi Holocaust; there is also nothing to compare with the progressive emancipation and acceptance accorded to Jews in the democratic West during the past three centuries.[3]

Life was far more precarious for Jews living in Christendom than it was for Jews living within the Islamic Caliphate. It is crucial to recall that Zionism, and therefore Israel, is an Ashkenazim (European Jews), not a Sephardic (Middle Eastern Jews), creation. Islam was not anti-Semitic in the way Christianity was, and it is a mistake to project Christian anti-Semitism onto Muslims.

As if Jewish migration were not enough, the Jewish arrivals were European and wealthier than the local population. Using their wealth and connections they were able to purchase good land and eventually deprived the existing peasants of the fields they had traditionally cultivated. In these circumstances it is no wonder that they made poor decisions in terms of whom they sought as leaders and allies, namely Hajj Amin al-Husseini and, during World War II, Germany. They were, however, not driven by an irrational hostility to Jews in the European sense of anti-Semitism. They were driven by genuine grievances that deserve recognition and acknowledgement.

To the European powers there was nothing exceptional about this: they had been establishing colonies, dispossessing local populations and ruling them for centuries. The Arabs of the Middle East ruled by France were able to establish self-governing representative institutions with fewer problems than those under British rule. But a complicating factor in the case of Palestine was the British support for Jewish immigration and the nationalist aspirations of this group. The Zionist arrivals went about building the institutions and infrastructure they knew to be necessary preparations for statehood. The Jews of Palestine, the Yishuv, moved quickly to create their own, separate institutions of statehood. They elected their own assembly, the Vaad Leumi, built up a strong trade union and labour movement, the Histadrut, established schools, universities, medical services and legal system, and in June 1921 set up an underground defence organization, the Haganah. They ignored, or were unaware of, Arab grievances. For the most part they saw the Arabs as obstacles and regarded them with contempt, hostility and fear. They were, after all, Europeans, as well as Jews. The British – especially the army – viewed both the Arabs and Jews of Palestine with, at best, disdain and, at worst, contempt.

The Arab population was at a disadvantage because any response they made to British policies – and to the Zionist movement they supported – was interpreted as oppositional and uncooperative. This British attitude was exacerbated by the willingness of the more radical and extreme Arab nationalist leaders to foment unrest among their own people and resort to violence against the Jewish population. Arabs were divided by family and clan, and by traditional religious, cultural and economic differences between Christians and Muslims reinforced by the previous Ottoman system of self-governing autonomous confessional units. These divisions prevented them from forming a representative body and meant that they were unable or unwilling to come up with positive proposals to further their goal of national independence: as a result, they were always on the defensive. The Jewish arrivals, on the other hand, seized whatever opportunities British policy offered. Some Zionist leaders recognized the desirability of seeking accommodation with the Arabs but others, more extreme, were determined to achieve their goals by the use of violent means. Some, led by Vladimir Jabotinsky and known as Revisionist Zionists, rejected any attempts to negotiate with local Arab leaders and advocated the removal of the Arab population.

The vast majority of Zionists openly stated that their goal was the establishment of a Jewish national home in Palestine. As Europeans, they saw nothing untoward in this; ethno-cultural-religious groups had been asserting their rights to national identity throughout the previous half-century. The Arab sense of grievance was felt most keenly on the occasions of Muslim and Jewish high Holy days when crowds took to the streets of Jerusalem and other towns to observe religious rituals. The Western Wall of the Temple was a particularly sensitive site as it is the location of the last remnant of the temple built, according to Jewish scriptures, by King Solomon in the tenth century BCE and is thus sacred to Jews. And on the raised level behind the wall, the *Haram al-Sharif* (noble sanctuary), the name given to the Temple Mount, is located the furthermost mosque (from Mecca), the al-Aqsa mosque and the shrine, the Dome of the Rock, where Muslims believe Mohammed ascended into the seventh heaven and is thus sacred to Muslims. The religious hierarchies of both groups were therefore justifiably fearful of the intentions of one another, and fiercely guarded against any infringement of their traditional rights and practices. They correctly recognized in these observances, if not a political agenda, certainly the political overtones and implications for the future of Jerusalem and the holy sites. Frequently these activities got out of hand and riots occurred.

The first major Arab–Jewish riot under British rule occurred in Jerusalem in April 1920 during the Muslim pilgrim festivity of Nabi-Musa, which coincided in that year with Easter and the intermediary days of Passover.[4] This riot is illustrative of events that were to become a pattern that has continued to the present. The Jerusalem riot, which lasted four days from 4 April to 7 April, followed rising tensions in Arab–Jewish relations over Zionist immigration, which had spilled over into skirmishes at Jewish settlements in the Galilee. On 1 March 1920, during a gun-fight in defence of Tel Hai, a settlement in the Upper Galilee, Joseph Trumpeldor, a Zionist activist and member of the local Jewish self-defence team, and others were killed.

At about the same time, a coup in Damascus installed Emir Faisal as king of Syria. On 4 April 1920 between 60,000 and 70,000 Arabs congregated in Jerusalem's Old City square. Anti-British and anti-Zionist speeches were delivered by nationalist and religious leaders, including 22-year-old Hajj Amin al-Husseini and Jerusalem mayor Musa Kazem Pasha al-Husseini, to Muslim pilgrims gathered at the Haram al-Sharif prior to their journey to the tomb of

Moses near Jericho. Rioting then broke out and Arab gangs attacked Jews in the Old City. The British military administration's erratic response failed to contain the rioting, which continued for four days. Nine people were killed, including five Jews, and 244 were injured, 211 of whom were Jews. The leaders of both sides were arrested, but all were later released.

A military commission of enquiry into the riots on 1 July 1920 concluded that the Zionists were largely responsible for the disturbances because their impatience to achieve their ultimate goal and their indiscretions had substantially increased the sense of disappointment and frustration among the Arab population. The commissioners singled out Hajj Amin al-Husseini and Jabotinsky in particular for aggravating the sense of distrust between the British, Jews, and Arabs. These admonitions spurred Zionists to build an autonomous infrastructure and security apparatus parallel to that of the British administration. Believing that the British were unwilling to defend Jews from continuous Arab violence, Zionists proceeded to set up the Haganah in June 1921.

In return for assurances about keeping the peace, the British High Commissioner, Sir Herbert Samuel, appointed Hajj Amin al-Husseini as Mufti (senior religious leader) of Jerusalem to succeed his father. Musa Pasha al-Husseini was replaced as mayor by Ragheb Bey Nashashibi. Whether or not it was the purpose of the Zionist high commissioner, these appointments exacerbated the simmering rivalry between the Husseini, Nashashibi and other 'notable' Arab families. Shortly after, in 1921, Hajj Amin was elected president of a newly established Supreme Muslim Council and within a short time had established himself as the most powerful Muslim in Palestine. He went on to become the leader of the Palestinian Arab nationalist movement. He did so partly by exploiting Muslim sensibilities toward the sanctity of Jerusalem and its sacred shrines like Haram al-Sharif and the threat to them posed by the actions of newly arrived over-zealous Jewish/Zionist immigrants.

Following the Nabi Musa riots, High Commissioner Samuel urged Colonial Secretary Winston Churchill to clarify the meaning of the Balfour Declaration. In early June 1922 Churchill presented his White Paper to Arab and Jewish delegations in London. Churchill's statement did little to clarify British policy or to reassure either party. Although around 25,000 Jewish immigrants had arrived in Palestine since British occupation, the colonial secretary asserted that the government had never 'at any time contemplated, as appears to be feared by the Arab Delegation, the disappearance or the subordination of the Arabic population, language or culture in Palestine.'[5] But there was nothing in the White Paper about British support for Arab national aspirations, simply a ruling out of Arabs' worst fears of Jewish nationalism on the grounds that it was impracticable in all of Palestine.

And while Zionists may have been disappointed that the White Paper limited Jewish immigration, stating that it should not 'be so great in volume as to exceed whatever may be the economic capacity of the country at the time to absorb new arrivals', Churchill went on to assert that it was 'essential' that the Jewish community, which at that time numbered about 80,000 (or about 10 per cent of the total population of Palestine), 'should know that it is in Palestine as of right and not on sufferance. That is the reason why it is necessary that the existence of a Jewish National Home in Palestine should be internationally guaranteed, and that it should be formally recognized to rest upon ancient historic connection.' This document was hardly reassuring to Arabs, and it was rejected by the Arab delegation. The Jewish delegation accepted it because it did not preclude the eventual establishment of a Jewish state in Palestine.[6]

After the initial post-war surge of Jewish immigration, there were a few years of relative calm in Palestine. In some years, Jewish emigration even exceeded immigration. However, Arab and Jewish religious sensibilities over Jewish activities at the Western Wall in Jerusalem remained volatile. The issues revolved about customary religious practices, access and, ultimately, ownership. One of the responsibilities of the Mufti of Jerusalem was ensuring that traditional forms of prayer and worship were observed in the vicinity of the Western Wall and protecting the shrines on the Haram al-Sharif from Jewish encroachment. Although the majority of Zionists lived in Tel Aviv and country towns rather than in Jerusalem, Jewish religious zealots sometimes utilized the wall to rally nationalist sentiment.[7] Rumours contributed to fear and suspicion on both sides. In September 1928 small-scale violence again took place during Yom Kippur prayers.

On 15 August the following year, 1929, in a sequence of events that were repeated in similar fashion by Ariel Sharon in 2001 with much the same outcome: members of the Revisionist party escorted by a heavy police presence assembled at the wall shouting 'the wall is ours'.[8] The next day, after an inflammatory Muslim sermon, serious violence against Jews in Jerusalem, Safed and

Hebron led to hundreds of Jews and Arabs losing their lives or being injured. During the week of riots, 133 Jews were killed and 339 were wounded (mostly by Arabs), 116 Arabs were killed and 232 wounded (mostly by British-commanded police and soldiers). An official inquiry reached similar conclusions to previous investigations, and the subsequent White Paper issued in 1930 recommended that land sales to Jews and Jewish immigration be suspended. The Zionist-led hostile reaction was so great that the recommendations were never put into effect.

During the 1930s developments in Europe once again played an important role in shaping events in Palestine, this time leading Zionist leaders to think about the feasibility of partition. Denied more suitable alternatives, thousands of Jews sought refuge in Palestine from rising and increasingly virulent anti-Semitism, especially in Germany. In 1936 the followers of Sheikh Izz al-Din al-Qassam, killed by the British the year before, called a general strike in Jaffa and Nablus to protest the increased inflow of Jews, and as a response to Jewish companies and farms exclusively hiring Jewish labour. Hajj Amin al-Husseini, then president of the newly formed Arab High Committee, a coalition of political parties, was also prominent. Yet again London responded with an inquiry, this time a royal commission chaired by Lord Peel. In its report, issued in July 1937, the commission called for the partition of Palestine into an Arab state (to be joined to Transjordan) and a smaller Jewish state. Jerusalem, and the immediate surrounding towns including Bethlehem, together with a corridor to the coast at Jaffa, was to remain a British mandate. Haifa was also to remain under English rule.

Following vigorous debate among themselves, Zionists accepted the concept of partition but demanded more advantageous boundaries for the Jewish state. They recognized that there was little chance of Christians allowing Jerusalem to be included in a Jewish state. Arab leadership was divided, but the Husseini family, who totally rejected the notion, succeeded in silencing the Nashashibi family, who were attracted to it. Strikes and Arab violence against Jews continued and violence escalated. In 1937 a strike escalated into a full blown rebellion with attacks on British and Jewish buildings and people. The Arab High Committee was dissolved and leaders of the Supreme Muslim Council were arrested. Between 1936 and 1939 fighting between Arabs, Jews and the British claimed several thousand lives and inflicted massive property damage. By 1938 the British had 20,000 troops trying to restore law and order.

More than 500 Jews were killed by Arabs, while between 4,000 and 5,000 Arabs were killed in Jewish and British attacks (and in attacks between rival Arab factions). In May 1939, cognizant of the need to cultivate regional Arab loyalty in what seemed an inevitable approach of war in Europe, the British released a White Paper designed to placate the Palestinian Arabs and end their revolt. The Macdonald White Paper declared that an undivided Palestine would be granted independence after ten years. Jewish immigration over the next five years was to be limited to 75,000, and Jewish land sales were greatly restricted. Whitehall justified its position on the grounds that the conditions of the Balfour Declaration had been fulfilled as a 'national home in Palestine for the Jewish people' had been established. British responsibility now, it stated, was to assist the majority population, the Arabs, gain independence; presumably this meant Arab statehood. The likelihood of a Jewish state reaching fruition under these circumstances seemed remote.

The Arabs stated that ten years was too long to wait, but they believed they had triumphed. Their revolt came to an end, so the British succeeded in that respect. The Jewish population was bitterly disappointed, but resolved to continue their, increasingly violent, struggle for a state. The outbreak of World War II in September 1939 strengthened their resolve; even this unpalatable British policy was preferable to a victory by Nazi Germany. David Ben-Gurion declared: 'We will fight the White Paper as if there is no war, and fight the war as if there is no White Paper.'[9] The war, and its aftermath, provided the opportunity for Zionists to achieve their goal of establishing a Jewish state in Palestine.

CHAPTER 3

The First Arab–Israeli War

The first Arab–Israeli War, fought between 15 May 1948 and early 1949, known by Israelis as the War of Independence, and by Palestinians as *al-Nakba* ('the Catastrophe'), was, in reality, the continuation of a civil war that had begun in November 1947 when the General Assembly of the newly formed UN, then located in Lake Success, New York, voted to partition the British Mandate of Palestine into a Jewish and an Arab state with an international enclave surrounding Jerusalem (including Bethlehem). The Palestinian Arabs could never have accepted Zionism as a just cause. They regarded the Israelis as foreign intruders who had invaded their land, and from their point of view they were right. Nor were they responsible for the destruction of European Jewry, for which they were now being asked to pay the price. Equally, the Zionists could not have accepted anything less than a Jewish state in Palestine. There were some among them who believed that there was enough room for everone, but so far at least they have been proved wrong.

So the war of 1948 was inevitable, and the issue of whether or not there would be a Jewish state established was decided by military force. It is not usual for a people to voluntarily give up their homeland to an incoming population. Nevertheless, both sides must share the responsibility for the outcome. As Meron Benvenisti notes, 'war is devoid of human values'. It is also important to remember that had the Arabs won the war of 1948–9 it is unlikely that they would have been any more concerned with the fate of the Zionists than Israelis have been with the fate of the Palestinians.[1]

At the outbreak of World War II the chairman of the Jewish Agency in Palestine, David Ben-Gurion, had resolved that the Agency would fight the British as if there were no war and to fight the war as if there were no White Paper. As the Nazi death camps continued their murderous tasks unabated, the Jewish Agency had agonized over how best to assist the Jews of Europe. In addition to offering to form Jewish fighting units with the British against the Germans in North Africa (27,000 Jews enlisted with British forces), their answer had been to organize illegal immigration from Europe and to work primarily toward building the political and military infrastructure necessary to establish a Jewish state in Palestine. In both ventures they had been opposed by the Arabs of Palestine and by the British authorities. Some attempts to transport illegal immigrants to Palestine ended in tragedy. In 1940 more than 250 lives were lost when the *Patria* sank and another 280 drowned a few weeks later when the SS *Bulgaria* capsized after being ordered back to Europe from Haifa. On 24 February 1942 the *Struma* was torpedoed with the loss of more than 760 refugees.

The Arabs of Palestine had remained somewhat apprehensive and quiet throughout the war. The mufti of Jerusalem, Hajj Amin al-Husseini, had fled overland to Germany, from where he broadcast appeals to his fellow Arabs to ally with the Axis powers against Britain and Zionism. The mufti failed, however, to rally Palestinian Arabs to the Axis cause. Although some supported Germany, the majority supported the Allies and many (approximately 23,000) enlisted in the British forces (especially in the Arab Legion). Increases in agricultural prices benefited the Arab peasants, who began to pay accumulated debts. British war activities, although they brought new levels of prosperity, weakened the old traditional social institutions – the family and village – by fostering a large Arab working urban class.

The end of World War II brought about a dramatic change in the state of affairs. The question of Palestine, internationalized by the mandate in the aftermath of World War I, again became the focus of international attention. During and immediately following World War I the oil resources of the Middle East and the strategic importance of Palestine emerged as major considerations for the victorious allies. The United States of America and the United Kingdom were concerned about the supply of oil for the war effort and for the reconstruction of post-war Europe. Both wanted to reassure the Arab world of their friendship.

In early 1945, following the Yalta conference, President Franklin Roosevelt had met with King Abdul-Aziz Ibn Saud of Saudi Arabia and promised him that no decision would be made concerning the future of Palestine without full consultation with both Arabs and Jews. Washington, however, did not want to become directly involved, certainly not militarily involved, in the growing troubles between Jews and Arabs in Palestine. The British government wanted to retain its control of Palestine, especially of the strategic oil port of Haifa. Post-war tensions soon emerged between the allies, and the US and UK both wanted to ensure that the Soviet Union did not project its power into the Middle East.

The Jewish Agency, and related Zionist organizations in the US and UK, took the initiative and renewed their diplomatic offensive to further the formation of a state. Proposals concerning the future of the displaced persons became an indispensable tool. The solution to the problem, the Zionists asserted, was to allow the displaced persons to go to the only place in the world where they would be welcomed and safe, namely a Jewish homeland in Palestine.

The British government opposed the notion for two principal reasons. The first was that it would in a sense feel like completing the work of Hitler, namely ridding Europe of its Jewish population, and the second was that the arrival of so many Jews in Palestine was opposed by oil-rich ally Saudi Arabia and other Arab states. Whitehall believed that securing a reliable and cheap source of oil with which to reconstruct the UK and Europe was far more important than the fate of a few thousand displaced persons, especially given the price the Allies had already paid to defeat an expanding Nazi Germany. Neither Britain, nor the US, felt they could afford to upset or alienate the oil-producing Arab states by proposing something they strenuously objected to and promised to resist with the use of force if necessary, thereby jeopardizing oil supplies to Europe. Nevertheless, the Zionists persisted, rallying supporters around the globe for the scheme. In this they were helped by developments in Palestine and other parts of the British Empire, as well as the mounting costs to the US treasury of supporting the displaced persons camps and American occupation troops in Germany. In 1947–8 the Palestinian Arab cause did have the indirect support of a number of senior members of the US state and defence departments who did not support the idea of a Jewish state, a view shared by the UK Foreign Office.

The British and US defence establishments were particularly anxious to prevent the migration into Palestine of European Jewish refugees or Jews from the Soviet Union. They imagined the new arrivals would be imbued with communist, or at the very least socialist, ideology. At a time when the Soviet Union was extending its power and influence into Greece and Iran, London and Washington did not want a Jewish state, especially one populated by communists, established in the eastern Mediterranean. They believed it would threaten the region's fragile stability and warned that future United States access to Middle East oil could be jeopardized. In Washington this position was overruled by the White House. The Soviet Union, however, welcomed the idea of partition and the founding of a Jewish state in Palestine. It saw it as a way of extending its influence into the region; Moscow believed that the predominantly socialist ideology of the Israeli leaders would provide the Soviet Union with an ally. A Jewish state would also hasten the departure of Britain from at least one area of the Middle East.

These post-World War II developments led neighbouring Arab countries to take a more direct interest in Palestine. In October 1944 Arab heads of state had met at Alexandria, Egypt, and issued a statement, the Alexandria Protocol, setting out the Arab position. They made clear that although they regretted the tragedy inflicted upon European Jewry by European dictatorships, solving the problem of surviving European Jewry, they asserted, should not be achieved by inflicting injustice on Palestinian Arabs. The covenant of the League of Arab Nations (or Arab League), formed in March 1945, appointed an Arab Higher Executive for Palestine (the Arab Higher Committee), which included a broad spectrum of Palestinian leaders, as spokesman for the Palestinian Arabs. In December 1945 the League declared a boycott of Zionist goods. The pattern of the struggle for Palestine was unmistakably emerging.

Following World War II, in Palestine the Jewish Agency also resumed its insurgency activities against British rule and the Arabs. The group known as Lehi ('Fighters for the Freedom of Israel', popularly referred to as the Stern gang after their leader Abraham Stern) had been active during the war. In November 1944 members of Lehi assassinated Lord Moyne, minister of state for the Middle East and an anti-Zionist, in Cairo. Moyne, a close personal friend of Winston Churchill, had been responsible for the terms of the 1939 White Paper limiting Jewish immigration to Palestine. Fearing a British negative backlash over Moyne's assassination, the Haganah arrested members of the two most prominent insurgency groups, Lehi and Irgun, handing over around 1,000 to the British authorities. This did not deter the Jewish terrorist groups who united to drive the British out by force. In particular, Lehi and *Irgun* were responsible for the bombing of trains and train stations, and the kidnapping and murder of several British troops and Arabs throughout Palestine. Probably the most infamous incident was the blowing up of the British headquarters in Jerusalem's Hotel David in 1947, where approximately 90 people were killed.

The British lacked the resources to fight a prolonged and determined resistance movement, although by the end of 1945 the British garrison in Palestine was strengthened to 80,000 personnel (50,000 troops, supported by 30,000 civilians) trying to keep the peace and defend themselves against terrorist attacks. The UK was virtually bankrupt. The United States was of little help, pressurizing the newly elected Labour government to allow Jewish displaced persons entry to Palestine but refusing to get actively involved in the larger Palestine question. Concerned over the conditions of the displaced persons and the ongoing costs of administering the camps, the new US president Harry S. Truman in November 1945 agreed to an Anglo-American Committee of Inquiry (AACI), which recommended in April 1946 that Britain authorize the immediate admission of 100,000 Jewish displaced persons to Palestine and that Palestine be placed under a UN trusteeship. Truman's request indicated that the United States intended to play a role in determining the future of Palestine.

The AACI painted a grim picture of Palestine at the time. The commissioners noted that in the nine years since the Peel Commission report:

> The gulf between the Arabs of Palestine and the Arab world on the one side, and the Jews of Palestine and elsewhere on the other has widened still further. Neither side seems at all disposed at the present to make any sincere effort to reconcile either their superficial or their fundamental differences. The Arabs view the Mandatory Government with misgivings and anger. It is not only condemned verbally, but attacked with bombs and firearms by organized bands of Jewish terrorists. The Palestine Administration appears to be powerless to keep the situation under control except by the display use of very large forces.[2]

The predicament was reflected in the large prison population: 'Apart from those convicted of terrorist activity, the number of Jews held on suspicion averaged 450 during most of the year 1945 and was 554 at the end of the year.

The aggregate of persons in the whole-time police and prisons service of Palestine in 1945 was about 15,000.'

The report described conditions in Palestine that read remarkably like a description of the West Bank today:

> In consequence of these conditions, the Holy Land is scarred by shocking incongruities. Army tents, tanks, a grim fort and barracks overlook the waters of the Sea of Galilee. Blockhouses, road barriers manned by soldiers, barbed wire entanglements, tanks in the streets, peremptory searches, seizures and arrests on suspicion, bombings by gangsters and shots in the night are now characteristic. A curfew is enforced, and the press of Palestine is subject to censorship. Palestine has become a garrisoned but restive land, and there is little probability that the tranquillity dear to people of good will, Jews, Moslems and Christians alike, will be restored until vastly better relations are established among the principal elements of the community, including the Administration.[3]

The AACI report, however, satisfied no one. Despite its balanced approach, it was unrealistic; neither Jews nor Arabs were going to accept a further period of foreign domination, however well intentioned. The Commissioners concluded:

> We have reached the conclusion that the hostility between Jews and Arabs and, in particular, the determination of each to achieve domination, if necessary by violence, make it almost certain that, now and for some time to come, any attempt to establish either an independent Palestinian State or independent Palestinian States would result in civil strife such as might threaten the peace of the world.
>
> We therefore recommend that, until this hostility disappears, the Government of Palestine be continued as at present under mandate pending the execution of a trusteeship agreement under the United Nations.

Finally, the report accurately but somewhat helplessly observed, 'in the light of its long history, and particularly its history of the last thirty years, Palestine cannot be regarded as either a purely Arab or a purely Jewish land.'[4]

The Jewish Agency welcomed that section of the Anglo-American report recommending immigration. The Arabs sought to pressure the British into preventing such a proposal, but Arab leadership had been decimated by the British during the Arab uprising prior to the war and during the war it had either fled or was imprisoned. Truman for his part angered the British by advocating that 100,000 Jews be allowed entry to Palestine, and ignoring the rest of the report. Given the subsequent course of events it is interesting to speculate on what might have eventuated had the UN been willing to take up the burden of a trusteeship of Palestine proposed by the AACI, rather than wash its hands of the matter.

Faced with even more troubling events in the 'Jewel in the Crown' of the British Empire, India, where Mahatma Gandhi was mounting a massive drive for independence, on 2 April 1947 the British reluctantly handed the future of Palestine to the fledgling United Nations for resolution. In August, India was partitioned into two independent states, India and Pakistan, a piece of political surgery that was followed by massive outbreaks of violence and a huge population exchange, a portent of what was to befall Palestine.

Palestine was the first world issue the United Nations was called upon to adjudicate. Members of the new body took their responsibility seriously, convening an eleven-nation Special Committee on Palestine (UNSCOP) in May 1947 (Australia, Canada, Czechoslovakia, Guatemala, India, Iran, Netherlands, Peru, Sweden, Uruguay and Yugoslavia). UNSCOP held hearings in the displaced persons camps, in the UK, in Palestine and in Arab states. It made a 2,200-mile fifteen-day tour of Palestine, a five-day trip to Lebanon and Syria, a one-day visit to the King of Transjordan in Amman, and a 2,700-mile seven-day tour of displaced persons camps in Germany and Austria. The Arabs in the Mandate area refused to cooperate with the Committee. The Arab Higher Committee also refused to cooperate with UNSCOP and demanded that the UN grant Palestine its independence.

In its report to the General Assembly on 31 August 1947, UNSCOP recommended unanimously that the British mandate should be terminated and that Palestine be granted independence. A majority recommended that Palestine be partitioned and constituted into an Arab state and a Jewish state, both to become independent after a transitional period of two years beginning on 1 September 1947. The city of Jerusalem was to be placed under the International Trusteeship System by means of a trusteeship agreement designating the United Nations as the administering authority. The three recommended entities – Arab state, Jewish state and internationalized Jerusalem – were to be linked in an economic union. This recommendation was supported by seven members of the committee (Canada, Czechoslovakia, Guatemala, Netherlands, Peru, Sweden and Uruguay). The minority – India, Iran and Yugoslavia – proposed an independent federal state, comprising an Arab state and a Jewish state, with Jerusalem its capital. Australia abstained.

The United Nations proposal to partition Palestine in 1947 was not a new idea; as noted earlier, it had first been put forward formally by the British government's Peel Commission in 1937. But the major impetus for the 1947 decision came from considerations in relation to the future of Jewish displaced persons who had survived the Nazi genocide directed against Jews. Of the pre-war European Jewish population of seven million, fewer than one million survived the war. By the end of 1945, more than 100,000 of the survivors were located in displaced persons camps in the western sector of Germany controlled by the United States, and a year later this figure had swelled to 250,000. The US Army, under Supreme Allied Commander General Dwight D. Eisenhower, was responsible for the administration of the displaced persons camps and within a short time neither the army nor the camp residents were very happy with each other. The options facing the Jewish survivors were bleak. As was the case prior to and during the war, few nations appeared willing to accept large numbers as immigrants. The first choice of many, the United States, was reluctant to lift its restrictive quota on immigrants. The UK, exhausted by the war effort, was not in a position to take many. Canada, South Africa, Australia and Latin American countries were not especially appealing destinations to many Jews. One group, however, was ready and willing to accept their fellow co-religionists, the Jewish Agency in Palestine.

The General Assembly constituted itself into an Ad-Hoc Committee to consider the two UNSCOP proposals. Between 25 September and 25 November the committee held 34 meetings. Both the Jewish Agency and the Arab Higher Committee, who had by now realized their error in not cooperating with UNSCOP, made presentations. On 25 November 1947 the Ad Hoc Committee passed what was essentially an amended version of the UNSCOP majority partition proposal for consideration by the General Assembly. The amendments slightly altered the boundaries and the populations of the two proposed states. Jaffa was to be an Arab enclave in the Jewish state, and the Arab population of the Jewish state was to be reduced. The final outcome was as follows: the Arab state was to occupy 4,500 square miles and contain approximately 800,000 Arabs and 10,000 Jews. The Jewish state was to be an area of 5,500 square miles and contain 538,000 Jews and 397,000 Arabs. With about 32 per cent of the population, the Jews would get 56 per cent of the territory; the Arabs would get 42 per cent of the land. The Jerusalem area, including Bethlehem, with 100,000 Jews and an equal number of Palestinians, was to become a *Corpus Separatum*, to be administered by the UN.

On 29 November 1947 the General Assembly, in UN Resolution 181, voted in favour of the partition of Palestine by a vote of thirty-three to thirteen, with ten abstentions. The Muslim countries (together with India, Yugoslavia and Greece) voted against partition. The United States and the Soviet bloc (together with several other nations, including France and Australia) supported partition. Although many construed partition as an American plan, Latin American and European nations supported partition in part because Catholics liked the special international status planned for Jerusalem.

It is now taken for granted that the passage of the UN partition resolution in November 1947 virtually assured a Jewish state in Palestine in that it liquidated the mandate, defined a legal framework in which the Yishuv could establish a state, and gave to the Haganah a definite goal around which it could rally its forces. The situation was not nearly so clear in early December 1947. In Sydney, a former governor general of Australia, Sir Isaac Isaacs publicly stated that the partition resolution 'had broken the express terms on which Britain had accepted the mandate', something he regretted.[5] The *Sydney Morning Herald* editorialized that: 'Time alone will show the wisdom of this momentous decision.' Under the banner headline: 'Palestine Crisis a Supreme Test for UNO', the *Herald* reported that there was considerable doubt and misgivings in diplomatic circles in New York as to whether the United Nations had the legal right to partition the country against the will of the majority. The newspaper raised the even more important question as to the practical means of enforcing the decision should the Arabs resort, as they did, to armed force and the matter went before the Security Council.

The *Herald* pointed out that the UN was not yet equipped to enforce its will. The paper warned that if the decisions of the General Assembly were challenged by war the whole fabric of collective security created to protect the world from the horrors of atomic warfare would fail. The *Herald* urged the

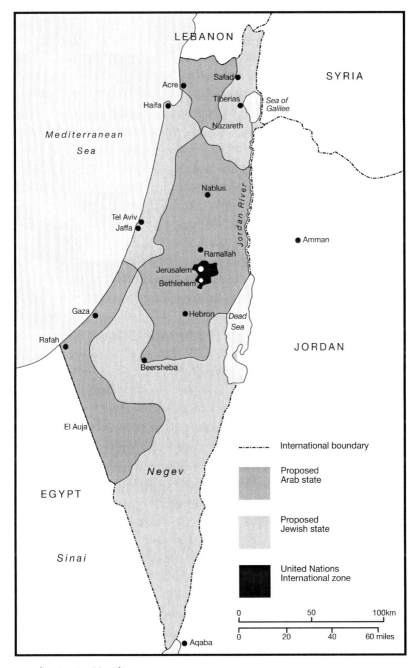

United Nations Partition Plan, 1947.

Arab states, despite their disappointment, to accept the decision, otherwise 'Armageddon may yet be fought on the plains of Palestine.'[6] The signs were ominous. A leading Arab spokesman in London stated that: 'UNO has set the Arabs and Jews in the Middle East irrevocably against each other and made war inevitable', and pointed out that the UN charter authorized member states to oppose aggression, by force if necessary.[7] Perhaps attempting to placate Arab hostility, world leader of the Jewish Agency, Chaim Weizmann, in a speech delivered in New York on 30 November, made the remarkable statement that there would be no mass migration of Jews from Europe to Palestine when the new Jewish state was created. On 4 December 1947 the British announced that they would depart from Palestine in August of the following year, but many predicted an earlier date, in May.

The next months were full of uncertainty and confusion. Jewish celebrations were matched by Arab determination to prevent partition's realization. Efforts by moderate Arab and Jewish leaders to prevent bloodshed failed. Murders, reprisals and counter-reprisals took place, killing dozens of victims on both sides. Both sides resorted to terrorist atrocities against each other, especially in the major cities, with little regard for noncombatants or women and children. In one series of attacks and retaliation, in December 1947, Jewish terrorists (Irgun or Lehi members) threw bombs at a group of Arab oil refinery workers in Haifa, killing six and wounding 42. The Arabs then rioted and killed 41 Jews and wounded 48 before being dispersed by British troops.

Two days later, Haganah members disguised as Arabs entered a village close to Haifa and killed approximately 60 people, including a number of women and children, to avenge the Jewish deaths in the port city. British forces, who were withdrawing in a state of virtual collapse, found it increasingly difficult to be even-handed. During the period December 1947 through January 1948, it was estimated that nearly 1,000 people were killed and 2,000 people were injured. By the end of March the figure had risen to 2,000 dead and 4,000 wounded. These figures correspond to an average of more than 100 deaths and 200 casualties per week – in a population of 2,000,000. During this initial stage up to 100,000 Palestinians, chiefly those from the upper classes, sought refuge abroad or in eastern Palestine. The British devoted their energies to preparation for their evacuation and refused to assume responsibility for implementing the partition plan. From January onwards operations became more warlike, with the intervention into Palestine of a number of Arab Liberation Army (ALA) regiments organized, trained and armed by Syria for the Arab League states. At first the ALA had considerable success and the Haganah was forced on the defensive.

The British, meanwhile, resigned to the emergence of a Jewish state, favoured uniting the Arab areas of Palestine with Transjordan into a 'Greater Transjordan' under King Abdullah, who became king in 1946 when Britain recognized Transjordan's independence. On 7 February 1948 Foreign Minister Ernest Bevin informed Jordan's prime minister in London that Britain would support Transjordan's annexation of the Arab part of Palestine when the British left, using the Arab Legion if necessary. The Jewish Agency, Abdullah and the British had a common interest in preventing a Palestinian state headed by al-Husseini. Abdullah had long sought to control Arab Palestine and there had been contacts over the years with officials of the Jewish Agency about their mutual interests.

Shortly before the UN partition resolution was approved, in early November 1947, Abdullah had met with senior representatives of the Jewish Agency, including Golda Meir, acting head of the agency's political department. An understanding was reached in which the Agency agreed to Abdullah's annexation of Arab Palestine; in return, Abdullah promised not to stand in the way of the establishment of a Jewish state. Another meeting was to have followed the vote on partition, but owing to the tumult in Palestine, it did not take place. There was one last meeting between Meir and the king just before the partition plan was to take effect, but by then the demands on the king to fight against the Jews were too great. The outbreak of hostilities provided him with an opportunity to cross the Jordan and annex central Palestine, whether or not a Jewish state came into being.

By late February the chaotic situation led Truman to the view that partition should be replaced by a temporary UN trusteeship. This encouraged the Arab League to believe that the Palestinians, with the aid of the Arab Liberation Army, could now put an end to the partition plan. On 19 March, in the Security Council, US ambassador Warren W. Austin called for a suspension of all efforts aimed at partition and asked for a special meeting of the General Assembly to approve a temporary United Nations trusteeship for a period of five years. Secretary of State George C. Marshall was afraid that partition might require implementation by the use of UN forces – he estimated upwards of 100,000 troops. Soviet troops would then be involved and they would probably remain, dangerously close to Greece, Turkey and the Arabian oil fields vital for the European recovery programme. The fact that the Soviets were looking for a warm-water port also added to the threat of Soviet military in the area. The only solution, Marshall believed, was to turn the matter over to the UN Trusteeship Council, where the Soviets were not represented, so the danger of Soviet military intervention would be avoided.

During April the Israeli forces, armed with a shipment of weapons that arrived from communist-controlled Czechoslovakia, took the offensive. Arab leader Adb al-Qadir al-Husayni was killed, and all the towns and villages within the designated Jewish state were occupied. Tiberias was captured on 18 April and Haifa on 22–3 April. Most of Haifa's 70,000 Arabs fled, many to Lebanon. By early May the Haganah also had control of Jaffa and most of eastern Galilee. But East Jerusalem remained in Arab hands.

By 2 May the Israelis had carved out for themselves a state roughly equivalent to that approved by the United Nations in November 1947. The Jews went ahead with plans to announce an independent state on 14 May. On the morning of 14 May 1948 the Union Jack was hauled down from Government House in Jerusalem for the last time and, as the British high commissioner, Sir Alan Gordon Cunningham, sailed out of Haifa at 11:30 pm that night, the mandate came to an end.

About 4 pm on the afternoon of Friday 14 May 1948, in the assembly hall of the Tel Aviv art museum, with a photo of Theodore Herzl, the founder of modern Zionism, on the wall behind him, stood David Ben-Gurion, the 61-year-old Polish-born head of the Jewish National Council. He read to the 350 assembled members and guests an announcement proclaiming the establishment and independence of Israel, 'by virtue of our natural and historic right and on the strength of the resolution of the United Nations General Assembly'.[8] The declaration of independence took the prime minister and minister of defence of the newly created provisional government seventeen minutes to read. As members of the council signed the declaration, the Palestine Philharmonic Orchestra played 'Hatikvah', which was the new state's national anthem. The declaration of independence did not define the borders of the new state, although it did extend 'an offer of peace and good neighbourliness' to the Arab states.

Eleven minutes later President Harry S. Truman extended de facto recognition to the new state. Truman's decision to do this to the new state has raised considerable controversy over the past 60 years. Many argue that it was motivated by political considerations rather than by calculations of the national interest. In later years Truman himself basked in the praise lavished upon him by Israelis and their supporters for his swift action. Yet when in 1965 I asked him about this decision he merely observed that 'something had to be done, so I did it', which accurately reflects the essence of the man. The same kind of comment may be made about the president's meeting with his former Kansas City haberdashery partner Eddy Jacobson in April 1948, in which he agreed to see Chaim Weizman and reassured the future Israeli president that the US would not back away from partition. This Truman–Jacobson meeting has been given considerable attention by historians, myself included. Yet when called upon to unveil a bust of Jacobson in Independence, Missouri, in 1965 to commemorate Jacobson's role, Truman said nothing about this meeting, or Israel. Again revealing his pragmatic approach to life, he simply stated: 'Eddy Jacobson was a good friend of mine. Always there when I needed him', and sat down.

Just before midnight the same day, 14 May 1948, King Abdullah of Transjordan, standing on the eastern side of the Allenby Bridge across the River Jordan, fired his revolver into the air, so signalling his army, the Arab Legion, to enter and occupy the area on the west bank of the river the UN had allotted to the Arab state. Early on the morning of 15 May troops from Egypt, Syria, Iraq and Lebanon, together with volunteers from Saudi Arabia and Libya, entered Palestine to support local Palestinian irregular forces and the Arab League's Arab Liberation army. The Arab League of Arab States informed the UN Secretary-General on 15 May that their aim was to create a 'United State of Palestine' in place of the two-state UN plan. They also claimed it was necessary to intervene to protect Arab lives and property. The first Arab–Israeli war had entered a new phase.[9] Three days later, on 17 May, the Soviet Union extended full *de jure* recognition of the new state, ensuring that the dispute between Israel and the Arabs would become entwined in the developing Cold War between the two super powers and their allies. (The US extended *de jure* recognition following elections held in January 1949.)

On 15 May the first of around 1,000 Lebanese, 5,000 Syrian, 5,000 Iraqi and 10,000 Egyptian troops, with a few Saudi Arabian, Libyan and Yemenite volunteers, crossed the frontiers of Palestine with the intention of establishing a unitary Palestinian state. The first all-out Arab–Israeli war had begun. Israel, the United States and the Soviets called the Arab states' entry into Palestine illegal aggression. The primary goal of the Arab governments, according to historian Yoav Gelber, was to prevent the total ruin of the Palestinians and the flooding of their own countries by more refugees.[10] On 26 May 1948 the Israeli Defence Forces (IDF) was officially established and the Haganah, Palmach and Irgun were absorbed into the army of the new Jewish state. As the war progressed, the IDF managed to mobilize more troops than the Arab forces. By July 1948 the IDF was fielding 63,000 troops; by early spring 1949, 115,000. The Arab armies had an estimated 40,000 troops in July 1948, rising to 55,000 in October 1948, and slightly more by the spring of 1949.

The war consisted of three short phases of violence, each followed by a truce. In the first phase, from 14 May to 11 June 1948, the Arab Legion captured Jerusalem but the Israeli forces defended their settlements and their territory against the Egyptians, Iraqis and Lebanese. The UN mediator, Folke Bernadotte, declared a truce on 29 May that came into effect on 11 June and lasted 28 days. In the second phase of fighting, from 8 to 18 July 1948, Israeli forces secured and enlarged the corridor between Jerusalem and Tel Aviv, capturing the road-side cities Lydda (later renamed Lod) and Ramle. Following the seizure of these cities, the Israelis forced the 50,000 residents to leave – the largest single exodus of the war. Israelis also captured the area in the north between Haifa and the Sea of Galilee. A second truce lasted from 18 July to 15 October. On 16 September Bernadotte proposed a new plan in which Transjordan would annex Arab areas including the Negev, al-Ramla and Lydda, Galilee would be allocated to Israel, Jerusalem internationalized, and Arab refugees be allowed to return home or receive compensation. The plan was rejected by both sides. On the next day Bernadotte was assassinated by the Lehi and was immediately replaced by his deputy, an American, Ralph Bunche.

The last phase of the war lasted from 15 October 1948 to 7 January 1949. In this final stage Israel drove out the Arab armies and secured its borders. Israel signed separate armistices with Egypt on 24 February 1949, Lebanon on 23 March, Transjordan on 3 April, and Syria on 20 July. Israeli casualties amounted to 6,000 killed (4,000 soldiers and 2,000 civilians). Arab losses are estimated at between 10,000 and 15,000 killed.

The new borders of Israel, as set by the agreements, encompassed about 78 per cent of mandatory Palestine west of the Jordan River. This was about 25 per cent more than the UN partition proposal allotted it (55 per cent). These ceasefire lines were known afterwards collectively as the 'Green Line'. Trans-jordan occupied and later annexed the thickly populated West Bank and East Jerusalem. The Gaza Strip was retained and administered by Egypt. The United Nations Truce Supervision Organization and Mixed Armistice Commissions were set up to monitor ceasefires, supervise the armistice agreements, prevent isolated incidents from escalating and assist other UN peacekeeping operations in the region.

The Arab–Israeli war of 1948–9 and its outcome still determine the direc-tion and dimensions of the contemporary Arab–Israeli conflict. Sixty years later most of the issues that caused that war have still not been resolved. Questions such as the borders of Israel, its ethnic make-up and its relationships with neighbouring Arab states remain unclear. Palestinian Arabs are still stateless, and more than half survive homeless, are prohibited from returning, and are unlikely to receive compensation. The future of the occupied or disputed terri-tories, the status of Jerusalem, the sharing of water resources and many other contested matters have not been agreed upon. For all these reasons and many more, it is essential to examine closely the events that preceded and made up the war of 1948–9.

By twentieth-century standards the war of 1948–9 was not a large-scale war. At the beginning of the war neither side had more than 30,000 troops, although by the end of the war Israeli forces had risen to around 108,500, and the Arab armies to around 60,000. The weapons used were mainly World War II-vintage rifles and light and medium machine guns. Few tanks were involved, and not many aircraft. The repercussions of the war, however, were enormous. Israel emerged possessing territory 50 per cent greater than that which had been allocated by the UN, but beyond that nothing was settled. No peace treaties were signed, merely a series of uneasy armistices. No Palestin-ian Arab state was established. Palestinian Arabs had no independent voice in these negotiations; their spokesman was King Abdullah, whose forces had occupied the area of Palestine west of the River Jordan stipulated by the UN as an Arab state.

The events leading to the first war set a pattern followed in all future dealings between the two main parties in the Arab–Israeli conflict. The Jews and Arabs of Palestine, in addition to mobilizing and utilizing their own re-sources, called upon their friends and allies outside Palestine for help. In the lead-up to the war, the (now) Israelis were, and in all subsequent wars have been, more successful in gaining material and moral support for their cause than the Palestinians. This was in part because the world Zionist move-ment, which formed the core of Jewish support for the new state, was highly organized and effective in influencing the political process, especially in the United States and the United Kingdom, and because Zionists skilfully tapped into a deep-seated apocalyptic strain within US Christians, which saw the creation and security of a Jewish state in the Holy Land as confirming a central tenet of their faith. Evangelical Christians saw supporting the 'chosen people' in establishing themselves on the land promised to them by God as a divine directive. Some of the fundamentalist Christian vision is, in reality, pro-foundly anti-Semitic. It has at its core a depiction of the Day of Judgment in which Jews will have to choose to accept Christ as their Messiah or, remain-ing Jews, be damned for eternity in hell. Nonetheless, since the foundation of the Jewish state, evangelical Christians have provided the foundation of US support for Israel because, according to their eschatology, the establishment of a Jewish state must immediately precede the Second Coming of Christ.

In furthering their cause Zionists also drew upon Western guilt over the destruction of European Jews in the Nazi Holocaust, although there is little evi-dence in the official records to indicate that this significantly influenced UK or US policy-makers in 1947–8. The enormity and horror of the Holocaust still per-vades any discussion of Israel and its policies, however. The reluctance of Chris-tian commentators to criticize Israel's policies reflects the extent to which the Holocaust became the moral compass of twentieth-century Europe and how the Jewish state has succeeded in nurturing a sense of guilt for the Holocaust in the European Christian subconscious. The Holocaust also overshadows the domes-tic and world view of Israelis. The searing memory of the Holocaust creates such anxiety on the one hand and determination on the other that it is sometimes difficult for Israelis to realistically assess the difference between the actual and imagined threats to the nation. The majority of Israelis and their supporters are unable or unwilling to concede the possibility that their vision may be distorted. To them, the risks are just too great.

Palestinian Arabs, on the other hand, were less successful in garnering support in the West, and the assistance they gained from their neighbour-ing Middle East states was given begrudgingly and inadequately. The leaders of the United States and Western Europe were too preoccupied with the reconstruction of Europe, securing the oil supplies of the Arabian peninsula and containing the Soviet Union to listen to the complaints of Palestinians that they were unjustly being made to pay the price of a Holocaust they did not perpetrate. The leaders of adjacent Arab states, most of whom were busy with their own relatively new and fragile nation-building activities, were jealous of each other and suspicious of each others' territorial intentions, and had little interest in or concern about Palestinian Arabs whom they regarded as having little merit.

In addition to the political and military realities on the ground, the first Arab–Israeli war gave birth to a number of myths – myths that continue to be played out today. The Israelis, like all nations, drew upon long-past legends and recent events to construct heroic 'foundation' myths to explain and justify the nation's existence, and to unify and mobilize its diverse population. The Palestinian Arabs also needed comforting myths to explain what for them was the disastrous outcome of the events of 1945–8. The 1948 war provided many opportunities for participants of both sides to canonize the shedding of blood.

The most pervasive myth promoted by Israel following the euphoria of victory was the analogy of a Jewish David successfully defeating an Arab Goliath. Thus Jewish leaders were depicted as wisely accepting a less than desirable UN partition plan while the Arabs foolishly and stubbornly rejected it. The Arabs then sought to use their overwhelming strength to crush the infant Jewish state, which, after an unequal, heroic and desperate struggle, survived. To this image is added the story that in the course of the war hundreds of thousands of Arabs fled on orders from their leaders despite pleas from Jewish leaders to remain. Israel sought peace but was met with Arab intransigence, making a political settlement impossible. Thus Israel remains a small Jewish outpost in a huge hostile sea of Arabs set on destroying it. Finally, the myth concludes, throughout this period Israelis acted purely in self-defence against a pitiless, cruel and determined enemy. Recalling in particular the traumatic events of the previous decade, 'Never Again' became the nation's motto.

The Palestinian narrative has similar, if contradictory, myths. To them the Israelis are conquerors, who with the aid of the Western powers forcibly took their land, brutally expelled their people, destroyed their towns, villages, homes and livelihoods, and cruelly refused to allow their return. Palestinians describe the events as a great injustice and see themselves paying the price of Hitler's genocidal policies towards the Jews. Palestinians have no doubt that the Israelis were committed to a policy of transferring the Arab population out of all Palestine. They cite Plan Dalet, the Haganah's March 1948 master plan for fighting the war, which stipulated the expulsion of the Arab populations from the territory of the Jewish state, to support their claim. They saw the murder of between 120 and 254 unarmed villagers at Deir Yassin by Lehi on 9 April 1948 as a lesson awaiting all Arab villagers. To Palestinians it is the Israelis who are obdurate and who refuse to negotiate an acceptable solution that would allow both Jews and Arabs to live side by side peacefully.

In their grand narratives neither side sees fault in its own actions. Israeli historians blame the war, including the creation of refugees, on the Palestinians for refusing to accept the partition resolution of November 1947. They focus on the legitimacy of Israel's claims and ignore the inflammatory remarks by Revisionist Zionists threatening the expulsion of the Arab population. They also deny that there was any officially authorized policy of wholesale transfer of Arabs from the area of the Jewish state. Palestinian historians attach no blame to their bitterly divided leaders for their reluctance to cooperate with the British mandate authorities or to build up the infrastructure necessary for an independent state. They overlook their failure to develop a coordinated strategy of unified opposition, or to cooperate with UN committees until it was too late to influence the outcome. They blame the Zionists, the British, the United States and Transjordan for their plight.

The dominant Zionist account was for many years widely encouraged in the Western and Israeli media as well as in Israeli schools and universities. However, in the past two decades almost all the elements of Israel's foundation myths have been exposed and rejected by a younger group of Israeli scholars, collectively known as the Israeli revisionists or 'new' historians, who did not participate in the war of 1948.[11] In many cases they were shocked by inaccuracies in the accepted accounts revealed in released official Israeli and Western archival records, and some, no doubt, were offended by the injustices against Palestinian Arabs blatantly permitted in the name of Israeli nationalist chauvinism. As yet there are no Palestinian accounts that rely on Arab archival evidence rather than oral testimony to question the Palestinian myth of victimhood. The new Israeli historians, however, also shed light on the shortcomings of the Palestinian myths surrounding the war of 1948.

The new historians argue that British policy following the UN partition resolution in November 1947 was not hostile to the establishment of the Jewish state; instead it sought to encourage the creation of a unified Palestinian

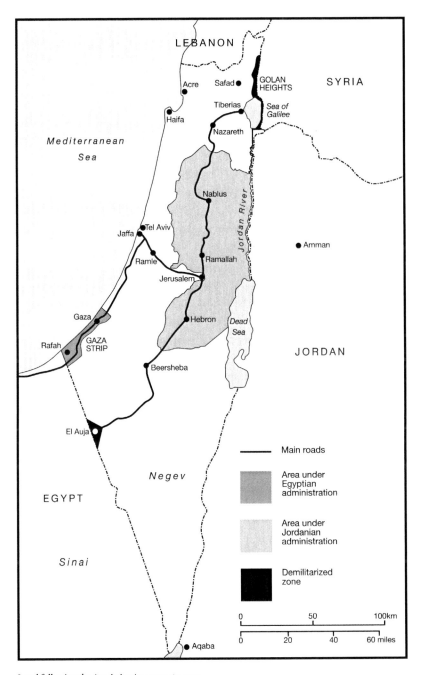

Israel following the Armistice Agreements, 1949.

Arab/Transjordan state – greater Transjordan. Rather than seeking to prevent the birth of Israel, British policy sought to endorse the agreement reached between the Jewish Agency and King Abdullah, whereby there would be no independent Palestinian Arab state.

They also question the extent to which Israel achieved its victory against overwhelming odds. They point out that although the 650,000 Yishuv were surrounded by 1.2 million Palestinian Arabs and nearly 40 million Arabs, within a short time of hostilities commencing in May 1948 they had a numerical advantage in armed forces. The Jewish armed forces were larger, better trained and technologically more advanced that those of their enemies. By the end of the war, Israeli troops outnumbered Arab forces by nearly two to one.

Perhaps the most contentious issue of the Israeli foundation narrative is the question of whether the 750,000 Palestinian Arabs who fled did so as the result of the conflict, or were expelled. Israel's first president, Chaim Weizmann, called the exodus a 'miraculous clearing of the land'. The new historians have pretty comprehensively shown that Arab leaders did not call upon the Palestinians to leave their homes. They do not entirely concur on the extent to which Israel's leaders ordered what might be called a systematic removal of the Arab population, but they do agree that Ben-Gurion wished to have as few Arabs living within the Jewish state as possible.

The new historians have also revealed that, rather than seeking to destroy Israel, even as it was being proclaimed, the Arab states were far from united when they invaded Palestine in May 1948. Indeed, as noted above, King Abdullah and the Jewish Agency had agreed to divide Palestine between them more or less along the lines of the partition resolution. The Israeli archives also reveal that the Arab states were willing to negotiate with Israel in 1949 to reach an overall political settlement. The key sticking points were Arab demands that refugees be allowed to return to their homes and that Israel make territorial concessions. Ben-Gurion considered the price of peace to be too high; he thought the 1949 armistice agreements met Israel's essential needs, and he was not prepared to allow the refugees to return.

The war of 1948 resulted in the consolidation of a Jewish state in Palestine, but it did not resolve the struggle between Jews and Arab Palestinians over mastery of the land. Indeed, it made it harder to find a satisfactory peaceful outcome. The war created new problems that were to provoke conflict for the next sixty years. We will examine some of these in the next chapter.

CHAPTER 4

The 1956 War

The armistices of 1949 signed at Rhodes ending the 1948 war lessened the intensity but not the course of the Arab–Israeli conflict. All the elements noted earlier that make up today's dispute were evidenced in the war of 1948–9, and they shaped events throughout the 1950s. No permanent peace was achieved. The unfinished business of the 1948 war included settling on terms of peace treaties, determining boundaries, the status of Jerusalem, questions of the return, compensation and reparations of refugees, and setting up economic arrangements between the participants. Each side blamed the other for the failure to reach agreement on any of these matters.

After the 1948–9 war all Arab nations maintained a state of hostility with Israel. Land routes in and out of Israel were blocked, and Egypt denied passage through the Suez Canal to Israeli-registered ships or to any ship carrying cargo to or from Israeli ports. Israel maintained access to, and trade with, the rest of the world by air and sea. The Jewish state, even as it sought to put in place the economic, political, social and diplomatic infrastructure essential to run an independent nation, feared the intentions of the adjacent Arab states. However, despite Israel's dominant narrative to the contrary, it is difficult to escape the conclusion that Israel shared responsibility for much of the uncertainty and turmoil that followed.

This chapter will briefly outline Israel's policy in relation to Palestinian refugees, to the armistice borders, and to Egypt and its neighbours, in the decade following Israeli independence, and it will outline the policies of the Arabs toward Israel. Differences over any one of these issues could have escalated into war; equally, none need have produced a war had the parties wished to avoid it. Why did war occur in 1956 and what was the outcome, intended and unintended? It is important to bear in mind that the Suez War took place at a critical point in the Cold War, and this chapter will demonstrate how the impetuous actions of Egypt, the Western powers and Israel provoked a war, and how the US and the USSR were drawn into the conflict.

The second Arab–Israeli war, widely known as the Suez War of 1956, was a by-product of the decline of the British Empire and an indication of the increasing importance the Cold War rivals, the US and the USSR, gave to replacing Great Britain in the Middle East. In the 1950s and '60s the Soviet Union in particular saw in Britain's weakness an opportunity to woo the Middle East's largest and most powerful, and arguably most strategically located, country into its orbit. The United States also sought to do so, but in a half-hearted way, preferring to concentrate on the Persian Gulf states rather than those of the Mediterranean Sea. Despite the unfinished business of the 1948 war, it is unlikely that Israel would have attacked Egypt had the British (and French) not attempted militarily to reverse Egyptian President Gamal Abdul Nasser's decision in mid-1956 to nationalize the Suez Canal. It was not an 'Arab'–Israeli war in any real sense; no other Arab states participated in the war. It was an opportunistic war for Israel, a chance to expand into the coveted Sinai. The consequence of Cold War rivalry and the 1956 war was to prolong the Arab–Israeli conflict for another 25 years.

In 1949 the victorious Israelis were in no mood to forgive or forget. They believed (wrongly as it turns out) that they had much more to worry about than the welfare or territorial concerns of their enemies, who appeared to them to show few signs of accepting defeat. Although Israel offered to accept a token number of refugees as part of direct peace negotiations (an offer the Arab states refused), the newly formed government was certainly not interested in facilitating the return of Palestinian Arabs who it was thought would act as a fifth column to undermine and destroy the state. Despite the passage of Resolution 194 by the UN General Assembly on 11 December 1948, which resolved that Palestinian refugees who wished to return to their homes and live at peace with their neighbours should be permitted to do so at the earliest practicable date, and that they should be paid compensation for loss of or damage to their property, Israel believed that the Arab states should accept the displaced Palestinians as immigrants. The Palestinians, dispossessed and bitter but without coherent leadership, could do little to regain or return to their homes as Israel consolidated its position in their former villages and towns.

Israel's leadership wanted peace, but not peace at any price. They were unhappy with almost every aspect of post-war relations with their neighbours, although there were deep disagreements within the cabinet over the means to achieve their goals. All agreed that the 1949 armistice lines with their UN-supervised demilitarized zones were unsatisfactory. At its 'waist' Israel was less than nine miles (14.5 km) wide from Transjordan to the Mediterranean Sea. This constriction had a profound effect on the thinking of Israel's military leaders. They believed that it made the state too vulnerable in the event of an Arab attack. The 'infiltration' of Palestinian Arabs into Israel – for whatever reason – had to be stopped, and any question of a large-scale return of Palestinians was rejected out of hand. Talks had taken place between Israel and Transjordan through March 1950, but Israeli prime minister Ben-Gurion rejected proposals from King Abdullah for a settlement and, following Jordan's annexation of the West Bank in April 1950, appeared uninterested in peace with Jordan. This attitude hardened when Abdullah was assassinated in Jerusalem in July 1951 and the king was replaced in 1953 by his young and inexperienced eighteen-year-old grandson Hussein ibn Talal, King Hussein.

Jordan's occupation of East Jerusalem, including the Jewish sector, was seen by Israel as an affront to be rectified. In December 1949 Ben-Gurion declared that Jerusalem was inseparable from Israel and was to be its capital. He rejected all proposals that did not include this provision. Attempts by the US, UK and France to limit further warfare with a tripartite agreement in May 1950 to restrict arms sales to both sides failed to halt incidents of violence. So did US and UN efforts to get cooperation between Israel and the Arab states over River Jordan water development schemes. In spring 1952 Israel attempted to change the status quo on the border with Syria. Ben-Gurion insisted that Israeli sovereignty extended into the Demilitarized Zone (DMZ) north of the Sea of Galilee, known in Israel as Lake Kinneret. In July 1953 Israel began to divert water from the River Jordan near the Benot Yaacov bridge, despite objections from the UN and Syria. The aim was to build a national water carrier to irrigate the Negev. And, on 6 May 1955, Israel declared that it regarded the blockade of its ships through the Straits of Tiran by Egypt as a *casus belli*.

The Arab states were in upheaval. No state in the region gave diplomatic or legal recognition to Israel. Israel's victory convinced young nationalists of the need to modernize the Arab states. The regimes in Syria and Lebanon were shaken by the influx of Palestinian refugees, who became a new factor in the politics of both countries. In March 1949, in Syria, the first of a series of military coups took place – probably with covert US assistance. In Transjordan, renamed the Hashemite Kingdom of Jordan in 1950, King Abdullah was assassinated by a disenchanted Palestinian refugee in July 1951. The king had annexed the West Bank in April 1950, and the new regime grappled with a potentially disruptive Palestinian population. In July 1952 a group of young Egyptian army officers threw off a decadent and inefficient King Farouk but were, by and large, indifferent to the fate of the Palestinians. In November 1952 the military also took over in Iraq. Militarily impotent, the Arab states could do little other than utilize economic weapons against Israel. In January 1950 an economic boycott was imposed and the Suez Canal was closed to Israeli shipping. In October 1954 the charismatic Gamal Abdul Nasser, the real leader of the young revolutionary officers, took over as President of Egypt. The primary objective of the young revolutionaries, however, was to remove foreign (that is, British) control from Egypt, rather than to challenge Israel.[1]

Israel's leaders believed their first priority was demographic; without a massive increase in population the country's chances of long-term survival appeared slight. For them, and to world Jewry, Israel was not merely another nation state. Centuries of 'exile' had come to an end and they found it hard to believe that all Jews would not wish to live in the security and normalcy of a reborn Jewish nation. The displaced persons of Europe were the first to arrive, followed by Jews from Soviet-occupied Europe. To facilitate the process of immigration – 'return' (*aliyah*) – in 1950 Israel's parliament (Knesset) passed the Law of Return, which stated that Jews immigrating to Israel were entitled to citizenship automatically – that is, without undergoing a naturalization process. Israel also 'rescued' Jews being 'expelled', virtually penniless, by the Arab states. Approximately 47,000 immigrants from Yemen and 113,000 (out of 130,000) from Iraq were airlifted en masse to Israel between 1949 and 1951. Similarly, the Jewish community of Libya was almost entirely relocated to Israel. A total of 586,269 Jews from Arab countries arrived in Israel. By the end of 1951 the population of Israel had increased to 1,404,400. Jews from Arab countries made up nearly 30 per cent of the entire population. Before 1948, almost 90 per cent of Jewish immigrants had arrived from Europe (Ashkenazim). This mix of the Ashkenazim from Eastern and Central Europe, who had played such a central role in building up the national home, with the non-European Jews (Sephardim and Oriental Jews), who were very different in language, customs and culture, was to create problems for Israel. In 1948 the Jews of Europe made up 75 per cent of Israel's Jews; by 1961 they represented only 55 per cent.

Israel's immigrants were housed wherever possible in the towns and houses abandoned by Arabs, or in huts and tents in transient camps (ma'abarot) little better than slums. The camps became a focus of economic and social ferment and towards the end of the 1950s and into the 1960s new towns and settlements were built to house these immigrants. Many were built on the sites of 'abandoned' Arab villages and tracts of land. The majority were moshavim, a cooperative system in which each family was responsible for its own holding. These development-towns were established across the country, from Mitzpe Ramon in the south to Kiryat Shmona in the north. The policy was to spread the population into sparsely settled areas, particularly along the borders. Settlements were established along the boundary with Jordan, where it was hoped that the chain of settlements would form a human barrier against infiltration by returning Palestinians.

The influx of immigrants provided military manpower and occupied vulnerable empty spaces, but it added to Israel's economic difficulties. By 1959, although Israel was feeding itself, the economy was struggling and the state depended upon outside assistance for infrastructure projects. The Export-Import Bank extended a US$100 million loan in January 1949, and the US government provided a series of grants-in-aid. Overseas Jews, especially those in the United States, also provided funds amounting to between US$60 million and US$100 million annually. In 1953 the Federal Republic of Germany (West Germany) signed an agreement to pay Israel DM3 billion (US$715 million), most of it in machinery and goods, over the next twelve years as partial reparations for material losses incurred by the Jews during the Nazi regime.

Responsibility for the future of the Arabs displaced during the 1948 war, although downplayed at the time, has remained one of the most intractable problems in resolving the Arab–Israeli conflict. At the end of hostilities early in 1949, the United Nations estimated that there were 726,000 Arab refugees from Israeli-controlled territories, about 70 per cent of the Arab population of

Palestine. In February 1949 the British estimated that about 320,000 Palestinians moved into, or already resided in, the eastern portion of Palestine, which was controlled by the Arab Legion, and into Transjordan. Approximately 210,000 were in camps in the Gaza region, 100,000 went into Lebanon, and 75,000 to Syria. A few went to Egypt and others to Iraq. Some 150,000 remained within the Jewish state. Although most were displaced, around 80 per cent of Palestinians remained within the boundaries of the former mandate. By 2008 the number of refugees and their descendants living in 59 United Nations Relief and Works Agency (UNRWA)-administered camps located in Jordan, Syria, Lebanon, the West Bank and Gaza Strip had risen to an estimated 4.3 million.

One might perhaps forgive the Palestinians for thinking that one of the most ironic turnarounds in history took place in July 2008. Dovish Knesset member Yossi Beilin called on the European Union to declare how many Palestinian refugees and their descendants European countries would be willing to absorb as part of any future peace agreement between Israel and the Palestinians. Those who had been displaced in Europe a generation ago were now arguing that those they displaced in Palestine should be allowed to migrate to Europe! Beilin acknowledged only a few Palestinians would be willing to go to Europe, but he complained that European countries had never indicated how many they would be willing to absorb. This was one of the first times for years that the highly sensitive issue of dealing with Palestinian demands for the 'right of return' of Palestinian refugees to Israel had been raised in Israel. The Jewish state flatly rejects these demands as a move that will indelibly alter the character of the country.[2]

At the time of the 1948 war, the Israeli government did not want the Palestinian Arab refugees to return to their homes; Prime Minister Ben-Gurion told the Israeli cabinet on 16 June 1948 that Israel should 'prevent their return'. Israel insisted it had no moral responsibility or legal obligation to restore the refugees to their property, or even compensate them for their losses. The official line was that they had brought their plight upon themselves by refusing to accept the UN partition plan and taking up arms to prevent its implementation. United Nations Resolution 194 of December 1948 regarding the Palestinian refugees was unacceptable to both sides. Israel insisted that any repatriation of refugees was dependent upon recognition of the state and upon directly negotiated peace treaties with the Arab governments, knowing that the Arabs would refuse these conditions. The Arabs were unwilling to accept resettlement schemes without acknowledgment of the refugees' right to return. The United States and the United Nations, working through its relief agency, the UNRWA, tried to alleviate the refugees' immediate situation.

Resolution 194 established a Palestine Conciliation Commission (PCC) comprised of representatives from the United States, France and Turkey to facilitate the repatriation or compensation of the Palestinian Arab refugees. The Commission's task was to work toward a peace settlement between Israel and the Arab states, to facilitate the repatriation, resettlement, and economic and social well-being of the Palestine refugees, and to determine the status of Jerusalem. The PCC, however, failed to achieve any of its goals, and these issues remain points of contention to this day. Both Israel and the Arabs rejected the UN position that Jerusalem should become an international city. The Jordanians and the Israelis came to a working arrangement by dividing the city between them, essentially disregarding the views of other nations. Israel later proclaimed Jerusalem its capital and gradually transferred government departments to the city.

For the Palestinian Arabs, the war of 1948–9 meant that Palestine was wiped off the map. Three-quarters of the land of Palestine was now part of Israel, and the rest (the West Bank) was absorbed by the Kingdom of Transjordan. Jerusalem became a divided city. Gaza was under Egyptian control. Entire cities and towns were taken over by Israel, Jaffa, Acre, Lydda, Ramle, Beit Shean and Majdal among them. Large parts of 94 other towns were also seized. More than a third of Palestinians had lived in urban centres prior to 1948; 90 per cent of them were uprooted. In all, a quarter of all buildings in Israel (100,000 dwellings and 10,000 shops, businesses and stores) formerly belonged to Palestinian Arabs. Arab agriculture – orchards, citrus groves, olive trees and other fruit orchards – was also destroyed with devastating effect. An indication of Israel's desire to remove all evidence of its former inhabitants can be seen in the fact that within a few months of the end of the 1948–9 war Israel set about drawing up a map in which all significant topographical features, including former Arab villages, would be given Hebrew names, the first step in creating 'facts on the ground'. Estimates of the number of villages destroyed and/or given Hebrew names range from 290 to 531.[3]

Bitter and resentful, the Palestinians remained in a kind of 'no-man's land', without a voice and unable to act independently to rectify their circumstances.

The mufti declared the existence of an 'All Palestine' state in the Gaza Strip in December 1948, but it was more a protest against the actions and ambitions of Transjordan's King Abdullah to speak for and incorporate the Palestinians into a greater Transjordan than anything else. It soon collapsed. A few Palestinians – intellectuals, businessmen and professionals – went to cities such as Beirut, Damascus and Amman. The majority, *fellahin*, unskilled workers and dispossessed peasants, fled to refugee camps set up with the help of the UNRWA in the vicinity of the neighbouring Arab capital cities or on old unused British or French army campsites. Camp conditions were primitive with little sanitation, no sewage and only basic medical facilities. Gradually small cement-block huts replaced the tents, and electricity and communal running water were supplied in the 1950s.

Opportunities differed depending upon where the refugees were. As part of his effort to extend his reach over the West Bank, King Abdullah allowed Palestinians to become citizens of the Hashemite Kingdom, but their hopes of independence were dealt a severe blow when the King forbade the use of the term 'Palestine' in any legal documents and pursued other measures designed to make clear that there would be no independent Palestine. In Syria, Palestinians were permitted to join the army and civil service and acquired most rights except citizenship. Many also left the refugee camps and were integrated into the general society. Those who went to Saudi Arabia and the Gulf States found work but little else. The Palestinians in Lebanon fared worst. The Lebanese government did not want the arrival of 100,000 refugees, who were mainly Sunni Muslims, to disturb the political religious balance of the state. Some, Christians or those with family connections, and later some Shia, were able to acquire citizenship in the 1950s, '60s and '70s, but the majority were denied civil rights and most professions were forbidden to them.

At the time of the 1949 armistice agreements there were around 150,000 Arabs living in Israel, most of them in the north. As members of a minority living in a state at war with Arab states, their lives have been difficult. Many accepted life in the Jewish state, others refused to cooperate with it, while the majority remained ambivalent, depending largely upon their personal circumstances. Prime Minister Ben-Gurion regarded the Arabs with hostility, a view shared by many future Israeli leaders. Israelis were obsessed by the idea of national vulnerability, and their hostility and prejudice toward the Israeli Arabs stemmed from their largely unjustified fear that they would act as a fifth column against them. Under the Nationality Law of 1951, Israeli Arabs were allowed to vote, run for office and, on paper, enjoyed equal rights with Jews, the notable exception being army duty. Arab women were given the right to vote. However, Israel often employed oppressive measures in an effort to encourage, or force, the Arabs to depart. They were placed under military rule and forbidden to move outside their areas without permits. Educational and employment opportunities were limited. They were forbidden to form their own political parties. Under the post-war Defence (Emergency) Regulations imposed, which were not lifted until 1966, Arabs could be exiled or arrested and detained without reason; villages and land could be expropriated by declaring an area a 'security zone'. Ten thousand Bedouin remaining in the Negev lost nearly all their cultivable land and pasture and were transferred to an area northeast of Beersheba, from which they were prevented from moving. In the 'triangle' in the Galilee that was originally, under the partition plan, to be located in the Arab state, some villagers were separated from their land, which was then expropriated as 'absentee' property.

The 1949 Rhodes armistice agreements had set up Mixed Armistice Commissions (MACs), consisting of an equal number of Arab and Israeli delegates, to help resolve border disputes peacefully under the supervision of a UN Truce Supervisory Organization (UNTSO). Except along the border with Lebanon, which was for the most part quiet, individuals and unorganized groups of Palestinian refugees from Jordan, Syria and the Gaza Strip frequently entered Israel after the cessation of hostilities in 1949. These incursions reflected, among other things, the artificiality or uncertainty of the armistice lines, which, although considered temporary, had often divided Arab villages or cut off villagers from their fields or wells. Thus, Palestinians crossed over into Israel to reclaim possessions, harvest their crops, steal, smuggle and, sometimes, to kill Israelis.

Although at first most of the incidents were relatively minor and both Israel and the Arab governments took measures to prevent them, violence escalated on all the borders, and a cycle of raids and reprisals began. While both sides argued about the facts and the rights and wrongs of events, raids, counter-raids, shootings back and forth, commando attacks, foraging expeditions and day-to-day incidents continued. The MACs were kept busy sorting out claims and counterclaims, censuring and making recommendations, while being powerless to stop the activity.

The Israeli response to what it considered acts of provocation and murder was retaliation, often massive, by regular army units. In the years between 1949 and 1956 Israeli forces killed between 2,700 and 5,000 Palestinians who had crossed the border from the West Bank into Israel. The majority were unarmed. Overall, according to Israeli historian Benny Morris, Israel's retaliatory raids did not act as a deterrent and were ineffectual in stopping infiltrators. They certainly bolstered Israeli morale, but they also strengthened Arab resolve.[4] The first major retaliatory raid, carried out by the newly formed 'Unit 101', commanded by Ariel Sharon, took place in October 1953 against the Jordanian village of Qibya. Fifty houses were destroyed and more than sixty Jordanians killed, including women and children. A shocked United Nations strongly condemned Israel. Nevertheless, another large attack against the Jordanian village of Nahhalin occurred in March 1954 to avenge the Arab ambush of an Israeli bus and murder of eleven Israelis at Scorpion's Pass in the eastern Negev. Fearful of Israeli retaliation, the Jordanian government attempted to prevent Palestinians from entering Israel. The king also worried that the Palestinians might seek his overthrow.

On the Syrian border, there were several crises arising in the DMZ, many of which were the result of conflicting views about the legal status of the zone. The Israelis claimed that the armistice arrangements allowed them complete sovereignty and freedom of movement within the DMZ. Israel, therefore, took over Arab land, extended Israeli cultivation and began to drain Lake Huleh over Arab and United Nations MAC objections. A particular source of tension involved fishing rights in the Sea of Galilee. Syrian gun positions on the north-eastern shore overlooking the lake fired on Israeli fishing boats and sometimes killed Israeli fishermen, while Israel employed armed patrol boats not only to protect the fishermen but also to prevent Syrian use of the lake. On 11 December 1955, without provocation, an Israeli unit, once again under the control of Sharon, attacked the Syrian gun positions, killing 50 Syrians. The Security Council censored Israel partly because of the scale of the attack, and partly because Israel had chosen to bypass the UN peacekeeping machinery.

On the Egyptian border, Palestinian and Egyptian infiltrators mined roads, blew up pipelines and bridges, murdered Israeli civilians and carried out deep penetration raids into Israeli territory. Initially the Israelis did not retaliate on a large scale. In February 1955, however, Israeli forces launched a massive attack against an Egyptian military post in Gaza, killing 38 and wounding 31. Egyptian president Nasser claimed that the Israeli Gaza raid compelled him to set up commando training camps for the refugees. In August 1955 these fighters, called *fedayeen* (those who sacrifice themselves), equipped and encouraged by the Egyptian government, began crossing the borders to spy, commit acts of sabotage and murder Israelis. Between September and November 1955, Israel drove Egyptian units from the demilitarized zone at al-Auja and took over complete control. The February Gaza raid in particular, however, had already convinced Nasser that Egyptian arms were not sufficient to retaliate in kind and provided a catalyst for him to seek arms wherever he could acquire them. In October 1955 Egypt and Syria agreed to a joint military command. The Israelis interpreted this alliance as an Arab preparation for war. Unceasing and punishing Arab raids into Israeli territory did not help calm Israeli apprehension.

In the absence of peace, tensions between Israel and Egypt increased. Moreover, the continuing Arab–Israeli conflict provided another arena for the rivalries of outside powers, especially the United States and the Soviet Union, as the Cold War extended into the region. Great Britain had emerged after World War II as the only European power of any importance in the Arab world, having influence and a large measure of control in Egypt, Iraq and Jordan, and important oil concessions in Iraq. In 1954 Egypt and Britain negotiated over the evacuation of British troops from the Suez Canal Zone, and the British agreed in October 1954 to evacuate their troops within twenty months. An important clause in the agreement, however, said that in case of enemy attack on a member of the Arab League or on Turkey, Britain or its allies could reoccupy the Canal Zone.

As Britain's presence in the post-war Middle East diminished, Washington determined it would become the most important Western player on the scene. Up to 1945 the United States had not been very much involved in the region, except for Christian missions, educational efforts and relatively small oil interests. World War II had provided opportunities for various forms of economic and military involvement and led to a growing concern about, and dependence upon, Middle East oil, but the United States would probably have been satisfied to leave diplomacy and policy initiatives to the British. Cold War rivalries brought the United States into the Arab–Israeli conflict.

In 1947 the British government notified the US that they could no longer maintain their strong presence around Greece and Turkey. Washington responded with the announcement of the Truman Doctrine, extending economic and military aid to the two countries. This step was the first indication of American determination to check the spread of communism in the Middle East. In 1948 Iran also received a small economic and military allocation. As pressures mounted with the victory of the Chinese communists in 1949, the Berlin blockade in 1948–9, and the invasion of Korea in 1950, the policy of containment was extended to the Arab states of the Middle East, now considered of vital geo-strategic importance to the free world because it contained two-thirds of the free world's oil reserves.

Accordingly, the United States sought to neutralize the Arab–Israeli conflict and, if possible, to convince Arabs and Israelis to make common cause with the West against the threat of Soviet encroachment. In May 1950, in a vain and empty attempt to maintain stability in the region, the United States, Britain and France signed a Tripartite Declaration declaring their opposition to the use or threat of force. They pledged to take action within and outside the United Nations to prevent violations of Middle East frontiers or armistice lines. Further, they reiterated their opposition to the development of an arms race. However, the three powers also stated that they would consider arms requests given an assurance that the purchasing nations would not use them for acts of aggression against other nations, essentially emasculating the Declaration.

The change of regime in Egypt in 1952 coincided roughly with the transition in the United States from the Democratic Truman administration to that of a Republican president, Dwight D. Eisenhower.[5] Initially relations between the two countries were cordial. Eisenhower promised a 'new look' at US foreign policy. Egypt solicited American help in negotiations with the British for evacuation of the Suez Canal Zone. The US intervened on Egypt's behalf, helping secure Britain's agreement to withdraw from the Sudan and to evacuate the Canal Zone bases. Meanwhile, Washington had been providing Egypt with technical aid. Now, this aid was supplemented with further economic assistance, and the promise of military aid as well.

The Eisenhower administration realized that the Arab states did not share US concerns about communism and decided against attempting to create a Middle East version of NATO. Washington, instead, began to focus on the 'northern tier' nations – Greece, Turkey, Iran and Pakistan – bordering the Soviet Union, which were more receptive to American proposals. In 1954 the administration sought to bring the pro-British Hashemite monarchy of Iraq into this scheme, and in April extended it military assistance. In early 1955 Iraq and Turkey signed a mutual cooperation pact open to all members of the Arab League. Britain joined this alliance in April 1955 and, later in the year, Iran and Pakistan also became members, forming the Baghdad Pact. Oddly, given their initial enthusiasm, the Americans did not join, hoping to avoid Egyptian criticism and Israeli demands for a similar defence commitment from Washington.

By this time the US had decided not to sell military equipment to Egypt. In November 1954 President Eisenhower had offered Nasser $13 million in economic aid and $27 million in military aid in return for Egyptian concessions in the British withdrawal arrangements, but the Egyptian president had alienated Eisenhower and his Secretary of State John Foster Dulles by his determined advocacy that the Arab world should become self-reliant. Following Israel's February 1955 Gaza raid, Nasser was determined to secure arms in order to deal with Israel as an equal, and so he turned to the Soviet bloc. In September 1955 Nasser announced a Russian arms purchase agreement with Czechoslovakia worth approximately $400 million, to be paid for primarily with Egyptian cotton. Tanks, artillery, MIG jets and other aircraft, two destroyers, two submarines, minesweepers, rifles and guns were part of the arms package Egypt acquired. In one stroke, the Soviets leaped over the 'northern tier' and emerged for the first time as an important and powerful influence in the area. The Cold War was thus extended into the Middle East. Israel and Egypt both thought the other was building up offensive arms to attack.

The Soviets wanted a foothold in the Arab world to embarrass and challenge the West and outflank NATO. The Russians wanted to effect a shift in the international balance of power. Initially the Soviet Union supported Israel, but Israel's reliance on US economic aid, both private and governmental, and its denunciation of North Korea during the Korean War, brought about a change in Soviet thinking. Traditional Russian anti-Semitism also played a part in the shift. As Soviet relations with Israel worsened, Nasser's situation and outlook provided the Soviets with an opportunity to undercut the West and undermine the Baghdad Pact. Syria made its own arms deal with the Soviet bloc in 1956, and Egypt subjected Jordan to intense 'pan-Arab' pressure in an attempt to weaken its Western orientation. Partly in an effort to recoup influence after the Egyptian–Soviet arms deal, and partly out of a continuing desire to maintain good relations with the Arab states, Eisenhower and Dulles indicated they would provide economic assistance to Egypt to help build a dam at Aswan on the River Nile. Nasser considered the dam essential to combat the effects of poverty and a soaring population, and to develop Egypt economically, but he did not immediately accept Washington's offer. Lobbying efforts by American cotton interests in the South, by Jewish organizations and by supporters of Nationalist China began to influence American policy-makers against the loan. American opinion about Nasser was changing, and Secretary of State Dulles was beginning to detest him. Dulles and others in the State Department had little patience with Arab nationalism and were increasingly frustrated, disappointed and angry at Nasser's 'neutralism' and unwillingness to follow the American game plan for the region. The last straw for Dulles was Nasser's recognition of communist China on 4 May 1956. On 19 July, without explanation, Dulles withdrew the loan offer. Official US statements questioned Egypt's ability to assure the success of the project or ever repay any debt that would be incurred, since the country's economy was being mortgaged to pay for Soviet arms. The World Bank more sanguinely interpreted the dam as a good investment.

An angry Nasser, in an emotional speech on 26 July, declared that in order to pay for the costs of building the dam, Egypt would nationalize the Suez Canal. In this dramatic gesture, the Egyptian president also struck at the remaining large symbol of Western imperialism operating on Egyptian soil. He thus set in motion the events that would lead to war in October 1956, when Britain, France and Israel operated in concert to try to bring about a 'regime change' in Egypt.

This abrupt and unexpected nationalization of the canal infuriated British Prime Minister Anthony Eden, who believed that Nasser was an upstart whose ambitions had to be checked. Eden was reluctant to abdicate Britain's imperial interests, and the Suez Canal was still seen as the gateway to the Far East and of strategic importance to British oil interests in the Persian Gulf. The spectre of Munich was never far from Eden's mind, and by the autumn of 1956 he was convinced that the time had come to deal decisively with Nasser.

The French also seized upon Egypt's actions as an opportunity for regime change in Egypt. France was attempting to deal with a volatile situation in its North African colonies of Morocco, Tunisia and Algeria. Nasser actively supported the rebellion in Algeria. The French were becoming increasingly sympathetic to Israel. The two countries had worked together on nuclear scientific projects in the early 1950s, and French and Israeli socialists shared common ideals. France's newly elected socialist Prime Minister Guy Mollet saw the removal of Nasser as the best way to protect and uphold French interests in the Middle East. Concerned about and angered at Nasser's support of the Algerian rebels, France had approved the sale of twelve Dassault Ouragan jet fighters to Israel in December 1954. After Soviet weapons began flowing in great quantities into Egypt in 1955, fourteen additional Ouragan fighters and twelve Mystère IV jet fighter-bombers were sold to Israel, arriving in the spring of 1956. The US encouraged the French to ship arms to Israel, and Dulles even requested Canada to provide Israel with American-licensed jets. Between 1956 and 1967 the French were the major military suppliers to Israel.

Israel's leadership was deeply divided over its policy toward Egypt and the Arabs. Border raids were becoming more severe and more destructive of life and property, and there was a desire to deal decisively with the fedayeen attacks. The Arab economic boycott and continued closing of the Suez Canal and the Gulf of Aqaba to Israeli shipping retarded Israel's economic growth. Israeli 'hawks', Ben-Gurion and those who agreed with him, wanted Israel to go to war against Egypt. Israel was spending about 7.2 per cent of its gross national product annually on military expenditure, and its military forces were shaped into an effective and vigorous army, especially under the leadership of Moshe Dayan, who was appointed chief of staff in 1953. These Israeli leaders argued that the best defence was strong, direct offensive action. They believed Israel's borders were unacceptable and insecure, and that the government could not afford to dismiss or ignore Arab threats or intimidation. To them the murderous fedayeen raids and constant harassment were just another form of Arab warfare against Israel. The 'hawks' insisted that retaliation take place after every incident.[6]

Moderates like Moshe Sharett, who had become prime minister in November 1953, believed that repeated censure in the United Nations, no matter how one-sided it seemed to Israel, and American disapproval were counterproductive and only encouraged the cycle of violence. They noted that retaliation did not necessarily discourage fedayeen raids, and they argued further that Israel's policies were creating a situation in which it would be impossible for the Arabs even to consider making peace. They were overruled, however, by the 'activists', led by David Ben-Gurion, Golda Meir and Moshe Dayan. Ben-Gurion replaced Sharett as Israeli prime minister in November 1955, retaining the defence portfolio. Israel's founding prime minister was determined to undertake a pre-emptive war against Nasser.

Ben-Gurion had already supported action to weaken Nasser's regime. In 1954 as the British prepared to withdraw, in what became known as the Lavon affair, Israeli agents had sabotaged American and British installations in Egypt to forestall the possibility of an Egyptian-American defence arrangement. By July 1956, the same month that Nasser nationalized the Suez Canal, Ben-Gurion instructed his general staff to draw up contingency plans for war and to concentrate initially on opening the Strait of Tiran at the entrance of the Gulf of Aqaba. Israel was more than ready for the collusion with Britain and France and that led to the 1956 Suez-Sinai war.

Following nationalization, the Suez Canal became a symbolic issue for Egyptians, Europeans and Americans. Egypt, supported by the Soviet Union, insisted upon its 'sovereign rights' and steadfastly refused to accept the idea of an international authority to run the canal. Britain and France, unwilling to recognize Egypt's sovereignty, were determined to undertake war to force the issue. As they planned military action against Egypt, they soon included Israel in their plans. Ben-Gurion, who had already begun preparations for a possible attack on Egypt to secure passage through the Strait of Tiran, embraced the idea. A larger military operation would remove Soviet arms from Egypt, destroy the fedayeen threat and, with any luck, remove Israel's arch-enemy, Gamal Abdul Nasser.

Meetings were held in September and October. On 21 October, Ben-Gurion, Peres and Dayan held joint talks with the British and French in France. The timing was propitious. The American administration would be preoccupied with the upcoming presidential election in the United States. The Russians were also distracted in Eastern Europe by unrest in Poland and Hungary. As part of the deception, the Israelis attacked an Arab League police fort at Qalqilya on 11 October in retaliation against Jordan for a fedayeen raid that had occurred the previous day. In that same month, Jordan had joined the Syrian-Egyptian military pact. Israel gave the impression that it was mobilizing to undertake a military offensive against Jordan.

Instead, in the later afternoon of 29 October, 1956, as part of the pre-arranged tripartite plan, Israeli paratroopers led by Raphael Eitan dropped at the Mitla pass in the Sinai Peninsula 30 miles (48 km) east of the Suez Canal. Simultaneously, additional forces under the command of Sharon set out overland to join them. The Egyptians responded and full-scale warfare erupted in the Sinai. Israel's aims were to capture the Sinai Peninsula in order to open the

Straits of Tiran to Israeli shipping, and to seize the Gaza Strip to end fedayeen attacks. Israel's chief-of-staff, Major General Moshe Dayan, was confident that the agreed coordinated British and French attack on Egypt would assist them in achieving these goals. The British and French on 30 October delivered an ultimatum calling for a halt to hostilities and a warning to Egypt to withdraw ten miles from the canal. For Egypt, of course, that would have meant a retreat from the canal, and on 1 November Nasser refused. The British announced that a combined Anglo-French force would land to halt the fighting and secure uninterrupted navigation of the Suez Canal. Within 100 hours Israeli troops had occupied the entire Sinai and taken Sharm el-Sheikh, opening the straits to Israeli shipping.

The war itself was mercifully short. Israeli forces entered the Gaza Strip on 1 November and Gaza City fell after a three-hour fight on the morning of 2 November. At 10 a.m. that morning the general commanding the Egyptian army 8th Division in the Gaza surrendered. By 3 November Israel's conquest of the Sinai and the Gaza Strip was almost complete. The Egyptians and Palestinians offered little organized resistance. British and French air and sea forces attacked Cairo and Port Said, inflicting considerable damage on the latter city, especially its oil storage facilities. Nasser responded by scuttling the 40 ships then in the canal, rendering it impassable. The Anglo-French force eventually arrived at Port Said on 5 November and attempted to secure the area. Britain (and France) faced widespread condemnation of their actions from NATO allies, the United Nations General Assembly and British Commonwealth countries. The Soviet Union threatened armed intervention on the side of Egypt if the attacks continued. A furious Eisenhower threatened Britain with dire financial consequences if it did not stop the invasion. In addition, Saudi Arabia began an oil embargo against the British and French. The French wanted to proceed until concrete military results were achieved, but before more operations could be undertaken, an exhausted and ill British prime minister, Eden, agreed to a ceasefire on the night of 6/7 November. The French reluctantly followed suit. The Israelis, who had conquered the entire Sinai and had taken control of the Egyptian positions at Sharm el-Sheikh overlooking the Strait of Tiran, also agreed to the ceasefire.

The Israelis suffered relatively light casualties: fewer than 200 soldiers were killed and 700 wounded. Egypt's losses were considerably higher with thousands killed and many more wounded, and more than 5,500 taken prisoner.

Almost all Israel's casualties were among the lightly armed troops led by Sharon, who recklessly attacked fortified Egyptian forces supported by heavy artillery and tanks at Jebel Heitan. British and French losses were light.

The 'successes' of the war were almost as short-lived as the war was brief. Under US and UN pressure, British and French forces withdrew from the Suez zone before Christmas, replaced by a newly created United Nations Emergency Force along the Egyptian-Israeli border. In early January 1957 Eden resigned, citing reasons of health. Nasser was not forced to disgorge the canal, which reopened under Egyptian control in early 1957. Despite triumphalist rhetoric from Ben-Gurion immediately following the Sinai conquest, Israeli troops left the Sinai and Gaza Strip in March 1957 after receiving from the United States a guarantee that it would ensure Israeli shipping unhindered passage through the Straits of Tiran and the Gulf of Aqaba.

Perhaps more lasting in terms of the continuation of the Arab–Israeli conflict were events that took place during the war near the Green Line separating Israel and Jordan and in the Gaza Strip. The Israeli military high command had expected that in the event of war with Egypt, Jordan would also commence hostilities against Israel. Such an eventuality did not take place. However, at the commencement of the war, a curfew was placed on the population of around 40,000 Israeli Arabs living in a group of towns and villages known as the 'Little Triangle' about 12 miles (20 km) east of Tel Aviv close to the Green Line with the West Bank. On the evening of 29 October Israeli border police at the village of Kafr Qasem shot and killed 48 unarmed Palestinian workers returning from the fields unaware that a curfew had been imposed. The massacre shocked both Israelis and Palestinians.[7]

Palestinians believe the massacre was part of a larger plan to expel the Arab population from Israel. This belief was reinforced by the transfer of between 3,000 and 5,000 Israeli Arabs of the Galilee to the eastern side of the River Jordan into Syria in the name of security. This transfer, which began on the following day, was conducted by the head of the Northern Command, Yitzhak Rabin, who exploited the attack against Egypt in the south to carry out the mass expulsion.

There were several attacks on Palestinian populations in the Gaza Strip during the course of the war that Palestinians believe were also designed to terrorize the population into fleeing the area. On 3 November, according to UNRWA reports, around 275 residents of the Khan Yunis refugee camp were killed by Israeli army units and a week following the ceasefire more than 100 refugees were slain at the Rafah camp.[8] The troops who carried out these operations were under the command of Eitan, a hero of the 1948–9 war, who later became the army chief of staff from 1978 to 1983. He was criticized by the Israeli Kahan Commission of Inquiry for his failure to try to prevent the September 1982 massacres at Sabra and Shatilla in Beirut. He later became leader of the right-wing Tzomet Party and minister of agriculture and environment in the Likud cabinet of Benjamin Netanyahu.

The 1956 war altered the balance of European power in the Middle East. The United States began to assume the role previously played by the United Kingdom and France. Ironically, although Eisenhower insisted that Israel withdraw from the Sinai in March 1957, the United States became more and more closely identified with Israel in the Arab popular mind, as the Soviet Union took advantage of the situation to reinforce its relations with the Arabs and particularly to consolidate its position in Egypt. The destroyed Soviet arms were quickly replaced, and Soviet aid also arrived for the building of the Aswan High Dam, which became a Russian showpiece in the Middle East. Henceforth, the Cold War encompassed the Arab–Israeli conflict.

As had been the case in 1948, however, the war resolved very little between Israel and the Arabs. The Suez war deepened Egypt's desire for revenge. In the absence of peace, the Middle East remained a powder keg. Israel did make some economic gains. The US and UN guaranteed freedom of passage through the Gulf of Aqaba, allowing Israel to receive oil shipped clandestinely from Iran. In addition, the UN agreed to station an emergency force (UNEF) in Egyptian territory at Sharm el-Sheikh and between Israel and Egypt in Gaza, removing the fedayeen problem from the Egyptian border. Although navigating the Gulf of Aqaba was to some extent a symbolic issue for Israel, the Israeli town of Eilat became an important port. The gulf provided a window on Africa and Asia, which became markets for Israeli goods, influence and expertise.

Although defeated militarily, Nasser emerged as a hero and as the symbol of pan-Arabism and its valiant stand against imperialism, colonialism and Zionism. It was a role he appeared to relish. In the next decade, Arab nationalism would be an important factor in the domestic politics of most Arab countries. An inflated sense of Arab solidarity led to further problems with Israel, as will be seen in the next chapter.

CHAPTER 5

Altered States:
The Wars of 1967 and 1973

The wars of 1967 and 1973 were pivotal in the Arab–Israeli conflict. The war of 1967 led not only to the Israeli occupation of the remainder of British-mandated Palestine east of the River Jordan, including East Jerusalem, but also to the colonization of the conquered areas in the form of Jewish towns, called settlements. The war of 1973 led to negotiations that began the process of undoing the outcomes of the 1967 war. Egypt regained the Sinai, but Syria's Golan Heights and the West Bank remained in Israel's hands. Palestinians and Arabs today regard the West Bank settlements and Israel's occupation of East Jerusalem among the major obstacles to a resolution of the conflict. They argue that Israel has no intention of withdrawing to the pre-June 1967 borders, something they regard as a core prerequisite for peace.

The Israelis acknowledge that the settlements are an obstacle to peace, but, they assert, not an insuperable obstacle. They blame the Palestinians for the continuation of the conflict. They argue that the Arabs and Palestinians refused Israel's offer to withdraw in 1967 in return for recognition and peace, as well as rejecting subsequent peace offers made by Israel at Camp David and Taba in 2000–1. Israelis allege that the Palestinians have consistently refused a two-state solution since 1937, when it was first proposed by the Peel Commission, through 2000 to the present, and, regardless of what they say, basically want an Arab state in all of Palestine. The majority of Israelis believe Palestinians have rejected all proposals put to them and have resorted to violence, despite Israel's best efforts to accommodate their demands. If Syria gave up its support of terrorism against Israel and extended diplomatic recognition to the state of Israel the Golan would be returned without delay; if the Palestinians had not resorted to violence in resisting the occupation, Israelis assert, they would have achieved statehood years ago.

Much of this story is sheer fabrication. If, prior to 1967, the Palestinians had failed to achieve a state in Palestine because, as Abba Eban so pithily put it, they had never missed an opportunity to miss an opportunity, it appears to many that since June 1967 it has been the Israelis who have never missed an opportunity to prevent the Palestinians from gaining statehood. Since its victory in its pre-emptive war in June 1967, Israel has been in a position to initiate a peaceful outcome if it chose to do so. It has not so chosen.

It is true that in June 1967 the Israeli cabinet formally decided to withdraw from captured Syrian and Egyptian territories, namely, the Sinai and the Golan Heights. But, as 'new' historian Avi Shlaim has shown, no offer was made to Jordan, or to the Palestinians in the territories, concerning the West Bank and Gaza Strip. In fact, the Gaza Strip was declared fully within the state of Israel. Within a very short time the offers to Syria and Egypt, which were never passed on to the Syrians or Egyptians by the Israeli government – or by Washington, which was informed of the decision – were withdrawn. No formal decision was ever made about the future of the West Bank. The cabinet decided that it would allow only local autonomy in the West Bank and Gaza, a status that they hoped would lead in time to international recognition of the River Jordan as Israel's security border, and as its political border as well.[1]

None of these decisions were made in response to Palestinian or Arab terrorism or Palestinian rejection of Israel's legitimacy. By mid-June the vast majority of Arab West Bank leaders had indicated to Mossad and IDF intelligence personnel that they were prepared to reach a permanent peace agreement with Israel on the basis of an independent Palestine, without an army.[2] All major parties in Israel supported the settlement enterprise. The debate within Israel was not over the establishment and presence of settlements in the occupied territories, but over what to do with the Palestinians whose lands were being confiscated. Shimon Peres and the Labor Party advocated that they be given home-rule and Jordanian citizenship, while others harked back to the 'transfer' idea. All sides agreed that rather than adopt a formal position on the status of the West Bank residents and risk international opposition, even condemnation, Israel should establish 'facts on the ground' and say nothing. Again it was hoped that in time everyone would accept the River Jordan as Israel's Eastern border.

The rationale for the establishment of settlements had been to ensure Israel's security, but by the 1980s the settlements had created entirely new security problems that continue to this day. From the outset, the settlements violated international law and, in the opinion of many, Israel's own laws. Within a few years the settlers, driven by economic self-interest in the form of government subsidies as well as by extreme nationalist and intense messianic religious ideology, involved almost all areas of Israeli life, and were supported by successive governments. The Israeli Defence Forces has become almost an army of the settlers. Not only does it protect the settlers at the expense of the Palestinians it is also supposed to protect, many senior commanders are increasingly under the influence of settler rabbis. Israel's courts also reflect the sway the settler movement holds in Israel. Settlers, and IDF soldiers, are rarely tried for crimes against Palestinians, and if found guilty receive lenient sentences, while more than ten thousand Palestinians, including women and children, are in prisons awaiting trial without indictment for specific crimes.[3] The United States, while publicly opposing them, provided funds to Israel that enabled settlements to expand.

Underlying Israel's efforts to retain the occupied territories is the fact that it never really considered the West Bank as occupied territory. To the Israelis, the Palestinian areas are 'contested' territory to which they have claims no less compelling than the Palestinians, regardless of international law and UN resolutions.[4] The use of the biblical designations of Judea and Samaria to describe the territories, terms now applied by the Labor party as well as the Likud, reflects this view. That the former prime minister, Ehud Barak, endlessly describes the territorial proposals he made at the Camp David summit as expressions of Israel's 'generosity', and never as an acknowledgment of Palestinian rights, is another example of this mindset. The majority of Israel's leaders do not seem to recognize that Palestinians have a national right to statehood, as declared by the UN in 1947.

Immediately following the war, Israel's military advocate general, Colonel Meir Shamgar, recommended that the West Bank and Gaza Strip be regarded as 'disputed' rather than 'occupied' territory, as the two areas had not previously been an integral part of a sovereign state. This was a legal device to reject the applicability of the 1949 Fourth Geneva Convention relating to the occupation of conquered territory by separating the status of the people from the status of the land. Although the international community has overwhelmingly rejected Shamgar's interpretation, Israel has maintained it ever since.

The map of Palestine was redrawn once again in 1967. The new boundaries created by the June war of 1967 created the physical, political, economic and cultural environment in which the contemporary Arab–Israeli conflict has been waged for the past forty years. The critical issues causing conflict between Israel and the Arabs shifted in 1967. Israel decimated the armed forces of Egypt, Jordan and Syria, extended the area of territory under its control by three times, and assumed direct rule over an additional 750,000 Palestinians, totally changing the nature and extent of what up to that time had been a relatively contained conflict.

Until the mid-1960s the conflict between Israel and the Palestinians had been depicted by Israelis as a kind of David versus Goliath situation. References were made to population statistics and military capabilities; maps showing Israel's vulnerability were part of Israel's rhetorical arsenal to gain continued world, especially American, support for the Jewish state. These arguments were used to justify massive Israeli retaliatory border raids. The Palestinians, dispersed and dislocated, failed to gain the support of the world or even their Arab neighbours in their efforts to establish a Palestinian nation. They had little chance of success acting alone, as their ineffectual efforts only too clearly revealed. For all intents and purposes, they were a marginalized group of refugees who had resorted to terrorism and who, therefore, deserved and received little sympathy. The events of 1967 dramatically changed all that and shaped the issues that are currently being resolved.

To the Arabs the cause of the 1967 war is to be found in Israeli aggressiveness and expansionism, Israel's excessive retaliations and Israeli 'hawkishness' and determination to maintain military superiority. The Israelis see the cause of the war as the continued antagonism and inability of the Arabs to recognize and accept the political sovereignty of the Jews in Israel and their desire to avenge the defeats and humiliation of the previous wars. It is impossible to reconcile these conflicting views, but in many ways the causes of the war of 1967 are less important to an understanding of the contemporary issues than the outcome of that conflict.

Whatever the merits of these claims and counter-claims, there is little doubt about the outcome. Israel gained territory, but did not want to assimilate the people living in it. Nor did it achieve the security it thought the territory would bring. The war lifted restraints on the advocates of Greater Israel, and successive Israeli governments encouraged and supported the establishment of Israeli settlements throughout the conquered West Bank and in the Gaza Strip. The war also unleashed Palestinian nationalism, gave impetus to the Palestine Liberation Organization, and led to virtually unrestrained terrorist activity that culminated in two intifadas and continued rocket attacks directed against Israel. Had Israel withdrawn from the West Bank immediately after the 1967 war, in all likelihood the PLO would have been destroyed, and with it the possibility of a Palestinian state. The Arab states, certainly Jordan, would have agreed to suppress Palestinian resistance as the price for Israeli withdrawal and for Jordan regaining its territory. For 40 years, from 1947 to 1987, Jordan was Israel's ally in preventing the emergence of a Palestinian state.

There is a certain element of déjà vu about the rhetoric of the Israeli government in relation to the present dimensions of the conflict. Once again we are seeing maps depicting Israel's precarious security situation, in relation not only to a possible Palestinian state but also to the neighbouring Arab states, to justify the building of a 'security' wall, and not returning territory seized in 1967. Once again we are hearing that the Palestinians are terrorists who cannot be trusted as a reason why Israel cannot permit Palestinians to control contiguous areas as part of an autonomous Palestine.

Yet, if one reconsiders the situation during the years prior to 1967, it is clear that most of today's arguments appear little more than casuistry, as they did then. Israel's occupation of the West Bank and East Jerusalem were neither necessary nor desirable for the Jewish state's security and continued existence prior to 1967. The UN General Assembly in 1947 regarded the partition boundaries as sufficient to enable a Jewish state to thrive, and certainly did not authorize a single state – Jewish or Arab – extending from the Mediterranean to the River Jordan. Now, as then, the Palestinians, alone or supported by Arab states, are in no position to challenge either Israel's military superiority or its existence. Israel's neighbours, now as then, were incapable of defeating Israel in military conflict. Indeed, Jordan has never been interested in doing so. This chapter amplifies these issues.

In the summer of 1967 Israel believed it was in trouble. The Egyptians had closed the Straits of Tiran, expelled UN forces from the Sinai and mobilized troops on its border with Israel. Egyptian President Gamal Abdul Nasser called for war, a call echoed from Damascus. The prime minister at the time, Levi Eshkol, formed a unity government with the leader of the opposition, Menachem Begin, a man he despised and who had failed to win over the Israeli voters in five consecutive election campaigns. Together they forged a plan: to launch a pre-emptive strike against Egypt. Israel's surprise attack ended a decade of relative calm in the conflict.

The decade following the Suez–Sinai war was the longest period in the Arab–Israeli conflict without a major confrontation or war. The years between 1956 and 1967 saw a consolidation of previous gains in Israel and impressive growth economically, militarily, politically and culturally. In the Arab world, Nasser became the symbol of pan-Arabism, which reached its zenith in the late 1950s. On the other hand, an Arab 'Cold War' had developed. Some Arab countries, like Syria, followed Nasser's lead in embracing radical social and economic change and rejecting foreign commitments. Nevertheless, both Egypt and Syria accepted aid from the Soviet Union. Other Arab states, including those led by conservative monarchs like Jordan and Saudi Arabia, approached change more cautiously and identified financially and ideologically with the West. The almost total discrediting of Britain and France after the Suez debacle left the United States and the Soviet Union as the major superpower protagonists in the region. Increasingly, the ties between the Soviets and their allies, and those linking the United States and its Arab friends and Israel, assumed the model of a patron–client relationship. Soviet-American rivalry, one aspect of which was supporting the arms race between the Arabs and Israel, became a significant factor in the events leading to the Arab–Israeli war in 1967.

The comprehensive nature of Israel's victory and the wide-ranging consequences of the 1967 war have somewhat obscured the causes of this war. It is generally assumed that the June war was fought because in May Egypt closed the Straits of Tiran to Israeli shipping. Nasser's act was certainly the catalyst that led to Israel's pre-emptive attack, but it was far from the only cause of the war. Israeli leaders felt the need to put a stop once and for all to raids into Israel from the Jordanian-controlled West Bank by newly formed Palestinian militant organizations, and to settle water and boundary disputes with a belligerent regime in Syria. Despite the Western orientation of Jordan, the close relationship and military support provided to Syria and Egypt by the Soviet Union added urgency to their deliberations. Israel's leaders felt they were being caught up in the web of the Cold War, and, rather than trust to others (that is, the US), they believed their only course of action was to rely on their own military capabilities.

Although the Zionist goal of a Jewish state had been achieved, throughout the 1950s and into the '60s Israel's hawks wanted much more than the 1949 armistice agreements provided. In the mid-1950s Moshe Dayan, then chief of staff, had pressed for war with Egypt to capture the Gaza Strip and Sharm el-Sheikh, and he suggested capturing the West Bank. Yigal Allon, Israel's foreign minister, had also wanted to remedy what he regarded as the 'long-term mistake' made in 1948, that of not capturing and annexing the West Bank. Ben-Gurion in his first meeting with the British and French to plan the Sinai campaign in 1956 had outlined his great dream. Israel, he stated, would occupy the Sinai Peninsula, take over the West Bank and dismantle the Kingdom of Jordan, and reach the Litani River in Lebanon, establishing a Maronite state in northern Lebanon. The entire Israeli leadership, with the exception of Moshe Sharett, was excited by the idea of creating an 'iron wall' excluding Arabs, an idea first floated by the early hard-line Zionist Ze'ev Jabotinsky in the 1920s.

The 1956 Sinai campaign had accomplished few of the goals sought by Israel's hawks. Israeli shipping had been permitted through the Straits of Tiran up the Gulf of Aqaba to Eilat since 1956, but Arab hostility had intensified. In 1964 the Palestine Liberation Organization was created. Israel kept pressing Syria over water rights to the River Jordan and control of the northern DMZ, and it continued military attacks against Jordan in an attempt to deter PLO raids into Israel. This constant harassment alarmed Syria and its ally Egypt. In April 1967, in response to fears encouraged by the Soviet Union – as it turns out, quite unwarranted fears – that Israel was planning an attack on Syria, the Egyptian president moved 100,000 soldiers and 1,000 tanks to the Sinai border near the Gulf.

These troops did not, however, present a serious threat to Israel's security. Nasser asked United Nations Secretary General U Thant to remove its Emergency Force (UNEF) from the entrance to the Gulf of Aqaba. UNEF had been stationed along the Sinai border since 1957 to provide a peacekeeping buffer zone. Nasser had every legal right to make this request, but it was fool-ish of him to do so. Nor was U Thant wise in readily agreeing to remove all the UNEF troops without insisting upon a cooling-off period. Then, on 23 May 1967, knowing that it might very likely provide Israel with the trigger it needed to launch a war, Nasser made the fateful step of closing the Straits of Tiran. The closing of the straits did not represent an immediate threat to Israel, or to its economic health; only 5 per cent of Israel's trade went through the port of Eilat. Furthermore, only two weeks after a 1949 ceasefire had gone into ef-fect, Israel had acquired a small piece of the coast of the Gulf at Eilat, giving it the right to navigate the Gulf. Israel, however, seized on the 1967 closure as a *casus belli*. On the morning of 5 June 1967, in a brilliantly executed surprise attack, Israeli planes destroyed the Egyptian air force on the ground. The war had begun. The question is why?

The war was a Nasser gamble gone terribly wrong. In a cable sent to the White House situation room at 11:51 pm on 25 May, the CIA gave the follow-ing assessment of Nasser's action. Nasser, the CIA thought, was confident of Soviet support, believed that the US would take no action, and was convinced that the Israelis would seek UN intercession rather than attack Egypt. The CIA concluded that the Egyptian leader was: 'gambling with possible hostil-ities in the hope of extracting heavy concessions from the United States as the price of his keeping the peace.' The CIA pinpointed the key to his actions: 'He will try to obtain both wheat and money from the United States as the price for his avoiding war with Israel.' The intelligence community believed that Nasser was attempting to place Israel in the position of an aggressor, and 'his belief that Israel will go to the United Nations on the Aqaba Gulf issue, and will not attack, is the main element of his gamble.'[5] A desperate Nasser, unable to feed his people and faced with domestic political unrest, hoped for US wheat sales to rescue him from the possibility of civil war.

In a meeting of the National Security Council in Washington the day before, 24 May, it had been suggested that Nasser might in fact have 'gone slightly insane'! Presidential Special Assistant Walt Rostow sent a cable to President Lyndon B. Johnson later that night offering the reassuring news that Nasser was 'shrewd, but not mad'. Washington knew that Cairo (and Damascus) did not have the complete support the Soviet Union publicly promised. Nor did the CIA see Soviet calculation behind the crisis. Washington also knew that it could not support an Israeli pre-emptive military response to the closure of the Straits of Tiran; the US was unwilling to 'unleash' the Israelis by giving them a green light. After meeting with Abba Eban in the White House on 26 May, President Johnson handed the Israeli foreign minister a note that concluded: 'I must emphasize the necessity for Israel not to make itself responsible for the initiation of hostilities. Israel will not be alone unless it decides to go alone.' The president added in his own handwriting the comment: 'We cannot imagine that it will make this decision.'[6] By 30 May, however, Israel thought it had at least a yellow light from Washington. Interestingly, the Soviet Union issued the same warning, not to attack first, to Nasser.

However, Washington also knew that Israel did not believe anything useful would come out of the UN, and had nothing better to offer Israel than the fall-back position of examining all options with a view to preserving freedom of the seas and international peace and security. Johnson set about organizing an international convoy of ships to run through the straits, breaking Egypt's blockade, but he was unsuccessful. This was never going to be enough for the Israelis. Nasser, to prove his toughness, increased his inflammatory rhetoric, which only exacerbated the situation, and he and King Hussein signed a military pact on 30 May. Eshkol, too, had to prove to his public – especially to former prime minister Ben-Gurion – that he had 'a real moustache'. After three weeks of anxiety, uncertainty and an increasingly fearful population, on Sunday 4 June the cabinet adopted the recommendation of Dayan, newly appointed as defence minister, and voted for war. Nasser, and the Arabs, had to be taught a lesson: don't mess with Israel.

It would never have come to this if it had not been for the events of the previous year in Jordan. On 11 November 1966 three Israeli soldiers on border patrol near the Jordanian-occupied West Bank were killed by a mine. The Israelis believed the mine had been planted by PLO militants from Es Samu, a village of 4,000 Palestinian refugees, just south of Hebron. Israel assured King Hussein that they did not intend an attack on Jordan. Nevertheless, on 13 November a large Israeli force of between 3,000 and 4,000 soldiers, backed by tanks and aircraft, crossed into the Jordanian-occupied West Bank and headed for Samu. A battle ensued between the Israeli forces and a battalion of the Jordanian army. Three Jordanian civilians and fifteen soldiers were reportedly killed; fifty-four other soldiers and ninety-six civilians were wounded. The commander of the Israelis was killed and ten other Israeli soldiers were wounded.

Special Assistant Rostow reported to Lyndon Johnson that the raid was out of all proportion to the provocation and was aimed at the wrong target. The raid had set back progress toward a long-term accommodation with the Arabs.[7] The US had been attempting to support the Jordanian king as a means of stabilizing Israel's longest border. Hussein would now be under greater pressure to counter-attack, not only from the more radical Arab governments and from the Palestinians in Jordan but also from the army. Rostow was right. Facing a storm of criticism from Jordanians, Palestinians and his Arab neighbours for failing to protect Samu, Hussein ordered a nation-wide mobilization on 20 November.

The mine-laying was not the work of King Hussein; he had done everything he could to prevent such incidents. Deployment of the hellish device was the work of al-Fatah, a militant group within the recently established PLO. *Fatah*, meaning 'conquest', is an acronym whose letters in reverse stand for *Harakat al-Tahrir al-Falastini*, or 'Movement for the Liberation of Palestine'. After some years in a state of shock, Palestinians were beginning to speak with their own voices. Palestinian aspirations could not be indefinitely ignored by the Arabs or suppressed by the Israelis. Any hope that the Arab states would restore them to their former homes had evaporated, so they turned to their own military activities. Fatah was founded in the late 1950s by a group of Palestinian students in Cairo, including Yasser Arafat, a member of the Hajj Amin al-Husseini family. Fatah had undoubtedly participated in fedayeen raids before the Suez-Sinai war, but as the group languished Arafat moved to Kuwait where he became a successful engineering contractor. In the 1960s Fatah began to gravitate into the orbit of Syria, which saw it as a useful adjunct for its own agenda directed against Israel. In January 1965 Fatah members carried out their first significant raid against Israel from Syrian territory.

The first meeting of the PLO had taken place in May 1964 when about 400 Palestinians who made up the Palestine National Council convened at the invitation of King Hussein in the new Intercontinental Hotel in the Arab sector of Jerusalem. The meeting drew up the Palestine National Charter, which stated that the purpose of the organization was to liberate Palestine from its colonialist oppressors, the Zionists, through 'armed struggle' and provided for the formation of a Palestine Liberation Army (PLA). The formation of such an organization had been proposed at a summit meeting of the Arab League in Cairo in January of that year. Ahmad Shuqayri, an influential lawyer and Palestinian spokesperson in the service, respectively, of Syria, Saudi Arabia and Egypt, was elected chairman. Troops for the PLA were to be recruited from among Palestinians scattered through the Arab world. Shuqayri established a headquarters in the Old City of Jerusalem, imposed taxes on the Palestinian refugees and set up training camps.

Hussein was no friend of the PLO, however, as he was not interested in an independent Palestinian state. The king believed that the PLO intended to build up a state within a state in Jordan. He arrested many members and shut down PLO operations. He hoped the Arab states, particularly Egypt, would control the organization and its agenda. For his part, Nasser also had reservations about the organization and would not permit guerrilla bases in Egypt and Gaza. Toward the end of 1966, in an effort to assert greater control over Fatah and to strengthen Palestinian independence from the Arab states, PLO leader Shuqayri initiated a rapprochement with Fatah.

By the mid-1960s the Arab states were deeply divided ideologically over how to deal with Israel. The left-leaning Nasser and the socialist Ba'athist regime in Syria regarded the monarchies, Saudi Arabia and Jordan (and Yemen), as reactionary puppets of the West. But neither Egypt nor Jordan wanted to challenge or provoke Israel. Lebanese governments also made serious attempts to prevent incursions from their territory. These inter-Arab tensions were exacerbated by Palestinian guerrilla activity originating in Syria, Jordan and the Gaza Strip, and also by the escalating and ongoing Syrian-Israel and Egyptian-Israel border and maritime disputes.

In 1966 General Salah Jadid, a Ba'athist Alawite (a minority Shia sect considered heretical by the Sunni mainstream), took over in a military coup in Syria, the second within three years. Ba'athist political ideology combined leftist social and economic ideas with pan-Arabism. Jadid instituted radical domestic policies and was openly hostile to the West and to Israel. He substantially increased weapons shipments and other support for Fatah. While the Syrian army fired down on Israeli farmers from the Golan Heights, Fatah guerrillas struck at Israeli patrols and conducted a number of raids – largely ineffectual – just north of the Sea of Galilee.

Syria tried to prevent Israel pumping water from the Sea of Galilee by constructing canals to divert the headwaters of the River Jordan arising in its territory. Israeli artillery and planes made this too hazardous to continue, and Nasser refused to help Syria because of the anticipated Israeli reaction.

The Syrians abandoned the project, but tension increased on the Syrian–Israeli border. Dayan estimated that approximately 80 per cent of Syrian attacks on Israeli farmers were provoked by Israel. There were also disputes in the central and southern sectors over cultivation rights, with each side arguing that the other was violating the DMZ. Both appealed to the UN, but in Security Council debates Western nations called upon Damascus to prevent Fatah operations from Syrian territory and the Eastern bloc chastised Israel for its aggressive intentions against Syria.

The Soviet Union, concerned that it might be dragged into a wider conflagration, called for restraint from the Syrian leader. Although the Soviet Union had been equipping Arab regimes and the US under Johnson had moved from partial to almost total support of Israel, there was little chance of the Soviet Union or the US intervening in any hostilities in the region; the costs were too high and the outcomes too unpredictable. The Soviets encouraged Egypt and Syria to enter into a joint defence pact. They hoped the pact, which was signed in early November 1966, would restrain the Syrians and that Egyptian adherence would deter Israeli retaliation. This was a perilous agreement, and Israel's military leaders viewed it with alarm. Egypt had received Soviet weapons in March and a well-armed and trained Egypt supported by Syria was a daunting prospect. In April 1967 a major clash occurred between Israeli and Syrian tanks and planes, heightening tension even further. Six Syrian planes were shot down and Israeli planes contemptuously flew low over the suburbs of Damascus. Jadid asked Nasser for help, leading to Egypt's troop movements outlined above.

The Israeli authorities did little to lessen the anxiety, even panic, among the Israeli public created by the threatening declarations coming from Egyptian and Syrian leaders. The situation was very tense. On paper the odds looked overwhelmingly in favour of the Arab states. Egyptian forces in the Sinai, although deployed along defensive lines, numbered around 100,000 with almost 1,000 tanks and more than 400 aircraft. Syrian troops, also mobilizing, numbered between more than 60,000 men with 200 tanks and over 100 planes, while King Hussein's army numbered around 56,000 men with around 300 tanks. Most of Jordan's army (45,000 troops and 200 modern tanks) was deployed to defend the West Bank and East Jerusalem. General Moshe Dayan was called in as defence minister to bolster the apparently indecisive Eskhol. The fiercely nationalistic Dayan, a devoted disciple of Ben-Gurion, and the right-wing extremist Menachem Begin, who had also joined a national coalition cabinet, convinced their more moderate colleagues that the only chance of success, should it come to full-scale war, was a pre-emptive attack. By 20 May Israel had fully mobilized its forces of around 264,000 men (including more than 214,000 reserves) with around 1,300 tanks and an air force of about 800 combat aircraft by 20 May. The primary focus of Israel's plan of attack approved by Dayan was to strike through the Sinai desert to attack Sharm el-Sheikh and open the Straits of Tiran. Dayan did not want Israeli forces to occupy the Gaza Strip or to seize the Suez Canal as he thought these actions would compromise and prolong the war. As it turned out, in the flush of battle both those restrictions were ignored by the generals.

The 1967 War

The Six-Day War must rank as one of the most stunning demonstrations of the effective use of air power in military history. At 7:45 a.m. on 5 June 1967 Israel launched a pre-emptive strike against Egypt's air force. Because of a mixture of luck, Egyptian ineptitude and inefficiency, the attack was more successful than expected, catching the Egyptians completely by surprise. The Egyptian radar system had been shut down as the Egyptian High Command was in an aircraft flying to inspect Egyptian units in the Sinai. By the end of the day more than 300 of Egypt's 450 aircraft were destroyed and 100 Egyptian pilots had been killed.[8] Later the same day attacks were carried out destroying the Jordanian, Syrian and Iraqi air forces. By nightfall, Israel claimed to have destroyed 416 Arab aircraft. By contrast, in the first two days of fighting Israel lost only 26 planes, mostly through mechanical failure or accidents. These attacks guaranteed Israeli air superiority for the rest of the war. Israel's total air superiority greatly assisted Israeli ground forces. Attacking from the north through the Gaza Strip and from the south with fast armoured units, within four days Israeli ground forces, augmented by paratroopers, had defeated Egypt's well-equipped army in the Sinai and reached the Suez Canal. Two thousand Egyptian troops were killed in the Israeli assault and another 10,000 were killed in the chaotic retreat.

Israel was equally successful in the West Bank. The events of the previous months had placed King Hussein in an impossible position: if he joined with Egypt and Syria in an attack on Israel he risked losing the West Bank, but if he did not enter the war he risked losing his throne (and perhaps his life) to an uprising of a population caught up in nationalistic hostility to Israel. Faced with these options, the King chose the former, and on 30 May he signed a mutual defence treaty with Egypt and agreed to place his forces under Egyptian command.

Despite assurances from Eshkol delivered through the UN that no action would be taken against the Kingdom unless conflict was initiated by Jordan, on the morning of 5 June, acting under false information of early Egyptian successes provided by Nasser, Jordanian troops began shelling targets in West Jerusalem, Netanya and the outskirts of Tel Aviv. The Israelis did not respond at first, but on 6 June when the Jordanians occupied small areas of West Jerusalem Israeli units attacked Jordanian forces in the West Bank, and the air force destroyed the small Jordanian air force. By the evening of that day, Israeli troops had surrounded Jerusalem, but did not enter the city itself. In heavy fighting the next day, Israeli brigades entered the Old City, capturing the Western Wall and the Temple Mount. Israeli soldiers also occupied Mount Scopus, Ramallah and Jenin. In the south, Israeli forces seized Judea, Gush Etzion and Hebron. When Hussein ordered his forces to withdraw across the River Jordan, Dayan ordered his troops to capture the rest of the West Bank. Israel's occupation of the West Bank was not an original aim of the war, it was an unintended consequence.

Given Israel's remarkable and quick success, Syria was reluctant to join hostilities. But on the basis of Nasser's false claims of early Egyptian victories it, too, initiated hostilities against Israel. However, by the evening of 5 June the Israel air force, which had been shelling Syrian artillery positions in the Golan Heights for four days prior to the outbreak of war, attacked and destroyed two-thirds of the Syrian air force, essentially eliminating it from further action. Rather than launching a major ground offensive into Israel as planned, Syrian artillery instead began a massive shelling of Israeli towns in the Hula Valley. Under the cover of air protection, by the evening of 9 June Israeli brigades had broken through to the plateau of the Golan. Syrian forces fled, and on 10 June Israeli troops occupied the area to what became the ceasefire line, known as the 'Purple Line'.

In what became one of the most contentious issues of the war, on 8 June Israeli air and sea forces attacked and nearly sank the USS *Liberty*, a United States Navy electronic intelligence vessel, just outside Egyptian territorial waters off Arish, killing 34 US servicemen and wounding 171. Israel claimed the attack was a case of mistaken identity, but recent evidence casts considerable doubt on this claim.

By 9 June, Jordan, Egypt and Syria agreed to a Security Council call for a ceasefire. On 10 June, when Israel's offensive against Syria ceased, Israel controlled all of the Sinai to the Suez Canal, the symbolically vital area of East Jerusalem and the strategic Golan Heights. The fighting had lasted six days. It was a spectacular demonstration of Israeli military power. The Arab states were totally humiliated. More than 21,000 Arab soldiers were killed and 45,000 wounded. Israel lost less than 1,000 soldiers, with around 2,500 wounded.

Israelis and Jews worldwide were ecstatic at the speed and comprehensive nature of their victory. Israelis regard the major outcome of the 1967 war to be the state's continued survival, and many Israeli leaders today argue that any significant alteration to the end result would seriously threaten Israel's security. To most Israelis the war reunited the ancient 'Land of Israel' with the modern state of Israel, completing its Jewish character. The Arabs, especially the Palestinians, saw Israel's conquest as further evidence of Israel's expansionist ambitions and were determined to seek a reversal of their defeat.

War planners had not expected such a decisive triumph. The war itself had transformed Israeli political goals into an outcome entirely unintended. The government was divided over its war aims and it improvised as the war progressed. The plan had been to destroy the Egyptian forces and capture and hold the Gaza Strip and the eastern Sinai until Nasser agreed to open the Straits of Tiran. In the north, following the destruction of the Syrian air force, the plan had been merely to capture the demilitarized zones, while in relation to Jordan only minor modifications in Jerusalem were envisaged. There were no plans to capture the West Bank; indeed the government opposed it. The complete collapse of the enemy had been unexpected. This military development led Israel to launch its takeover of the Golan Heights on the fourth day of the war. Whether Israel's occupation of the Sinai, the West Bank, Gaza Strip, the Golan Heights and East Jerusalem was an intended or unintended outcome of the war, with the exception of the Sinai, for 27 years Israel refused to return any of the conquered areas to either Jordanian or Palestinian control. An unintended consequence of the war for Israel was the control of approximately 1.3 million Arabs.

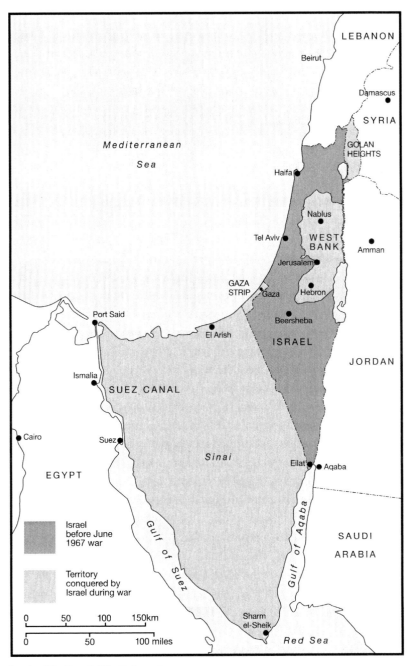

Israel and the Occupied Territories, 1967.

No one had planned what to do next. What was clear was that Israel could now negotiate, if it so desired, from a position of great strength. The first thing the government did was to annex East Jerusalem and the surrounding area on 18 June. The following day the cabinet unanimously agreed to negotiate a peace settlement with Egypt in which Israel would withdraw from the Sinai to the international borders if Egypt agreed to guarantee freedom of navigation in the Straits of Tiran, the Gulf of Aqaba and the Suez Canal, consented to the demilitarization of the Sinai, and countenanced the Gaza Strip remaining within Israel's borders. The cabinet also decided upon a peace settlement with Syria. Israel would return to the international border if Syria accepted the demilitarization of the Golan Heights and guaranteed the free flow of water from the sources of the Jordan into Israel. The Israeli plans explicitly excluded withdrawal from the West Bank or the Gaza Strip. The question of peace with Jordan was deferred. These decisions were relayed to the US administration, but it appears that the Americans did not tell Cairo and Damascus about them. The proposals were certainly kept secret in Israel, and the military strongly opposed them. In any event, within a few days the offers to return the Sinai and the Golan Heights were reversed.[9]

The cabinet decided to maintain military control of the West Bank, but left the status of the Palestinian residents indeterminate. They were not to become Israeli citizens, nor were they to remain Jordanians. The problem was demographic: how could Israel keep the West Bank without turning into a bi-national state? Some 300,000 Palestinians already lived in Israel proper, increasingly embittered by their status as second-class citizens. The Jewish population in 1967 was 2.7 million; the combined Arab population west of the River Jordan was 1.3 million (500,000 in the Gaza Strip and 800,000 in the West Bank). In the absence of a decision, Dayan, by now a national hero with the status of a demigod, Allon, and assorted right-wing and religious fundamentalist militants and squatters, were able successfully to establish dubious 'facts on the ground' – settlements and so-called outpost positions that multiplied over the years through formal and semi-informal arrangements.

Reflecting on the outcome of the Six-Day War, distinguished Israeli writer Amos Elon wrote in 2002 that right-wing and religious fundamentalists endowed the war with a metaphysical, pseudo-messianic aura.[10] Although at the time they were still a relatively small minority, they pushed for the formal annexation immediately of all 'liberated areas'. Squatters were gradually legalized, lavishly subsidized and eventually hailed as national heroes. If the British Empire was born in a fit of absent-mindedness, Elon noted, the Israeli colonial intrusion into the West Bank was undertaken under similar shadowy circumstances. Few people took the settlements seriously at first. Some deluded themselves that they were bound to be temporary. Those responsible pursued the goal of expanding the settlements consistently. The few who protested against them on political or demographic grounds were ignored. They were no match for the emerging coalition of religious and political fundamentalists. The Knesset never voted on the settlement project.

The settlements were at first financed mostly through non-governmental agencies: the United Jewish Appeal (UJA), the Jewish Agency and the National Jewish Fund (NJF). Although Washington mildly protested the settlement project, it took none of the legal and other steps it might have taken to stop the flow of tax-exempt contributions to the UJA or NJF that financed the settlements on land confiscated for 'security' reasons from its Palestinian owners. For all practical purposes, the United States served as a ready partner in the settlement project. The National Coalition cabinet remained in power. Levi Eshkol died soon after the war and was succeeded by the Ukrainian-born, American-raised hardliner Golda Meir, who became known for her smug maternalism and later remembered, among other things, for her infamous remark, 'Who are the Palestinians? I am a Palestinian.'[11]

The Six-Day War may have been forced on Israel, but as Amos Elon observed, the war's Seventh Day, which began on 12 June 1967, was the product of Israel's choice and lives on to this day. Israel, he wrote, enthusiastically chose to become a colonialist society, ignoring international treaties, expropriating lands, transferring settlers from Israel to the occupied territories, engaging in theft and finding justifications for all of this.[12]

Israel's leaders were blind to the Palestinian presence in the region. They dismissed the aspirations of more than a million Palestinians in the West Bank and Gaza Strip as of limited political importance. The Palestinians had been remarkably passive; they had allowed the West Bank to be conquered in a few hours without firing a single shot. They were shocked and paralysed by the war. The number of dispossessed people living in United Nations Relief and Works Agency (UNRWA) refugee camps swelled to 1.5 million, including 650,000 in thirteen camps in Palestine, Jordan, Syria and Lebanon.[13] As noted earlier, soon after the war Palestinian leaders in the West Bank, including intellectuals, notables, mayors and religious leaders, told two senior Israeli intelligence officers – one of whom was David Kimche, who later served as deputy director of Mossad and director general of the Israeli Foreign Ministry – they were ready to establish a demilitarized Palestinian state on the West Bank and sign a separate peace with Israel. Dayan never submitted the report Kimche wrote to the cabinet. It probably would have been rejected anyway. Dayan believed it would be possible to maintain the status quo on the West Bank and in Gaza for generations. The PLO at the time was still a fairly marginal group. Dayan – and nearly the entire political and military establishment – was convinced that not only the Palestinians but also Egypt and Syria would be unable to present a military threat for decades.

The failure to reach an agreement over the West Bank at this time seems all the more tragic, since there were still relatively few settlers (less than 3,000) and they would not have been able to veto all concessions, as they do today. The Palestinians over the ensuing years became radicalized by the increasingly humiliating occupation regime and by the large-scale expropriation of Palestinian land for the exclusive use of Israeli settlers. At that time the PLO was not recognized internationally, and neither Hamas nor Hezbollah existed. The later creation of Hamas was, in fact, encouraged by the Israelis as a counterweight to the PLO. An autonomous Palestinian entity, at peace with Israel, would not have removed the PLO from the scene, but its impact might have been considerably weakened. Alternatively, in a peace settlement with Jordan the Palestinian issue might have reverted to what it had been before 1967: mainly a Jordanian problem.

The Arab response to their defeat was dramatic. Nasser's immediate response to Egypt's crushing collapse was to melodramatically announce his 'resignation', but mass demonstrations of the people 'forced' him to stay on. Egypt and Saudi Arabia did come to their senses in Yemen and ended their fighting there. Jordan's King Hussein offered a full peace in return for withdrawal from the West Bank, but Israel's exultant leaders replied in the negative. Arab leaders felt the only way they could respond was with defiance.

At a summit held in Khartoum between 28 August and 2 September 1967, eight Arab heads of state agreed on three 'no's' with Israel: no peace, no recognition, no negotiations. The resolutions adopted called for the continued struggle against Israel, the creation of a fund to assist the economies of Egypt and Jordan, the resumption of interrupted oil sales to the West, and insistence on the rights of the Palestinian people to their own country. This obdurate stance did nothing to advance the cause of peace. Israeli leaders interpreted these dictums literally as indicating a total rejection of Israel by the Arabs. Despite the 'three no's' of Khartoum, direct negotiations with Jordan began soon after the Six-Day War, by 1970 with King Hussein himself. Even while Meir was publicly lamenting that the Arabs would not sit down 'like decent human beings and talk', her representatives were secretly meeting the king. Hussein flew his own helicopter to Tel Aviv and was taken by Dayan on a tour of the city by night.[14] He was ready to make peace with Israel if Israel withdrew from much of the West Bank as well as from East Jerusalem, and if the Muslim and Christian holy places in the Old City were restored to Jordan. The king was ready to grant concessions to Israel along the narrow coastal plain and at the Western Wall in the Old City of Jerusalem. Israel would not hear of it. When told of Allon's plans, Hussein indicated that for such far-reaching concessions the Israelis would have to negotiate with the PLO. In retrospect, it is tragic that no agreement could be reached with Palestinian leaders in the West Bank, or with Jordan in the late 1960s and early 1970s.

Within weeks of war's end, the Soviet Union, determined to revive its influence and the confidence of its allies, began re-arming Syria and Egypt. The Soviets shipped more than 200 crated MiG fighter jets in two weeks. The US made no unilateral effort to begin a peace process. Washington appeared happy that Israel had humiliated the Soviet Union's main clients in the region and felt no urgency to intervene. The Arab–Israeli conflict was becoming a proxy conflict between the superpowers, a testing ground for their hardware.

Both superpowers turned to the UN to reach an acceptable diplomatic solution. In November 1967 the Security Council passed Resolution 242, a masterpiece of diplomatic ambiguity that became the key document in future attempts to arrive at a peaceful solution to the conflict. UN Resolution 242 proposed (in so many words) the idea of peace in return for territory – without specifying which should come first. It also introduced a rather new and startling principle in international law: the inadmissibility of the acquisition of territory by conquest. The resolution's first article called upon Israel to return occupied territories (but not 'the' territories). The second article recognized the right of all states in the region to live in peace within secure and recognized borders. Other important points included freedom of passage through international waterways and a just solution to the 'refugee' problem. Resolution 242 was accepted by Israel, Egypt and Jordan, but not by Syria, and was a notable milestone in its implicit acknowledgment by these Arab states of Israel's existence and its expectation of a negotiated settlement. There was no machinery to implement the resolution, however, except through the good offices of a special UN mediator, Dr Gunnar Jarring, whose task was to try to facilitate talks among the parties. The Israelis wanted explicit recognition through direct negotiations before any withdrawal; they had no intention of withdrawing from all the occupied territory. The Arabs insisted on Israel's withdrawal from all the occupied territory, including East Jerusalem, which the Israelis had annexed shortly after the conclusion of hostilities, and insisted upon negotiations through intermediaries. The resolution did not address the escalating arms race. Even more significant in both the short and long run was the absence of any specific reference to the Palestinians, except for the provision that there should be a just solution to the refugee problem.

The war of 1967 did not bring peace to the region, or security to Israel. It did hasten a virtual alliance between Israel and the United States that the majority of Israelis believe has proved invaluable to Israel. Others, a minority, believe it has led Israel to lose its soul. Washington began to view Israel as a strong and valuable ally in the region and in 1968 approved the first major sale of offensive weapons to Israel. The absence of a negotiated settlement, however, made another round in the Arab–Israeli conflict almost a certainty, especially when the injury done to Arab honour, pride and self-respect was added to the loss of territory. Egypt, using its new Soviet military equipment, began shooting at the Israelis dug-in across the Suez Canal as early as 1968. Nasser wanted to destroy the line of massive earthwork fortifications, the Bar Lev line, built by the Israelis. This harassment escalated into what is known as the 1968–70 War of Attrition. Egyptian shelling was comparatively ineffective, but Israeli bombardments were so severe that Egypt had to evacuate several towns. Daring Israeli raids into Egypt destroyed radar equipment, anti-aircraft missile sites, bridges and electricity plants. By 1969 the Israeli air force was using drones to photograph and monitor Egyptian, Syrian and, later, Jordanian troops. In July 1969 the Israeli air force bombed the Nile Valley inside Egypt. President Nasser asked the Soviets for help in defending Egyptian air space. The Soviets responded quickly, sending batteries of surface-to-air missiles (SAMs) with Soviet crews, and squadrons of MiG-21s with Soviet pilots and ground crews. At first Israel refrained from engaging the Soviet-piloted MIGs, but in July 1970 the Israeli air force shot down four or five Soviet MIGs in a dogfight off the Suez Canal. Washington became concerned that things might get out of hand and negotiated a ceasefire in the form of the Rogers Plan, which went into effect on 7 August 1970. This plan called for a freeze of Egyptian and Israeli deployments.

Palestinians too, became more militant in the years following the 1967 war. The old leaders of the PLO were completely discredited. New active leadership was required to lead the inhabitants of the festering camps in Jordan and Lebanon and the Palestinians now living under Israeli occupation. Ahmad Shuqayri resigned as chairman in December 1967. In July 1968, at a meeting of the Palestine National Council (PNC) in Cairo, the PLO covenant was amended and the fedayeen were named as the nucleus of the armed struggle. This statement had implications for Jordan as well as Israel. The PLO functioned as an umbrella organization coordinating the activities of diverse small groups. Within two years Fatah had emerged as the most important of these, and in 1969 the PNC elected the Fatah leader, Yasser Arafat (Abu Ammar), chairman of the executive committee.

Fatah became the largest and most popular Palestinian party for several reasons. Unlike some of the smaller blocs within the PLO, Fatah steered clear of close identification with any one Arab country. Indeed, its doctrinal vagueness also enabled it more easily to attract followers. The organization at the start also had an appeal to several Muslim activists, who equated the religious cause with the national cause and who desired in the name of Islam to liberate Palestine. Some factions, however, like the Popular Front for the Liberation for Palestine (PFLP), led by Dr George Habash, a Greek Orthodox Christian born in Lydda (now Lod, Israel), and the Democratic Front for the Liberation of Palestine (DFLP), led by Nayef Hawatmeh, a Jordanian Christian, became overtly Marxist–Leninist in their ideology. These radical activists believed that there had to be fundamental social and economic changes in the Arab world itself, and especially that there had to be revolutionary change in the conservative Arab states like Jordan and Saudi Arabia even before the liberation of Palestine.

The PFLP, DFLP and other splinter groups such as the PFLP-General Command, led by Ahmad Jibril, adopted the tactic of hijacking airplanes in 1968 and initiated other terrorist attacks against civilians outside the Middle East in order to draw attention to the Palestinian cause. Terrorism was condemned by the world community, which seemed powerless or unwilling to do much about it, but it served the Palestinian cause by encouraging the passage of resolutions in the UN General Assembly and other forums that recognize as legitimate the aspirations of the Palestinian people and their right to self-determination. Although there was always diversity and fragmentation over questions of ideology and tactics within the PLO, Yasser Arafat was unable or unwilling to prevent the actions of his more extreme rivals.

The Arab states did not entirely welcome the new Palestinian militancy. Nasser was cautious, and King Hussein was even less keen about their actions. The Palestinians despised Hussein and his moderate and temporizing policies and the PLO became a serious threat to Jordan's political stability. It prevented King Hussein from considering any negotiated settlement with Israel that did not include the PLO, and both indirectly and directly it undermined the monarchy. In June and again in September 1970 the King survived assassination attempts by Palestinians.

The PLO became so much like a state within a state in Jordan that eventually there was a showdown with Hussein. This occurred after Palestinians hijacked three airplanes and landed them at Amman (Jordan's capital) in September 1970 and subsequently blew them up on the tarmac, making the king appear impotent. The king ordered his loyal Bedouin troops to destroy the PLO. Around 3,000 Palestinian fedayeen were killed, and the Jordanian army turned back Syrian tanks poised to support the PLO. Hussein reasserted his control, but he could not have succeeded without the support of Israel, which, at the request of the United States, had threatened to intervene to prevent a major Syrian incursion. At that time the Syrian air force commander was Hafez al-Assad, later Syria's president, who, afraid of Israeli–US intervention, refused to provide air cover for the Syrian tanks. By July 1971 Hussein had expelled PLO terrorists and fighters from Jordanian territory. This crisis provided another example of the underlying common interest between King Hussein and Israel. It also demonstrated to the United States that Israel could be a reliable, effective American ally in the region.

Another important result of these events was the spawning of a new terrorist group called Black September, an arm of Fatah. Its first act was the murder of the Jordanian prime minister, Wasfi Tell, in Cairo in November 1971. The next year, at the 1972 Olympic Games in Munich, Black September was responsible for the deaths of eleven Israeli athletes. Another result of the showdown in Jordan was that the PLO moved to Lebanon, where their military and political activities became a significant factor in the Lebanese civil war that began in 1975 and in the unraveling of that fractured country.

The Palestinian cause was soon being described as the 'crux' of the issue in the Arab–Israeli dispute. Not only in the United Nations but in the capitals of the world, as well as in the deliberations of regional and international conferences, the right of the Palestinian people to self-determination was recognized. Palestinian nationalism had certainly become a reality. This was especially true after 1967 for several reasons: the absence of a negotiated settlement between the Arab states and Israel; the failure of the Palestinians to achieve repatriation or resettlement (except in Jordan) within the Arab world; the continued occupation of the West Bank and Gaza Strip, first by the Arabs and then by Israel; and finally the success of the self-generated Palestinian resistance. This situation fostered and nurtured the feeling of a separate identity among the Palestinian people, and what was originally perceived by many as a refugee problem did indeed become the problem of Palestinian nationalism.

The 1967 war galvanized the Palestinian sense of national identity. The Palestinians had been relatively quiescent during the previous nineteen years, looking to Nasser and other Arab leaders to liberate Palestine. They now realized they would have to rely upon themselves and, under Yasser Arafat as chairman, the restructured PLO, which was becoming a major force in the region's politics. In 1974 the Arab League recognized the PLO as the sole representative of the Palestinian people, and in November 1974 Arafat spoke before the UN General Assembly, confirming the PLO's international status.

In addition to mounting acts of terrorism, the PLO was creating an infrastructure for a state much as the Yishuv had done in the British mandate period. The PNC expanded its membership from 105 in 1969 to 293 in 1977, and 450 in 1989. The majority of these members were not part of guerrilla organizations, but rather represented mass organizations, trade unions and communities abroad. By the 1980s the PLO bureaucracy numbered around 8,000 Palestinians in noncombatant roles such as health care and education.

The PLO was only one reason among many that the Palestinian question added urgency to the Arab–Israeli dispute after 1967 and made the search for a settlement even more complicated than it already was. While supporters of

Israel insisted that the fundamental problem in the Arab–Israeli conflict was the inability of the Arabs to accept the sovereignty of the Jewish state, all Arabs, whether sympathetic or not to the plight of the Palestinians, could unite behind the Palestinian cause so as to force concessions from Israel to relinquish territory. The Palestinian issue took on a life of its own after the 1967 war, and that life would lead to another war in less than a decade.

The 1973 War

While Palestinian terrorists increased tension between Israel and its neighbours, they played little role in precipitating the war that broke out in October 1973. This war was fought to regain the Sinai. Nasser had died of a heart attack in September 1970. Vice-President Anwar al-Sadat, who took his place, had none of the stature or charisma of Nasser, but he was determined to regain the Sinai. He first tried diplomacy. In February 1971, in response to an initiative by UN intermediary Gunnar Jarring, Sadat declared that if Israel committed itself to 'withdrawal of its armed forces from Sinai and the Gaza Strip' and to implementation of other provisions of UN Security Council Resolution 242, as requested by Jarring, Egypt would then 'be ready to enter into a peace agreement with Israel'. In fact, he would have been happy to have the Israelis withdraw from the Suez Canal to the Mitla and Giddi passes (about 30 miles east of the canal) so that he could reopen and operate the canal. This was an extraordinary offer, one that gave lie to the Israeli argument that the Arabs would not talk to them of peace. Israeli prime minister Meir, however, insolently responded that Israel would not withdraw to the pre-5 June 1967 lines.[15] Despite pressure from the US administration of Richard M. Nixon, Meir would not budge. It was an opportunity arrogantly and tragically missed.

In July 1972 Sadat expelled almost all of the 20,000 Soviet military advisers in the country, hoping in vain that the US would interpret this as an act of conciliation. When nothing came of these initiatives, in late October 1972 Sadat reverted to the war option – the limited-war option of regaining part of the Sinai, not liberating all of the occupied peninsula. Even this was a high-risk venture because in the years following the 1967 war the United States had dramatically increased its military aid to Israel. At the same time, the Soviet president Leonid Brezhnev appeared to be helping Israel through his policy of allowing increased Jewish emigration from the USSR to Israel.

But the Egyptian president also had important domestic reasons to go to war. Egypt's economy was depressed and he knew that economic reforms would be highly unpopular among parts of the population. A military victory would give him the popularity he needed to lessen corruption and free up the economy. King Hussein of Jordan was reluctant to fully commit to a new war, however. The king did not trust Sadat. The Egyptian president was backing PLO claims to the West Bank and the Gaza Strip, and he promised Yasser Arafat that, in the event of a victory, the Palestinians would be given control of those territories. Hussein still saw the West Bank as part of Jordan and wanted it restored to his kingdom. Furthermore, during the Black September crisis of 1970 in Jordan, Syria had intervened militarily on the side of the PLO, leaving Assad and Hussein estranged from each other.

As early as April and May 1973, a full six months before the actual combined Egyptian/Syrian attack on the Sinai and Golan fronts, Israeli intelligence services had begun to pick up clear signals of Egypt's preparations for war. They knew that Sadat had the necessary divisions prepared to cross the Suez Canal, he had the bridging equipment to facilitate his army's crossing, and he had SAMs to protect his own divisional crossings from the penetrating raids of the Israeli Air Force. By mid-1973 Israeli military intelligence was highly aware of Arab war plans. They knew that the Egyptian Second and Third Armies would attempt to cross the Suez Canal to a depth of about ten kilometres inside the Israeli side of Sinai. Following the infantry assault, Egyptian armoured divisions would then attempt to cross the Suez Canal and advance all the way to the Mitla and Giddi Passes – strategic crossing-points for any army in the Sinai. Naval units and paratroopers would then attempt to capture Sharm el-Sheikh at the southern end of the Sinai. Israeli military intelligence was also aware of many tactical details of the Syrian war plan.

But Israeli analysts did not believe the Arabs were serious about going to war. Even when all the signs indicated that war was imminent, they continued to believe the Arabs would not launch an attack. Why? Hubris, basically. In the late 1960s and early 1970s the Israeli military believed that the 1967 war had been such an overwhelming victory that the Arabs would not be able to overcome Israel for a considerable period of time. Part of the reason for this Israeli complacency was Arab political and military deception. President Sadat frequently and publicly declared his intention to attack Israel. He called 1971 'the Year of Decision' – but 1971 came and went without an attack. In 1972 he continued to make threats of his aggressive intentions towards Israel but he took no action. By 1973 Sadat had become, in the minds of Israeli Intelligence, the boy who cried 'wolf'.[16]

Final Egyptian planning was done in absolute secrecy. Sadat could not afford to have the timing of the planned Egyptian crossing of the canal leaked. The Soviets thought Egypt had little chance in any war. They warned that any attempt to cross the heavily fortified Suez would incur massive losses. The Soviets, who were then pursuing détente, had no interest in seeing the Middle East destabilized. In a June 1973 meeting with US President Nixon, Brezhnev proposed that Israel pull back to its 1967 border. The Soviet leader said that if Israel did not, 'we will have difficulty keeping the military situation from flaring up', indicating that the Soviet Union was having difficulty restraining Sadat.[17]

On the night of 25 September 1973, ten days prior to the Arab attack, King Hussein secretly flew to Tel Aviv to warn Israeli Prime Minister Golda Meir of an impending Syrian–Egyptian attack. Surprisingly, this warning fell on deaf ears. Mossad chief Zvi Zamir insisted that war was not an Arab option. He would later remark that, 'We simply didn't feel them capable of war.'[18] Aware that an attack was impending, Meir, Dayan and General David Elazar met at 8:05 a.m. on the morning of Yom Kippur, 6 October. After lengthy discussion, the prime minister decided there would be no pre-emptive Israeli strike. 'If we strike first, we won't get help from anybody', she said.[19] European nations, under threat of an Arab oil embargo and trade boycott, had stopped supplying Israel with munitions. As a result, Israel was totally dependent on the US to resupply its army and was particularly sensitive to anything that might endanger that relationship. After Meir had made the decision not to strike first, a message arrived from US secretary of state Henry Kissinger: 'Don't pre-empt.'[20]

The attack did not begin as the Israelis expected at 6 p.m. that day – it began at 1:55 p.m. Israel was woefully unprepared. If Israel's initial success in the 1967 war was due to Egyptian recklessness, as Ahron Bregman notes, at the outbreak of the 1973 war it was the Israelis who were foolish and inept.[21] Under the protection of their Soviet-supplied surface-to-air missile (SAM) batteries and a massive hour-long artillery barrage, 8,000 Egyptian troops crossed the Suez Canal, easily overcoming Israeli defences, and within six hours five infantry divisions and 400 tanks had crossed the canal and established a bridgehead about ten kilometres into the Sinai. At the same time the Egyptian air force successfully struck Israeli airfields, command posts, radar stations and artillery positions with negligible losses. Israeli military intelligence had seriously underestimated the lethal effectiveness of the Soviet-made Sagger anti-tank missiles, which the Egyptian infantry used to devastating effect against Israeli armoured counter-attacks, as well as the SAMs, which both the Egyptians and Syrians used with similar effect against the Israeli air force. In the first 24 hours of the war, around 300 Israeli tanks and 30 aircraft were destroyed. On 7 October the Egyptians consolidated their positions. The following day Israeli tanks counter-attacked, but were repulsed with heavy losses.

On the Golan Heights 1,400 Syrian tanks and more than 1,000 artillery pieces faced 177 Israeli tanks and 50 artillery pieces. Israel fought a tenacious battle and turned near-defeat on 6 October to a recapture of almost all of the Golan by the evening of 7 October. But Syria's rapid advance towards the Sea of Galilee and Israel's northern settlements unleashed a fear of invasion that Israelis find hard to forget. The tide in the Golan began to turn as Israeli reserve forces were able to contain and, beginning on 8 October, push back the Syrian offensive. By Wednesday 10 October the last Syrian unit in the central sector had been pushed back across the Purple Line, that is, the pre-war border. Then a decision had to be made – whether to stop at the 1967 border, or to continue into Syrian territory. The Israeli High Command spent the whole of 10 October debating this until well into the night. The prime minister was in no doubt, the Purple Line had to be crossed and the attack would be launched the next day, 11 October.[22]

From 11 October to 14 October the Israeli forces pushed into Syria, conquering a further twenty-square-mile box of territory in the Bashan. From there they were able to shell the outskirts of Damascus, only 25 miles (40 km) away, using heavy artillery. Pressure mounted on King Hussein to send his army into action. He found a way to meet these demands without opening his kingdom to Israeli air attack. Instead of attacking Israel from their common border, he sent an expeditionary force into Syria. He let Israel know of his intentions, through US intermediaries, in the hope that Israel would accept that this was not a *casus belli* justifying an attack on Jordan. Dayan declined to offer any such assurance, but Israel had no intention of opening another front. Iraq also sent an expeditionary force to the Golan, consisting of some 30,000 men, 500 tanks and 700 armoured personnel carriers. The Iraqi divisions were a strategic surprise for the IDF, and the combined Syrian, Iraqi and Jordanian counter-attacks prevented any further Israeli gains. However, they were also unable to push the Israelis back from the Bashan salient.

In an attempt to relieve pressure on the Syrians, Egypt launched a large mechanized offensive in the Sinai on 14 October, but without SAM cover about half the advancing 400 Egyptian tanks were destroyed by the Israeli air force. The next day, Israeli infantry counter-attacked against Egyptian forces and after heavy fighting managed to cross the Suez Canal into Egypt. Using rebuilt World War II pontoon bridges to cross the canal and with air support, by 22 October an Israeli division was soon well within Egypt, about 62 miles (101 km) from Cairo.

Very quickly the USSR recognized the need to rearm its Arab allies and began doing so. It also mobilized its Mediterranean fleet. Washington reassured Israel that it would replace its lost weapons and on 22 October began ferrying shipments of arms to Tel Aviv. The war looked as if it could very easily escalate into a superpower contest, something neither the US or USSR wanted. On 22 October the UN Security Council passed Resolution 338 (14-0) calling for a ceasefire, largely negotiated between the US and Soviet Union. It called upon 'all parties to the present fighting' to 'terminate all military activity immediately'. It came into effect twelve hours later, at 6:52 p.m. Israeli time. During the night, with US acquiescence, Israeli troops in Egypt continued their drive south, and trapped the Egyptian Third Army east of the Suez Canal, presenting Secretary of State Kissinger with a tremendous opportunity – Egypt was totally dependent on Washington to prevent Israel from destroying its trapped army, which now had no access to food or water. Kissinger realized that the position could be parlayed into allowing the US to mediate the dispute, and push Egypt out from under Soviet influence.

As a result, the United States exerted tremendous pressure on the Israelis to refrain from destroying the trapped Egyptian army. In a phone call with Israeli ambassador Simcha Dinitz, Kissinger told the ambassador that the destruction of the Egyptian Third Army 'is an option that does not exist'.[23] In the meantime, Brezhnev sent Nixon a letter in the middle of the night of 23/24 October. Brezhnev proposed that American and Soviet contingents be dispatched to ensure both sides honour the ceasefire. He also threatened that if the two superpowers did not act jointly, the Soviets would take unilateral steps to prevent Israel acting arbitrarily. In short, he was threatening to intervene in the war on Egypt's side. The Soviets placed seven airborne divisions on alert, and an airlift was marshalled to transport them to the Middle East. Several air force units were alerted. The Soviets also deployed seven amphibious warfare craft with some 40,000 naval infantry in the Mediterranean.

A conciliatory response was sent to Brezhnev, and a message was also sent to Sadat asking him to drop his request for Soviet assistance, threatening that if the Soviets were to intervene, so, too, would the US. The Soviets reconciled themselves to an Arab defeat. The next morning the Egyptians agreed to the American suggestion, and dropped their request for assistance from the Soviets, bringing the crisis to an end. On 23 October Syria announced it had accepted the ceasefire, and the Iraqi government ordered its forces home.

On 24 October the UN Security Council passed Resolution 339, serving as a renewed call for all parties to adhere to the ceasefire terms established in Resolution 338. The ceasefire did not end the sporadic clashes, nor did it dissipate military tensions. Egypt's Third Army, cut off and without any means of resupply, was effectively a hostage to the Israelis. Egypt indicated it was willing to enter into direct talks with the Israelis, provided that the Israelis agreed to allow non-military supplies to reach their army and agreed to a complete ceasefire. Organized fighting on all fronts ended by 26 October.

Talks between Israel and Egypt began on 28 October. Sadat agreed to a Kissinger-brokered agreement. United Nations checkpoints replaced Israeli checkpoints, non-military supplies were allowed to pass, and prisoners-of-war were exchanged. A summit in Geneva followed and, ultimately, an armistice agreement was worked out. On 18 January 1974 Israel signed a pullback agreement to the east side of the canal, and the last of its troops withdrew from the west side of the canal on 5 March.

On the Syrian front, Kissinger's shuttle diplomacy eventually produced a disengagement agreement on 31 May 1974. It stipulated an exchange of prisoners-of-war, Israeli withdrawal to the Purple Line and the establishment of a UN buffer zone. The agreement ended the skirmishes and exchanges of artillery fire that had occurred frequently along the Israeli–Syrian ceasefire line. A UN Disengagement and Observer Force (UNDOF) was established as a peace-keeping force in the Golan.

The peace discussions at the end of the 1973 war were the first time that Arab and Israeli officials had met for direct public discussions since the end of the 1948 war. On a geographical and operational level, the end of the war saw Israel with territorial gains in the Golan Heights and the encirclement of the Egyptian Third Army. The Arab side succeeded in surprising Israeli and worldwide intelligence agencies both strategically and tactically. Some commentators see this as one of the outstanding plans of deception mounted in the course of military history. For the Arab states (and Egypt in particular), the psychological trauma of their defeat in the Six-Day War had been healed. In many ways, it allowed them to negotiate with the Israelis as equals. The initial success greatly increased Sadat's popularity, giving him much firmer control of the Egyptian state and the opportunity to initiate many of the reforms he felt were necessary. Conversely, however, the war helped convince many in the Arab world that Israel could not be defeated militarily, thereby strengthening peace movements. The war effectively ended the old Arab ambition of destroying Israel by force.

The 1973 war had a stunning effect on the population in Israel. Following their victory in the Six-Day War, the Israeli military had become complacent. The shock and sudden defeats that occurred at the beginning of the new war dealt a terrible psychological blow to the Israelis, who had thought they had military supremacy in the region. In Israel, the casualty rate was high. On a per capita basis, Israel suffered three times as many casualties in three weeks of fighting as the United States did during almost a decade of fighting in Vietnam.[24]

A protest against the Israeli government started four months after the war ended. Anger against Dayan, in particular, was high. Shimon Agranat, president of the Israeli Supreme Court, led an inquiry into the events leading up to the war and the setbacks of the first few days. The resulting Agranat Commission published its preliminary findings on 2 April 1974. Although a number of senior military and intelligence officers were held responsible, it cleared Meir and Dayan of all responsibility. As a result of what appeared to be a whitewash, public calls for their resignation (especially Dayan's) became more vociferous. Finally, on 11 April 1974 Golda Meir resigned. Her cabinet followed suit, including Dayan, who had previously offered to resign twice and was turned down both times by Meir. Rabin, who had spent most of the war as an adviser to Elazar in an unofficial capacity, became head of a new government, which was seated in June.

In reaction to US support of Israel, on 17 October the Arab members of OPEC (the Oil Producing and Exporting Countries), led by Saudi Arabia, decided to reduce oil production by 5 per cent per month. Two days later, President Nixon nonetheless authorized a major allocation of arms supplies and US$2.2 billion in appropriations for Israel. In angry response, Saudi Arabia declared an embargo against the United States. The Saudis were later joined by other oil exporters and the embargo was extended to the Netherlands and other states, causing the 1973–4 oil crisis. This concentrated the minds of everyone, and set the Arab–Israeli conflict on a course of negotiations that we look at in the next chapter.

CHAPTER 6

Peace Gained, Peace Lost

During the 1973 war the Arab armies had seriously challenged the whole Israeli security philosophy of secure and defensible boundaries. Until 1967 Israel's defensive policy was based on the necessity of maintaining the capacity to mount a pre-emptive strike. From 1967 to 1973 the concept of 'secure borders' had been borders that could be defended without a pre-emptive strike. The defence establishment had believed that the territories occupied in 1967 gave Israel the depth of territory that made this possible. It was a serious error of judgement; the Arabs succeeded, however briefly, in imposing their will militarily on Israel.

The history of the conflict since 1973 has revealed only too clearly that topographical obstacles, strategic depth and security zones – or, since 2002, a concrete wall – cannot, of themselves, provide security. Security can only be gained through mutual acceptance of, and by, one's neighbours. Reciprocal respect between Arabs and Israelis, as exemplified by Egypt and Israel in 1979, make the creation of so-called 'secure' borders unnecessary. Without recognition of the legitimate rights of each other, allegedly secure borders will not be sufficient. The use of overwhelming military firepower will certainly not achieve lasting security. If Israel's leaders learned these basic lessons surrounding the concept of 'secure borders' in 1973, they were not prepared to say so for a number of years. This chapter details the prospects briefly offered by peace and how they were dashed in Lebanon during the decade or so following 1973.

Many Israelis regard the three-week 1973 war as more consequential than the war of 1967. The tank battles fought between Israel and Egypt were the largest since World War II, and the losses on both sides were massive. Almost 15,000 Egyptians and Syrians and more than 2,600 Israelis were killed in battle. Israel's victory was far from conclusive. Egyptian pride and honour was restored and Israel's over-confidence shattered.[1] The United States played a critical role in ending the war and in producing the peace. Washington worked with the Soviets in the UN to obtain a ceasefire. Washington could not contemplate an Egyptian–Syrian victory, as this would reinforce Arab reliance upon Soviet arms. The Soviets could not be seen to benefit from the war. Equally, the US did not want to be seen by the Arab states as unconditionally supporting Israel. Sadat was not to be humiliated. Nixon and Kissinger were determined that an evenhanded United States, rather than the Soviet Union, should become the dominant superpower in the Middle East. The end of the war opened a lengthy period of negotiations that resulted in the first peace treaty between Israel and an Arab state, Egypt, in 1979. Israel agreed to withdraw from the Sinai captured twelve years previously in 1967. For the first time negotiations appeared to offer more than war. Discussions between Israel, Syria, Jordan and the Palestinians did not make much progress, however, and in the 1980s violence once again took over.

The Camp David Peace Accords

In calling upon the warring parties to end the fighting, the UN Security Council, in Resolution 338 of 22 October 1973, decided that negotiations between the parties concerned should begin under 'appropriate auspices' to establish 'a just and durable peace in the Middle East'. The appropriate auspices were the United States and the Soviet Union. The United States and the Soviet Union stepped in to contain their 'clients'. In December the two powers invited Egypt, Jordan, Syria and Israel to a peace conference in Geneva. This conference, held on 9 January 1974, was the first time that foreign ministers of the United States, the Soviet Union and Middle Eastern states met at the same table. Syria refused to attend because the PLO was not invited due to opposition by the US and Israel. Tensions remained high; during the meeting, which lasted only one day, not a single word was directly exchanged between Arab and Israeli delegates. There was little progress and the conference was adjourned inconclusively. Kissinger immediately began working with the Egyptian president to sort out disengagement agreements, and to discuss approaches to end the oil embargo imposed by the Arab states during the war. Disengagement agreements were signed between Egypt and Israel on 18 January 1974 and between Syria and Israel on 31 May.

The Arab states realized that the threat of oil embargos and price increases was more effective in furthering their cause than military action against Israel. By this time the US regarded Israel as a strategic asset in the region. But Kissinger did not want US support for Israel to alienate the neighbouring Arab states. He was determined to set American–Egyptian relations on a more stable basis, and Sadat was eager to cooperate. Kissinger and Sadat hoped that they could draw Jordan into peace negotiations with Israel. However, negotiations proceeded slowly. On 10 April 1974 a disgraced and disillusioned Golda Meir resigned and Rabin, chief of staff during the 1967 war and former ambassador to the United States, took over as prime minister of Israel in early June. Rabin was cautious and hard-line, and his task was made more difficult by the fact that his senior Labor colleagues, Peres and Yigal Allon, both wanted his job. Rabin believed Israel could not be seen as acting from weakness. His reluctance to move forward was helped by the fact that the 1973 war, unlike that of 1967, which revitalized it, seriously damaged Israel's economy. Living standards were drastically reduced, a situation made even more galling by the soaring revenues coming in to the oil-rich Arab states.

In September 1975, following a number of informal, secret meetings in which the US agreed to build and man early warning radar stations in the vicinity of the Giddi and Mitla passes on behalf of Israel and Egypt, Israel reluctantly endorsed a second Sinai disengagement agreement. Israel agreed to withdraw from the Abu Rodeis oilfields and the two passes, which would be included in a demilitarized buffer zone under the control of UN forces. Rabin also insisted upon a memorandum of understanding between the US and Israel, in which the US pledged ongoing support for Israel. In a separate secret agreement Washington agreed that it would not recognize or negotiate with the PLO without prior consultation with Israel, or deviate from UN resolutions 242 and 338 as the sole basis for peace negotiations. The second Sinai agreement (Sinai II) was very specific and limited. It did not refer to the West Bank or the Golan Heights, and was not intended as a first step toward a comprehensive peace settlement.

In elections held in 1977, Labor's 29 uninterrupted years in government in Israel came to an end. Menachem Begin became prime minister in May, leading the newly formed conservative coalition, Likud. The Likud opposed returning any territory to Egypt. Given his strong hawkish views about the inviolability of the territories occupied since 1967 and his deep distrust of and animosity toward Arabs, Begin seemed the most unlikely person to agree to any surrender of territory.

Sadat was determined to press ahead, however, to gain the remainder of the Sinai. The Egyptian president believed that, although Israel could not be defeated militarily, it could be forced to negotiate the return of the Sinai. Several secret meetings had been taking place involving such intermediaries as Jordan's King Hussein, King Hassan II of Morocco and President Nicolae Ceausescu of Romania. On 9 November 1977 Sadat declared to a surprised Egyptian National Assembly that he was ready to go to the Israeli Knesset itself to discuss peace. Under intense international scrutiny, a shocked Begin had little choice but to extend an invitation to him to do so. Sadat arrived in Israel on 19 November 1977, and in his speech to the Knesset he announced that he was prepared to accept and live in permanent peace with Israel 'based on justice'.

The Egyptian knew Begin would not meet all his terms, especially those demanding that Israel withdraw from all territories occupied in 1967 and recognize the right of the Palestinians to self-determination. Little came of the private talks the two leaders held, but the visit did, as Sadat hoped it would, break down some of the psychological barriers between Israel and Egypt that stood in the way of reaching a settlement. The two agreed to meet in December at Ismailia, Egypt. As expected, he rejected the idea of a Palestinian state in the West Bank and Gaza Strip, agreeing only to limited home rule for the Palestinians, by which he meant 'administrative autonomy', in the form of elected municipalities, with the Israeli army maintaining law and order. Nevertheless, two committees were formed – one political and one military – to discuss the terms of a peace treaty. Plans were submitted and rejected by both sides, and talks dragged on fruitlessly for the next seven months.

Sadat's initiative had bypassed both the United States and the Soviet Union, but in August 1978 President Jimmy Carter invited Begin and Sadat to Camp David, the presidential retreat in Maryland. Carter hoped that, if he could enlist Soviet support, he could facilitate a comprehensive settlement of the Arab–Israeli conflict based on the 'land for peace' formula implicit in UN Resolution 242. Several meetings took place at Camp David; Carter called the negotiations one of the most frustrating experiences of his life but eventually, as a result of his persistence and dedicated personal involvement, two accords were signed on 17 September 1978. Begin agreed only after Carter threatened to cut off all aid to Israel, and then promised to increase it.

The accords signed at Camp David have formed the basis of all subsequent peace negotiations. They consisted of two agreements. The first, 'A Framework for Peace in the Middle East', called upon Egypt, Jordan, Israel and 'representatives of the Palestinian people' to negotiate the question of the West Bank and the Gaza Strip. A self-governing Arab authority was to replace the Israeli military forces for five years while talks took place on the 'final status' of the two areas. The second accord, 'A Framework for the Conclusion of a Peace Treaty between Egypt and Israel', was a draft proposal for a peace agreement to be negotiated and signed within three months. This provided for a phased Israeli withdrawal from the Sinai over three years and a full restoration of the area to Egypt. Israeli ships were to be allowed free passage through the Suez Canal. The United Nations would oversee provisions of the accords so as to satisfy both sides. The accords omitted the issue of Jerusalem and the future of the Golan Heights.

Begin was willing to make concessions to achieve peace with Egypt because the ideological and national reasons for retaining the West Bank, Gaza and Jerusalem did not apply to the Sinai. But he adamantly refused to consider an independent Palestinian state, repeating his position that the 'final status' of the territories could be no more than autonomy for the Palestinians. Sadat came to terms with Israel in 1978 and 1979 because he wanted to free up resources that had been devoted to waging war in order to reconstruct and widen the Suez Canal and to free Egypt from the Soviet orbit. To both Israel and Egypt, the future relationship with the United States was an important, if not the overriding, consideration.

Washington was willing to pay for loyalty. Separate agreements provided massive American economic and military aid. Israel was to receive US$3 billion in military and financial assistance, approximately US$800 million of which was to assist the relocation of Israel's two Sinai airbases to the Negev. Egypt was to receive US$2 billion in tanks, planes and anti-aircraft weapons. All this was in addition to the existing 1979 foreign aid allocation for the two countries of US$1 billion to Egypt and US$1.8 billion to Israel, an increase of around 200 per cent in US aid. The United States wanted to create a kind of 'coastal barrier' of friendly Western-orientated states stretching from Turkey through Lebanon, Israel, Jordan and Egypt to limit Soviet influence in the eastern Mediterranean and the Middle East. A peace treaty between Israel and Egypt was a key element in this strategy. Washington was confident that the Christian-based Lebanese government would support the formation of such a grouping.

Almost immediately, disagreements surfaced as to what exactly had been decided upon at Camp David. Begin insisted that new settlements go ahead on the West Bank and in the Gaza Strip, and claimed that the accords permitted him to do so after a three-month moratorium. Carter said that Begin had agreed that no new settlements would be established during the five-year transition period. For his part, Sadat claimed that any agreement should be linked to the issue of the occupied territories, and he stated that a peace treaty between Egypt and Israel could be signed only after a timetable for Palestinian self-rule had been finalized. He was careful not to endorse the formation of an independent state of Palestine. Both leaders were under intense domestic political pressure not to make concessions. Only after Carter visited Cairo and Jerusalem, in early March 1979, did the Israeli and Egyptian cabinets approve compromises he suggested. On 26 March 1979, on the White House lawn with Carter as witness, Sadat and Begin formally signed a treaty embodying the general provisions of the framework agreement. This was a watershed in the Arab–Israeli conflict.

The Camp David accords and the Israel–Egypt peace treaty split Egypt from Arab opinion; it was seen as a separate peace designed to neutralize Egypt from the anti-Zionist struggle. The majority of Arabs saw this as a way of preventing joint Arab action to dislodge Israel from the Arab territory and as weakening the legitimate right of the Palestinians for a national home. A few days after the signing ceremony, nineteen members of the Arab League met in Baghdad, Iraq, and, on 31 March, outlined political and economic sanctions against Egypt. By early May all the Arab countries except Oman and Sudan, close allies of Sadat, had severed diplomatic relations with Egypt. In addition, Egypt was suspended from the 22-member Arab League, expelled from the Islamic Conference, and ousted from a number of Arab financial and economic institutions such as the Federation of Arab Banks and the Organization of Arab Petroleum Exporting Countries (OAPEC).

Egypt gained specific benefits from the peace treaty with Israel, but other major Arab states were never going to throw their weight behind it, or the Camp David accords. Even the pro-American royal family of Saudi Arabia – a country in which Islam pervades social customs, dominates the political structure and legitimizes the regime – could not endorse an agreement with Israel that did not mention Jerusalem. Iraq's ruler, Saddam Hussein, who claimed to be the champion of Arab nationalism, could not support accords that omitted any reference to the recovery of Palestine. Likewise, Syria could not subscribe to negotiations that did not refer to the Golan Heights. Syrian president Assad felt betrayed and turned to active intervention in the chaos enveloping Lebanon to press Israel. Similarly, King Hussein of Jordan, with his Palestinian subjects, could not approve an accord that was unacceptable to the majority of his people and his three powerful neighbours. These Arab leaders did not favour the accords, therefore, since to have done so would have endangered their own political survival, because of the ideological and spiritual importance of the issues to their people. By signing a peace treaty with Israel, Sadat demonstrated that Pan-Arabism was no longer – if indeed it ever had been – anything more than a toothless tiger. Overall, the Camp David agreements increased Arab suspicion of Israel and the United States, and the other Arab states refused to be drawn into the process. This hostility, in turn, hardened Israeli attitudes toward the Arabs.

The future of the West Bank, Gaza, the Golan Heights and East Jerusalem remained the major unresolved issues. The Palestinians had been largely over-looked and ignored in the Israeli-Egyptian negotiations. In 1978 the 1.3 million Arab inhabitants of the West Bank and Gaza Strip did not regard themselves as part of Israel in any way. They differed in language, religion and culture from the Jews of Israel. Neither of these two worlds sought harmony with the other. Although religious and nationalistic Jews described the region as Judea and Samaria, the inhabitants were Arab in all their loyalties. Israeli 'doves' argued that although Israel would be smaller in size if the West Bank and Gaza Strip were returned to Arab sovereignty, a major reason for the Arab world's military, economic and psychological hostility to Israel would be destroyed, thereby creating a much more secure Israel. Israel would then be freer of the oppressive burden of its military priorities and diplomatic problems and, if peace resulted, would be able to trade and invest in Arab markets to great economic advantage.

During the 1970s it was beginning to dawn upon Israel's leaders that the state's relationship with the Palestinians was more of an existential threat to the state than its relations with other Arab states; not in terms of the PLO's military capacity, but in terms of shaping the future character of the Jewish state. While the Palestinians were regarded merely as refugees and under Jordanian authority, they did not present a problem for Israel, even when advocating the destruction of Israel and carrying out terrorist activities. That situation had changed with the 1967 war and developments after the 1973 war. PLO leader Yasser Arafat had made a number of overtures to Kissinger but the US Secretary of State ignored them. He and Israel preferred the Jordan option. So did King Hussein.

Israeli leaders and King Hussein, who were already close and often met secretly, believed they could resolve their issues between themselves. Golda Meir and Rabin agreed with the king that the only answer to the question of the future of the Palestinians was to have them remain under Jordanian jurisdiction. In March 1972 Hussein had proposed an Israeli withdrawal from the West Bank and Gaza Strip in return for a peace treaty with Jordan. The king wanted a federal United Arab Kingdom consisting of the East and West Banks (including the Gaza Strip) of the Jordan. Amman would be the capital of the federation and an East Bank region, called Jordan, and East Jerusalem would be the capital of the West Bank and Gaza, called Palestine. Each region or province would have its own legislature and legal system.

Knowing that no other Arab states supported or trusted the King, and unwilling to give up Israeli control of settlements in the West Bank and Gaza, Israeli prime minister Meir rejected the initiative. The PLO and Egypt also rejected the scheme. Had Israel accepted the scheme and withdrawn from the West Bank, Hussein would have made peace immediately, and the PLO would have been virtually eliminated as a political force. Arafat commented: 'Sometimes I think we are lucky to have the Israelis as our enemies. They have saved us many times.'[2]

In April and May 1974 radical groups within the PLO mounted a series of spectacular terrorist missions. In April, in the northern Israeli town of Qiryat Shemona, members of the Popular Front for the Liberation of Palestine (PFLP, founded by Greek Orthodox Christian George Habash) killed eighteen Israelis – eight of them children; in May, in the village of Ma'alot in Galilee, militants of the Democratic Front for the Liberation of Palestine killed twenty of the ninety children they were holding hostage. These attacks hardened the re-solve of the Israeli government against the Palestinians, although it could scarcely deny the existence of a Palestinian people. Arafat, unwilling or un-able to control the extremists in his organization, weakened the credibility of the moderates within the PLO. His inactivity also added weight to the argu-ment that the PLO was a terrorist organization that should not be negotiated with.

By mid-1974 Arafat was saying he would accept a Palestinian state on any part of liberated Palestine, rather than demanding all of Palestine. The Pales-tinian National Council, at its twelfth meeting in June 1974 in Cairo, shifted from calling for the liberation of all Palestine to setting up an independent national authority 'over any part of Palestinian territory which was liberated.'[3] Elements within the Palestinian cause, like the PFLP and the DFLP, as well as Habash's former associate, Ahmad Jibril, who formed his own splinter group backed by Syria, opposed this pragmatic approach. They believed it weakened the Arab revolutionary struggle to regain all of Palestine – which included Israel. Arafat and the majority of West Bank Palestinians preferred the option of the limited goal of regaining the West Bank and Gaza, but Arafat's leader-ship was not secure enough for him to speak out against the factions calling for the liberation of all of Palestine. Israel exploited these divisions, claiming it did not know who spoke for the Palestinians.

In fact, the Israeli Labor government thought the Palestinians were finished politically. Moshe Dayan strongly advocated creating facts on the ground by establishing Jewish settlements throughout the West Bank that would lead, through creeping annexation, to a strong Israel stretching from the Jordan to the Suez Canal. Moderate Israelis, on the other hand, wanted to with-draw from much, if not all, of the occupied territories and to seek peace with the Arabs in order to preserve the Jewish and democratic character of Israel.

The situation was compounded by the fact that the PLO would not accept UN Resolution 242 because it referred only to Arab refugees and did not rec-ognize the Palestinian rights of self-determination. As noted above, at Israel's insistence the United States required acceptance of Resolution 242, recogniz-ing Israel, as a precondition to negotiations. Israeli analysts insisted that the June 1974 modification in Arab policy was only to substitute a two-stage for a one-stage process in the destruction of Israel, and that a so-called national authority would be a launching pad for the achievement of that aim. Rabin, like Meir, refused to recognize the PLO as anything other than a terrorist organization committed to the destruction of Israel and refused to negotiate with it. On 28 August 1974, at one of the many meetings held inside Israel to discuss the future of the West Bank with the new government of Rabin, King Hussein suggested a phased partial Israeli withdrawal (of about five miles) followed by a complete withdrawal and peace treaty. Rabin's fragile domestic alliances would not allow him to agree. Another opportunity was missed.

At a meeting in Rabat in October 1974, the Arab League endorsed PLO claims to speak as 'the sole legitimate representative of the Palestinian people'. The summit also established the Palestinian Authority (PNA or PA), proposed earlier in the year. At this point, the UN General Assembly once again stepped in. In November 1974 it called for a full debate on the 'Question of Palestine' and invited the PLO leader as representative of the Palestinian people to take part in it. On 22 November Arafat spoke before the General Assembly, which passed Resolution 3236 affirming the right of the Palestinian people to self-determination, national independence and sovereignty. This was a far greater triumph for the PLO, and for the more moderate elements in that organization, than any achieved by the extremists and their terrorist acts. Rabin, however, refused to recognize the resolution, or the legitimacy of the PLO.

As the 1980s began, developments in the Persian Gulf region and in Lebanon intruded into the conflict. In 1979 the Shah of Iran's government collapsed and was replaced by a government led by the formerly exiled Ayatollah Ruhollah Khomeini. War broke out in September 1980 between Iran and Iraq, raising worldwide concerns about the stability of the Persian Gulf region and the future flow of oil. Additional uncertainty was created in October 1981, when Anwar Sadat was assassinated by Muslim extremists opposed to the Egyptian leader's domestic policies and to the peace treaty with Israel. Sadat's successor was Hosni Mubarak, former commander of the Egyptian air force, a vice-president since 1975 and reputedly Sadat's closest adviser. Mubarak pledged to uphold the peace treaty with Israel, but any further movement toward a comprehensive settlement stalled, as the newly elected US Republican administration of Ronald Reagan settled in and as Mubarak attempted to deal with internal economic and political problems. Meanwhile, in Israel, Menachem Begin's mandate was extended in general elections in 1981, and he turned his attention to the situation on Israel's northern border.

Lebanon and the Arab–Israeli Conflict

For the first twenty years following the establishment of Israel, Lebanon had played little part in the conflict over Palestine. The former French mandate contains an impenetrable number of mutually exclusive ethnic and religious groups – Maronite Christians, Greek Orthodox, Greek Catholics, Sunni and Shi'ite Muslims, the Druze and a host of others – that by and large follow the dictates of their feudal-like lords (*zaims*) or their individual or confessional leaders. The Bekaa Valley and the mountain area in the east are populated largely by a mixed Muslim population with close ties to neighbouring Syria. The Mount Lebanon region is the traditional home of Maronite Christians, Druze and Shi'ites. Large numbers of Sunni Muslims live in the coastal areas, including Beirut, along with Maronites, Druze and Shi'ites. Shi'ite Muslims, the poorest among the many definable groups in the population, live largely in the south, close to the border with Israel.

For most of the second half of the twentieth century the various groupings jostled for political and economic power working within an outdated framework known as the National Pact, created in 1943, that provided for a balance of power in favour of the Christians, who were at the time a slight majority of the population. By the early 1980s, however, the Muslim population exceeded that of the Christians, who nonetheless still maintained an increasingly uneasy balance of power and Western orientation in foreign and economic policy.

Lebanon was drawn into the Palestinian-Israel situation by the presence of the large numbers of Palestinian refugees who fled to the country (in the mid-1980s almost 400,000 out of an estimated population of 2.6 million). In 1968, in retaliation for PLO attacks originating in Lebanon, Israel bombed some Palestinian refugee camps and destroyed thirteen civilian aircraft in a commando raid at Beirut airport. Their message was clear: if the Lebanese government would or could not control the Palestinians, Israel would do it for them.

In November 1969, in Cairo, Nasser met with high-ranking Lebanese officials, Yasser Arafat and Arab League executive members, and oversaw an agreement that effectively endorsed PLO freedom of action in Lebanon to recruit, arm, train and employ fighters against Israel. The Lebanese Army protected their bases and supply lines. Following the PLO expulsion from

Jordan in 1970, Palestinian militias, numbering around 15,000, created 'a state within the state' in southern Lebanon. For the residents of south Lebanon, Arab and Christian, PLO rule was a nightmare. The border area became a launching site for Palestinian rocket and guerrilla attacks against Israel, which were followed by punishing Israeli bombing reprisals. Few Israeli towns were hit, but Lebanon was becoming virtually a 'front-line' state as far as Israel was concerned. More than 150 Lebanese towns and villages were constantly under attack from Israeli forces.

PLO attacks against Israel from Lebanon increased during the period of Secretary of State Kissinger's shuttle diplomacy and the disengagement agreements of 1974 and 1975, when it appeared that the United States and the belligerent countries were ignoring the Palestinian cause. Palestinian attacks also increased after Anwar Sadat's trip to Jerusalem in November 1977 and, as Israel and Egypt began to negotiate, Lebanon became the base of PLO attacks.

By 1975 relations between assorted Lebanese groups and the Palestinians had degenerated into open warfare. Various rival feuding Lebanese groups were already fighting one another for power as the country became caught up in a bloody civil war essentially between Muslims and Maronite Christians. The Maronites felt no Arab solidarity with the Palestinians, and did not want to be drawn into a dispute they regarded as none of Lebanon's business. In 1976 the Lebanese Christian leadership formed the Lebanese Front, a political coalition, with a military arm combining four Christian militias known as the Lebanese Forces. The Lebanese Front and Lebanese Forces were dominated by the Phalange, a Maronite party founded in the 1930s and led by Pierre Gemayel.

Responding to calls from the Lebanese Front, on 1 June 1976 Syria intervened on the side of the Christians. Syria's President Assad welcomed the opportunity to do so, and in the following months the Syrian presence grew to about 27,000 troops. Assad's goal was to make Lebanon a Syrian client and to achieve this he was prepared to weaken the PLO. In October the Arab League deployed an Arab peacekeeping force (usually called the 'Arab Deterrent Forces'), incorporating into its ranks the Syrian forces. Rabin accepted Syria's military presence in Lebanon but indicated Israel would not tolerate the deployment of Syrian troops south of the Litani River.

Israel had been in contact with Phalange leader Pierre Gemayel. The Gemayel family welcomed Israeli assistance in their fight against Muslim factions. Some Israeli leaders, especially after the Likud victory in 1977, began to think about creating and supporting a strong unified Christian Lebanon as a way to crush the PLO and, perhaps at the same time, to solve the problem of the West Bank. They argued that if the PLO was eliminated in Lebanon, its influence in the occupied territories would wane and Palestinian leaders would emerge who were willing to reach an agreement acceptable to Israel. They believed PLO funds, patronage and physical threats – as well as the assassination of those who cooperated with Israeli authorities – had prevented moderate Palestinians from emerging as an alternative to the PLO. They did not acknowledge that Israeli policies that included the expulsion or deportation of those advocating Palestinian independence also deprived them of the opportunity to deal with acknowledged leaders and opinion-makers.

Some in Likud revived the notion that southern Lebanon was, in fact part of *Eretz-Israel*, just like the West Bank, which they were now referring to as Judea and Samaria. Past Zionist luminaries like Theodore Herzl, Vladimir Jabotinsky, David Ben-Gurion and, more recently, Moshe Dayan had spoken of Israel extending to the Litani. Israel, they believed would be more secure, gain more land for settlement and, more importantly, obtain an additional source of vital water. These notions were fanciful, but extending Israel's northern border into southern Lebanon had been part of the Zionist dream since World War I. However, occupying Lebanon, with its ethnic and religious factionalism, was nowhere near as straightforward as establishing settlements in the West Bank, and was to cause more grief than any other venture in Israel's history.

By 1977 Israel was supporting the Christians with arms and training. As the Lebanese army disintegrated into small militias in 1976, Major Saad Haddad, a Greek Catholic commanding an army battalion of about 3,000 men in the south, had founded a group known as the Free Lebanon Army. Mainly made up of Christian Lebanese, this was initially based in the towns of Marjayoun and Qlayaa in south Lebanon and it fought against the PLO. In March 1978 PLO terrorists commandeered a bus on the Israeli coastal highway south of Haifa and more than 30 people were killed. Israel responded with a major invasion of Lebanon (Operation Litani), designed to destroy the PLO military infrastructure. Israel occupied most of the area south of the Litani River, resulting in the evacuation of at least 100,000 Lebanese, as well as approximately 2,000 deaths.[4] Israel backed the Free Lebanon Army, which now gained control over a much wider area. Although the Israelis withdrew three months later, they established a nine-mile wide 'security zone' under Major Haddad's control. In addition, UN troops (UNIFIL, United Nations Interim Forces in Lebanon) were sent to southern Lebanon.

Neither UNIFIL nor Haddad was able to prevent the PLO, which was in virtual control of many villages and camps, from developing into a conventional army replete with a growing arsenal that included long-range weapons and rockets. On 18 April 1979 Haddad proclaimed the area controlled by his force 'Independent Free Lebanon'. The following day he was branded a traitor to the Lebanese government and officially dismissed from the Lebanese Army. The Free Lebanon Army, renamed the South Lebanon Army (SLA) in May 1980, closely allied itself with Israel in combating the PLO. In return, Israel supplied the organization with arms, uniforms and other logistical equipment. Between 1977 and 1982 Israel sold more than US$118 million worth of arms to the Lebanese Christians. Begin stated it was to help prevent a Christian 'genocide' at the hands of the Muslims. In all of this, Israel and Syria had a tacit understanding that Israeli and Syrian forces would not provoke or attack each other in Lebanon.

In response to the PLO's somewhat ineffectual long-range rocket attacks into northern Israel, the Israeli air force continued its strikes on Palestinian refugee camps. The fighters themselves were able to avoid the attacks but innocent civilians were killed. Despite the hard-line rhetoric of the Palestine National Charter, Arafat and the mainstream PLO claimed they had turned to diplomacy, not terrorist attacks, to achieve their aims. Nonetheless, in response to rocket attacks that killed six Israelis in northern Galilee, Begin decided to escalate and, on 17 July 1981, the Israeli air force struck PLO targets in Beirut, killing 350. US president Reagan sent an American mediator, Philip Habib, to secure a ceasefire. Habib was shocked and outraged at the number of deaths caused by the Israeli airstrikes. The shaky ceasefire he arranged held into early 1982, with no PLO incursions and no Israeli strikes. In December 1981 an increasingly belligerent Likud government annexed the Israeli-held portions of the Golan Heights. At this time an estimated 6,000 PLO armed fighters were located in the south of Lebanon, with another 9,000 in Beirut and north. The PLO was armed with jeeps, mortars and artillery pieces, including long-range Soviet and French guns, Soviet Katyusha and North Korean rockets and shoulder-launched missiles, and around 80 Soviet tanks. It built a network of anti-aircraft guns.

Israel Invades Lebanon

By the spring of 1982 Begin's cabinet began to seriously consider an invasion of Lebanon. There were several reasons for this timing. Israel was just completing its withdrawal from the Sinai, so there was little likelihood of interference from Egypt. The main impetus for an invasion came from Defence Minister Sharon who had been in charge of the 20,000 troops required to forcibly remove the Jewish settlers evacuated from their homes when Egypt regained the Sinai. Sharon and Begin wanted to compensate their right-wing supporters with a show of strength against the Palestinians in Lebanon. They erroneously believed that Israel could strengthen its regional position by destroying the PLO (and with it the idea of a Palestinian state) and Syria in Lebanon, and installing a friendly (Maronite Christian) regime. Also, Israel felt it could act with relative impunity as the Arab world was distracted and divided over the Iran–Iraq war. In June 1981 Israel had even bombed Osirak in Iraq, where a nuclear reactor was being constructed.

On 4 and 5 June 1982 Israeli F-16 fighters bombed Palestinian refugee camps and other PLO targets in Beirut and southern Lebanon, killing 300 and wounding 500 people. The pretext for the Israeli air raids was provided by the near-fatal shooting on 3 June of Shlomo Argov, Israel's ambassador to London. His attackers were not the PLO, as Israel claimed publicly, but members of the Abu Nidal group, an anti-Arafat Palestinian faction operating independently of the PLO. Begin knew this but kept it from his cabinet colleagues.[5] For the first time in more than ten months, the PLO responded by launching artillery and mortar attacks on civilian centres in northern Israel. The following day, 6 June, 30,000 Israeli troops began an invasion of Lebanon.

The official explanation for the invasion, termed 'Operation Pines', or 'Operation Peace for Galilee', was that Israel would eliminate the PLO in southern Lebanon and create a secure area up to 25 miles (40 km) north of its border. However, Sharon, a hero of the 1973 war and Israel's leading hawk, planned much more than that. The real purpose of the invasion was to weaken or evict the PLO and impose Bashir Gemayel, Pierre Gemayel's son and head of the Christian Phalange party, as president of Lebanon in order to get Lebanon to sign a peace treaty with Israel and bring the country into Israel's sphere of influence. Bashir Gemayel, who headed the Lebanese Forces, believed in Christian hegemony in Lebanon and vehemently opposed the PLO and

Syrian presence. Over time he had developed a personal relationship with Ariel Sharon. The Israelis had come to view Bashir as a powerful and potentially successful political leader, and as a real ally.

The Israeli forces invaded in a three-pronged attack. One group moved along the coastal road to Beirut, another aimed at cutting the main Beirut–Damascus road, and the third moved up along the Lebanon-Syria border, hoping to block out Syrian reinforcements or interference. Within four days they were at the outskirts of Beirut. On the way, the Israeli air force brought down some 86 Syrian planes in air battles without loss, outflanked Syrian ground forces and, using US-supplied helicopter gunships, destroyed a number of modern surface-to-air missile sites installed by the Soviets in the Bekaa Valley.

Confronted with this situation, President Assad of Syria called for a ceasefire on 11 June. During the ensuing siege of Beirut, the PLO withstood Israel's military and political pressures. For seven weeks Israel attacked the city by sea, air and land, cutting off food and water supplies, disconnecting the electricity, and securing the airport and some southern suburbs. Thousands of civilians were killed and suffered alongside the PLO guerrillas. Israel was roundly accused of indiscriminately shelling the city.

The US finally brokered a UN-sponsored peace agreement. Syria agreed on 7 August; Israel, Lebanon and the PLO agreed by the 18th. On 21 August, 350 French paratroopers arrived in Beirut, followed by 800 US Marines and additional French and Italian peacekeepers (for a total force of 2,130), to supervise the removal of about 6,500 Fatah fighters from the capital by sea and then overland to Jordan, Syria, Iraq, Sudan, North and South Yemen, Greece and Tunisia. President Reagan's envoy to Lebanon, Philip Habib, provided an undertaking to the PLO that Palestinian civilians in the city's refugee camps would not be harmed.

Bashir Gemayel was elected Lebanese president on 23 August but immediately backed away from too close an association or public assertion of friendship with Israel. On 10 September the multi-national peacekeeping force began to withdraw, but on 14 September the newly elected president was assassinated at his headquarters. Syrians or Palestinians were suspected. The Israelis immediately re-entered West Beirut to 'keep the peace', but between 15 and 18 September, in an area controlled by the Israelis, Christian Phalangists, avenging the death of their leader, were permitted by the Israelis to enter the refugee camps of Sabra and Shatila. Hundreds of defenceless Palestinians were massacred. Israelis later accepted indirect responsibility for the shocking incident and Sharon was forced to resign as defence minister. As a result of this tragedy, Reagan agreed to the return and expansion of the multi-national peacekeeping force. Amin Gemayel, Bashir's brother, became president. He was less charismatic than his brother but more amenable to pluralism in Lebanon. Seeking to mend fences, he did little as the factions jockeyed for power.

The Israelis encouraged a peace accord between themselves and the Phalange in return for their withdrawal, which would have made Lebanon the second Arab country to recognize the Jewish state. The American government, especially Secretary of State George Shultz, supported this idea and brokered such an agreement, which was initialled by Israel, Lebanon and the US on 17 May 1983. It called for an end to the state of war between Israel and Lebanon and withdrawal of Israeli troops. Israel insisted, however, that the agreement was dependent upon the departure of Syrian troops. President Assad, who had not been consulted, vehemently opposed the pact and refused to budge. The United States, by closely identifying itself with Christian predominance, had simply ignored what the Lebanese themselves had been fighting about since 1975.

The Western presence was greatly resented by almost all the Lebanese and the 'peacekeeping' forces were constantly under attack. On 18 April 1983 a pro-Iranian group bombed the American Embassy in Beirut, killing more than 60 people, including many CIA operatives. In October 1983 a terrorist driving a car filled with explosives blew up the US Marines' barracks, killing 247 men. The French contingent's compound was also bombed. By March 1984 the United States had left Lebanon; on 5 March, under pressure from Syria and Muslim militias, the Lebanese National Assembly cancelled the March 1983 accord with Israel.

More ominously, on 16 February 1985 Shia Sheik Ibrahim al-Amin proclaimed a resistance movement called Hezbollah, an umbrella organization of several Shi'ite groups inspired, funded and supplied by Iran. Hezbollah supported Iran's Islamic ideology and preached the eradication of Western influence in Lebanon and the Middle East, Holy War against Israel, and the creation of an Islamic state in Lebanon. The Shi'ites, previously largely ignored, wanted a greater role in the governance of the country commensurate with their increasing numbers. They also became more radicalized, particularly in the south and in the southern suburbs of Beirut where many had migrated, first because of their enmity toward the PLO, and then because of Israel's prolonged occupation after the 1982 invasion. Over the next fifteen years, Hezbollah militia waged a guerrilla campaign against Israeli forces occupying southern Lebanon and their South Lebanon Army allies.

Israel withdrew its troops in June 1985, but left a residual force occupying its self-declared security zone. It is estimated that close to 18,000 Lebanese, Palestinians and Syrians were killed during the Israeli invasion of Lebanon, with differing estimates of the proportion of civilians killed. Local estimates indicated that more than 5,500 people, both military and civilian, were killed in the Beirut area during the conflict, while nearly 10,000 military personnel (PLO, Syrian and others) and 2,500 civilians were killed outside the metropolitan area. Approximately 675 Israeli soldiers were killed.

The senseless Israeli invasion had a number of negative, unintended consequences. Israel not only failed to achieve its objectives, it set in motion a train of events that further worsened the situation in Lebanon: the Christian regime was weakened rather than strengthened; Western hostages were seized by Lebanese factions; some Westerners were killed; politicians continued their bickering; the militias became little governments unto themselves. Violence and anarchy reigned, and Lebanon slid into economic and political chaos. Syria continued to occupy the country militarily, and its hold on Lebanon became even firmer than it had been throughout the Civil War. The war also strengthened Syrian ties with the Soviet Union, as the Soviets installed improved surface-to-air missile systems in Syria to replace those destroyed by the Israeli air force.

Israel's northern settlements were no more secure than before the war. Although the PLO 'state within a state' infrastructure in Lebanon was destroyed, the war exacerbated the conflict between the two peoples. The war against Lebanon exposed weaknesses and divisions within the Israeli armed forces, and shocked some of the more moderate Israeli leaders. Israelis were incensed by the heavy Israeli casualties, alleged disinformation of government leaders and the public by military and political advocates of the campaign, and lack of clear goals. This culminated in a large protest rally in Tel Aviv, organized by the 'Peace Now' movement, following the 1982 Sabra and Shatila massacre. Organizers claimed 400,000 people participated in the rally, and it became known as the '400,000 rally'. Other estimates put the figure much lower. A shattered Begin resigned in August 1983 to be replaced by the even more extreme Yitzhak Shamir. The cost of the war – estimated at one million (US) dollars a day – and the promotion of West Bank settlements (costing almost as much) substantially contributed to a two-fold increase in foreign debt and a three-fold increase in inflation, which by 1983 had risen to 150 per cent. Israel's image was tarnished in world public opinion. Israel became even more dependent upon US economic assistance, although the National Unity government formed after elections in July 1984 continued to reject US-backed Jordanian peace proposals that called for an Israeli withdrawal from the West Bank.

Nor did things turn out as the PLO leadership hoped. Within the PLO, Arafat was blamed for the defeat of the Palestinians, while radical groups attacked him for his diplomatic efforts rather than relying upon the military option to achieve a Palestinian homeland. In November 1983 the Iran-based Shi'ite group AMAL, and a Fatah faction backed by Syria, forced Arafat to depart Tripoli in northern Lebanon to set up a new PLO headquarters in Tunis. Arafat retained the support of the Palestine National Authority, but the PLO remained fractured and weakened.

Fifteen months later, in February 1985, Arafat joined with King Hussein in calling for a United Nations conference to oversee a peace agreement previously proposed by the Jordanian monarch: the creation of a Jordan-Palestine confederation in the West Bank following Israeli withdrawal in return for a treaty with Israel. Arafat saw this as a mechanism to obtain PLO participation in negotiations with Israel and stopping Israeli settlements, and Hussein saw it as a way of gaining PLO acquiescence in regaining the West Bank. Repeating their often-stated positions of refusing to negotiate with the PLO, both Israel and the US opposed the idea. The negative responses of Israel and the US, in turn, had unintended flow-on effects. 'Rejectionist Front' elements within the PLO felt justified in renewing their terrorist activities in the second half of 1985. PLO extremists assassinated three Israelis in Cyprus in late September, and this prompted an Israeli air attack on Arafat's headquarters in Tunis a week later. Violence escalated.

On 8 October, the Palestine National Front, a militant group headed by Abu Abbas, hijacked the cruise ship *Achille Lauro* in the Mediterranean and killed an American Jew before surrendering. These events confirmed the views of Israel's extremists. Ultra-nationalists not only increased their demands for more settlements and the annexation of the West Bank, but also called for the forceful removal of the Palestinians. Arafat, they argued, could not control the PLO or claim to speak for the Palestinian people. Arafat's opponents within the PLO forced him to withdraw his planned offer of recognition of Israel. King Hussein abandoned the joint plan with Arafat and instead began his own discussions with Israel for an international conference. Hussein's proposal was also rejected by Israel. Israel's leaders did not have the wisdom, or desire, to choose a path of compromise with either the Palestinians or Jordan.

Israel's calamitous invasion of Lebanon, 'anchored in delusion, propelled by deceit', continued to cast a long dark shadow over future relations with Lebanon, Syria, the Palestinians and Jordan.[6] It required only a spark to ignite the further violence, which is traced in the next chapter.

CHAPTER 7

The First Intifada,
and the Oslo Accords

In December 1987 Arabs and Israelis once again turned to violence. The outbreak of the uprising that was soon called the *intifada* (shaking off) was initiated by Palestinian civilians, mainly young ones, throwing stones and iron bars at Israeli soldiers who responded with rubber bullets, tear gas and tanks. Thousands of Palestinians died in six years of fighting, and several scores of Israelis lost their lives. The intifada did not achieve its goal of an independent Palestinian state. The outcome was simply to further embitter both sides, although a mutual Israel–Palestine recognition agreement was reached in September 1993. This chapter examines the course and implications of the first intifada and subsequent events.

The First Intifada

On the afternoon of 8 December 1987, at the Erez crossing between the Gaza Strip and Israel, an Israeli army tank transport ran into a truck carrying Palestinian workers back into the occupied Gaza Strip, killing four and seriously injuring seven. Three of the four killed were from the Jabalya refugee camp, home to 60,000 refugees, adjacent to Gaza city and the crossing. Word quickly spread that the incident was deliberate, a vengeance attack by the driver for the death of his brother killed by Palestinians two days previously. This false rumour added to the camp population's feelings of impotence and anger. Following the funeral procession the next day, a massive spontaneous demonstration erupted against the Israeli military camp located in the camp. Within a few days local leaders from a number of local Palestinian resistance groups had orchestrated riots in other camps in Gaza. Tyres were burnt, stones, bottles and iron bars were thrown at Israeli soldiers by hundreds of demonstrators. The soldiers fired tear gas and live bullets into the demonstrators, killing a seventeen-year-old and wounding several others. Large protest demonstrations spread throughout the Gaza Strip and the West Bank.[1] Things quickly got out of control; out of control of the Israeli authorities and out of control of PLO leaders in far away Tunis.

Within a couple of weeks it had become clear that local Palestinians had taken things into their own hands and embarked upon a mass movement of opposition to Israeli occupation across all the occupied territories. Palestinians regarded it as a national uprising against a colonial power that had been subjugating them since 1967. The Unified National Leadership of the Uprising (UNLU), as the local leaders of Fatah, the Popular Front, the Democratic Front, the Palestine Communist Party and Islamic Jihad coordinating the intifada called themselves, set out their goals in a series of leaflets. The first, issued on 10 January 1988, ended with the call: 'Let the whole world know that the volcanic uprising that has ignited the Palestinian people will not cease until the achievement of independence in a Palestinian state whose capital is Jerusalem.'[2]

The more specific goals set out in later leaflets give some idea of life under Israeli rule. UNLU demanded the removal of the IDF from cities, towns and refugee camps, the repeal of Emergency Regulations such as administrative detention, deportation, the demolition of houses and other collective punishments, the release of prisoners, the halting of expropriation of land and the establishment of new settlements on Arab land, the dismantling of all municipal village and refugee camp councils, and the holding of democratic elections in the West Bank and Gaza Strip. The UNLU made one other demand: Ariel Sharon must leave the house he had so provocatively occupied in the Moslem quarter of the Old City of Jerusalem to show that Jerusalem belonged to the Jews.

The uprising was a new kind of warfare and it came as a complete surprise to the Israelis, and to the PLO leadership in Tunis. It was to last six years and had a dramatic effect on the Arab–Israeli conflict. By the end of 1987, twenty years of Israeli occupation of the West Bank and the Gaza Strip had done little to further the chances of peace. Successive Israeli governments had continued an 'iron fist' policy of expropriating Palestinian-owned property for 'security purposes', establishing fortifications, roads and settlements, encouraging Israeli citizens to move to the occupied territories. More than 55 per cent of the West Bank and 30 per cent of the Gaza Strip had been expropriated. The majority of Palestinians in the Gaza Strip lived in small cement brick houses in eight refugee camps lacking sanitation and basic necessities. Israel's promises of improved apartments and houses went largely unmet. The lives of residents were made the more miserable by the high level of unemployment and the humiliations and delays imposed on them by IDF soldiers at checkpoints. Israel had not only created settlements and military outposts as physical facts on the ground, it had moved to integrate the West Bank into the Israeli economy and had done so at the expense of Palestinian farmers and workers. Thousands of the 850,000 living in refugee camps in the West Bank and Gaza Strip travelled daily through checkpoints to fill Israel's need for low-paid workers. As Palestinian anger grew so did the bellicose response of Jewish settlers backed by the Israeli military. Palestinian frustration and sense of abandonment increased daily.

The Palestinian population in the Gaza Strip and the West Bank were increasingly aware that they were on their own and no closer to gaining independence. A generation of Palestinian youths had grown up living with severely curtailed civil rights and in political limbo. The PLO leadership was distant, dispirited and impotent. The Arab nations at successive summits did little more than pass pious resolutions of support for Palestinian sovereignty while pursuing their own, more important, agendas. The Arab summit held in Amman in November 1987, preoccupied with the Iran-Iraq war, did not even mention the issue of the Palestinians' future. Israeli inflexibility and intransigence made sure that little changed to challenge their creeping annexation as they forcibly expropriated Palestinian-owned land for 'security' purposes, fortifications, roads and more and expanded settlements.

At first, the army was confident that it could quell the 'unrest', as it termed the uprising, using intimidating force. They were supported by the Likud and Herut parties in the National Unity government, especially Prime Minister Yitzhak Shamir. Shamir placed the blame for the agitation solely on 'terrorists', and advocated that Israel take a military hard line against the young unarmed demonstrators. By the end of December 1987 almost two dozen Palestinians had been killed, five of them children under the age of sixteen, and around 320 were wounded – two-thirds of whom were aged between seventeen and twenty-one. During the same period around 55 Israeli soldiers and 30 civilians were injured by thrown objects.[3] Rioting spread to Jerusalem. Foreign Minister Peres, recognizing that Israeli occupation of the Gaza Strip had helped create the conditions leading to the violence, urged dismantling the thirteen Jewish settlements in the Gaza Strip, removing their 3,000 Jewish settlers, and demilitarizing the area as part of peace negotiations with the Palestinians. This wise suggestion got nowhere.

During the next year, the young refugees were joined by farmers and villagers, women and, intermittently, workers, trade unionists and university students. Israeli authorities employed a range of harsh tactics in an attempt to quell the uprising. They cut electricity and telephone lines, and imposed more than 1,600 curfews on villages, towns and cities, some of which covered five or more days; it has been estimated that around 60 per cent of Palestinians were subjected to curfews. Approximately 25,000 olive and fruit trees were uprooted, 526 houses were demolished and a countless number had one of their few rooms sealed off with corrugated iron sheets to punish families whose sons or daughters were suspected of participating in the uprising. About 400 refugees were killed and more than 11,500 were wounded (almost two-thirds of whom were under fifteen years of age).[4] In the first eighteen months of the intifada, about 50,000 were arrested; around one in eight adults in the territories were imprisoned by administrative order. Universities, colleges and schools were closed, restrictions were placed on Palestinians transporting harvests to markets – yet nothing Israel did stopped the rock-throwing, the Molotov cocktails, the harassment or the Palestinian flag-waving demonstrations.

In February 1988 a new militant fundamentalist group, the Islamic Resistance Movement (*Hamas*) joined the intifada. Hamas, an Arabic acronym of *Harakat al-Muqawama al-Islami*, meaning zeal, was set up by Sheikh Ahmad Yassin, a quadriplegic cleric, as an offshoot of the Muslim Brotherhood. Hamas was opposed to secular and Western influences; its goal was to establish a state in Palestine on the basis of the Sharia, or Islamic, law. It was a small but dedicated group of volunteers (around 200) from the Gaza camps and was soon playing a prominent role in the uprising. Hamas, like Islamic Jihad, another radical Islamist militant group (founded in 1981), was encouraged by

Israel as a counter to weaken the more secular PLO. During the 1980s Israeli authorities had encouraged members of Islamic groups to take over welfare responsibilities of needy Palestinians in the West Bank and Gaza as a way of weakening the influence of the PLO. The number of mosques in the occupied territories had more than doubled in the previous twenty years. One unanticipated outcome of this policy was a greater radicalization of the Palestinian population.

Seven months into the uprising, perhaps seeing a threat to his own kingdom, and realizing that Palestinians, especially the younger generation, would never accept him as their spokesperson, on 31 July 1988 King Hussein renounced Jordan's legal and administrative claim to the West Bank, which in effect reversed the annexation decision made in 1950. Although Jordan continued to administer the daily affairs of the West Bank, the PLO gradually took some responsibility for funding these activities. The Jordanian monarch distanced himself even further from the PLO: on 7 August 1988 he stated that Jordan would not be part of a Jordanian–Palestinian delegation in any peace process.

Palestinian Declaration of Independence

Yasser Arafat took the diplomatic initiative. After meeting with King Hussein and President Mubarak in Aqaba in late October, he succeeded in having the 448-member Palestine National Council – essentially the Palestine parliament in exile – proclaim the independent state of Palestine by a vote of 253 to 46 at a meeting in Algiers on 15 November 1988.[5] The proclamation was also read in front of the al-Aqsa mosque in Jerusalem. The Declaration of Independence, although it mirrored the Israeli Declaration of Independence in its arguments, did not explicitly recognize Israel. However, it did explicitly accept UN General Assembly (partition) Resolution 181 of 1947, describing it as providing 'those conditions of international legitimacy that ensure the right of the Palestinian Arab people to sovereignty'.[6] An accompanying political communiqué, issued the same day, also referred to UN Security Council Resolutions 242 and 338.

The PNC statement called for an international conference on the question of Palestine, under the auspices of the United Nations, on the basis of UN Security Council resolutions 242 and 338 and 'the attainment of the legitimate national rights of the Palestinian people'. It demanded the withdrawal of Israel from all the Palestinian and Arab territories it occupied in 1967, including Arab Jerusalem, the annulment of all measures of annexation and appropriation, and the removal of settlements established by Israel in the Palestinian and Arab territories since 1967. It also called on the Security Council for protection for a limited period to enable the Palestinian state to establish itself and to reach a comprehensive political settlement and the attainment of peace and security for all on the basis of mutual acquiescence and consent. The council proposed that the future relationship between the two states of Palestine and Jordan should be a confederation. The communiqué further urged the settlement of the question of the Palestinian refugees in accordance with the relevant United Nations resolutions and guaranteed freedom of worship and religious practice for all faiths in the holy places in Palestine. Finally the communiqué affirmed its solidarity with the Lebanese nationalist Islamic forces in their struggle against Israeli occupation and 'its agents' in the Lebanese south.[7]

The Palestinian Declaration of Independence and its accompanying communiqué was a far-reaching, pragmatic compromise. In encompassing only the West Bank and Gaza, with East Jerusalem as its capital, the national council ceded the Palestinian claim to more than half the territory the UN's partition resolution had assigned to Palestine's Arab inhabitants. The declaration attracted immediate worldwide attention. Within three days, at least twenty-seven nations, mostly Arab and Muslim, extended recognition to the government in exile. On 18 November the Soviet Union recognized the proclamation of the Palestinian state, and on 21 November so did Egypt. By the mid-1990s, more states recognized the PNC declaration than recognized Israel.

The Palestinian communiqué renounced all forms of terrorism and, on 6 December 1988, Arafat stated he was ready to start negotiations leading to peace in the Middle East. When the US refused the PLO leader a transit-visa to speak to the UN General Assembly, the General Assembly took the unprecedented step of reconvening in Geneva. There, on 13 December, Arafat accepted Resolutions 242 and 338 without directly coupling them with demands for Palestinian independence. He also specifically stated that Israel had the right to exist in peace and security. The following day he was even more emphatic. During a press conference Arafat fully renounced – not just condemned – terrorism. 'Enough is enough. Enough is enough. Enough is enough', he repeated.[8] In the light of these declarations, President Ronald Reagan immediately authorized the start of diplomatic dialogue between the United States and the PLO.

Reagan also called for direct negotiations between the parties. The implicit position of the United States government was that the next stage must be face-to-face meetings between Israel and the PLO. This was a major change in US policy. Since 1967 the US had allowed Israel undue influence in setting the agenda and the choice of Arab participants in negotiations. Washington had accepted Israel's definition of the Palestinians as terrorists, had supported Israel's response to the intifada, and had backed Israel's efforts to exclude the PLO from direct negotiations.

As a result of US support, Israel was to a large extent protected from international pressure to withdraw from the occupied territories and to negotiate a settlement acceptable to the Palestinians and the Arab countries. American policy assisted Israel in pursuing a hard-line approach. Israel did not always welcome advice from the US, however. Indeed, Likud governments rejected US peace proposals that called for Israeli withdrawal from any part of the territories. Despite admonitions made by several American administrations that they were an obstacle to peace, Jewish settlements in the West Bank and Gaza became larger, more numerous and more entrenched.

Shamir called the PNC Declaration of Independence a sham and accused Arafat of a monumental act of deception. Israeli spokesmen objected that the proclamation did not mention Israel and made no reference to borders.[9] The same could, of course, be said of Israel's 1948 proclamation of statehood: it made no mention of the rights of Palestinians, nor did it, deliberately, specify the state's borders.

Throughout this period, despite pressure from Reagan, the new administration of George H. W. Bush, the PLO and other nations, Shamir refused to budge on the question of negotiating with the PLO or removing the West Bank settlements. Secretary of State James Baker indicated that the US regarded the PLO as the sole and legitimate representative of the Palestinian people, effectively repudiating the long-standing policy favouring the Jordanian option. In April and May 1989, Bush and Baker proposed an international conference to consider the future of the Palestinians, Israeli withdrawal from the West Bank and Israeli settlements. Shamir immediately rejected the plan, proposing instead a scheme that would lead to no more than Palestinian autonomy.

But within Israel few were happy with the prime minister's performance. He was too conciliatory for hardliners within Likud led by Sharon, and too hardline for Labor's Shimon Peres. Consequently, in March 1990 the Knesset passed a vote of no confidence in his government. For the next couple of years Israel's government was virtually dysfunctional.

In the early 1990s, Palestinians believed they faced a threat to the future of a Palestinian state almost as great as that presented by the Israeli war of independence and the 1967 war. In the first four months of 1990, more than 33,000 Soviet Jews arrived in Israel, the first of more than 330,000 to arrive in 1990 and 1991 (the number of former Soviet Union immigrants was to reach more than one million by 2000). Israelis welcomed Soviet Jewish immigration as validating Israel's purpose. The question was where would the new arrivals live and work in a population of about four million already severely burdened by unemployment, a long-running recession and a chronic housing shortage. Palestinians and others, including the United States, believed that the Soviet Jews would be encouraged to settle in the West Bank and the Palestinians would be forced to move across the River Jordan. Shamir's support for Israeli settlers in the West Bank, especially in and around the Old City of Jerusalem, and the sheer value of Jewish West Bank settlements (estimated at several billion dollars) lent weight to these fears. In May 1990 a concerned White House put on hold US$400 million voted by Congress for housing loan guarantees for Israel for Soviet Jewish immigrants. Shamir, however, who had forged a coalition with the minority hard-line parties of the Knesset and had formed another Likud-led government by 8 June 1990, promptly authorized two more Jewish settlements in the occupied territories, asserting that Israeli citizens had the right to live where they pleased.

Palestinian support for Iraq President Saddam Hussein following his invasion of Kuwait in mid-1990 and during the 43-day war waged against him by the US and its allies in January and February 1991, especially their joy when 40 Iraqi Scud missiles struck Tel Aviv, undermined and discredited PLO diplomatic efforts. Israel used the war to crack down even harder on the intifada. The Palestinians were subjected to an almost total curfew in the West Bank and Gaza, and deportations were increased in an attempt to end the Palestinian resistance. The Palestinian economy was virtually crippled as a result. The linkage drawn by Saddam Hussein contrasting the US coalition's use of force to drive Iraq from Kuwait and the lack of US resolve to force Israel to withdraw from the West Bank and Gaza, while it was ineffectual in splitting the Arab members of the coalition from the West, resonated in Washington. When, in 1991, Sharon, at the time Shamir's housing minister, oversaw the starting of 13,000 new units in the West Bank, Bush and Baker withheld US guarantees for US$10 billion in loans Israel had earmarked for the cost of absorbing the Soviet immigrants.

The end of the Cold War, the collapse of the Soviet Union, and the 1991 Gulf War heralded a shift in the dynamics of superpower rivalry in the region. For a variety of reasons the Soviet Union had not played a significant role in the Arab–Israeli conflict during the 1980s. However, in October 1991 Russian President Mikhail Gorbachev signalled a willingness to become an active participant by restoring diplomatic relations with Israel, which had been broken off in 1967, improving Soviet relations with Egypt and establishing diplomatic ties with conservative Arab Gulf states. The new Russian state achieved recognition of its continued interest in the Middle East by co-sponsoring, along with the United States, an international peace conference held in Madrid on 30 October 1991.

The Madrid peace conference was significant in that the parties conducted face-to-face talks for the first time in the history of the conflict. Bush and Gorbachev co-chaired, and Israel, Egypt, Syria, Lebanon and a joint Jordanian–Palestinian delegation attended. The starting point for negotiations was the 1978 Camp David 'Framework for Peace in the Middle East'. Bilateral talks between Israel and Syria, Israel and Lebanon, and Israel and the Jordanian–Palestinian delegation were held based on UN Resolution 242, with its principle of land for peace, and UN Resolution 338, which called for direct negotiations. The bilateral talks addressed the major issues, the conditions for signing peace treaties, the boundaries of Israel, the disposition of the occupied territories and the future of the Palestinians. The conference also set up a series of multilateral working groups to discuss broader issues affecting the Middle East as a whole. Despite the sense of excitement created by the gathering, Israeli obstructionism and evasiveness ensured that little progress was made. Shamir had no intention of allowing the peace talks to succeed.[10]

In June 1992 Shamir and the Likud were defeated in general elections held in Israel. The majority of Israelis were clearly ready for a new approach, realizing that the intifada, especially in the Gaza Strip, was not only an economic and military burden but an international public relations disaster. On 13 July

Yitzhak Rabin formed a Labor-led coalition government, reluctantly naming Peres, his old rival, foreign minister. According to historian Avi Shlaim, Rabin's election was important because, for the first time in its short history, Israel had a prime minister who did not see Jewish or Israeli history through a distorting, lachrymose lens and who called upon Israelis to overcome 'the sense of isolation' that had characterized Israeli thought for almost half a century.[11] Seeking to break the impasse, Rabin made several conciliatory gestures. He freed more than 800 political prisoners, halted most settlement activity, barred private Israeli building permits in the occupied territories, and reiterated the Labor party position of land for peace. Although he did not immediately alter the position of the Israeli government regarding Palestinian autonomy, he said that he would seek repeal of the six-year-old ban on contacts with the PLO. As a result, in early October 1992 President Bush agreed to send the delayed loan guarantee proposal to Congress, which approved it as part of the general US foreign aid bill.

The Palestinians, however, dismissed most of Rabin's actions as mere 'window dressing'. They had little faith in his desire for peace: he had, after all, been Israeli chief of staff in the 1967 war. Lack of progress at the ongoing peace talks and increasing frustration in the West Bank and Gaza led to escalating violence in late 1992, fanned by Hamas and other Islamic extremist groups like Islamic Jihad, as well as by the PFLP and the DFLP, which opposed the peace talks. It appeared that Arafat's influence was seriously on the wane as Fatah was challenged by rival groups. Hamas and other Muslim groups expanded their influence in the territories through their growing network of economic, social and educational institutions and seriously eroded the PLO's political base. In a massive over-reaction to an incident in which thirteen Israelis were killed by a small group of killers, in March 1993 Rabin sealed off the territories, thereby punishing 120,000 Palestinian day workers who travelled into Israel to work by depriving them of their livelihood.

By this time Palestinian workers had been incorporated into the Israeli economy as day-labourers. Most aspects of Palestinian economic activity, primarily agricultural, were dependent upon Israeli cooperation. This meant that Palestine had been unable to create a viable independent economy. Rabin's action also reinforced the idea of the 1967 border as a line of separation between the Israelis and Palestinians. Support for Arafat and the Tunis leadership of the PLO was further weakened. The PLO, no longer receiving funds from the conservative Arab states following the Gulf War, was unable to continue its welfare payments to the approximately 700,000 of the 1.8 million Palestinians who relied upon PLO assistance.

In July 1993 Rabin approved another attack on Lebanon. The Lebanese civil war had ended on 22 October 1989 with the signing of the Taif accord, so named because it was negotiated in Taif, Saudi Arabia. (It is also known as the 'Document of National Accord'.) The Taif accord recognized that Lebanon now had a Muslim majority, reasserted Lebanese authority in southern Lebanon (occupied by Israel) and legitimized the Syrian occupation. The agreement also provided for the disarmament of all national and non-national militias except Hezbollah, which was permitted to retain its arms as a 'resistance group' on the grounds that it opposed Israeli occupation in the south. Hezbollah kept up sporadic shelling of Israeli military positions in its self-proclaimed security zone, and in July 1993 one such attack killed a number of Israeli soldiers. On 25 July Israel responded with a week-long full-scale massive aerial and artillery bombardment of southern Lebanon. It is estimated that between 300,000 and 500,000 Lebanese civilians (around 10 per cent of Lebanon's population) were forced to flee their homes and villages. Hezbollah's retaliatory rocket attacks into northern Israel forced about 100,000 Israelis into bomb shelters. US Secretary of State Warren Christopher helped broker a ceasefire after seven days. Israel's efforts to deter the militants failed as the ceasefire was never fully observed. Intermittent exchanges of fire continued to take place between the IDF and Hezbollah militias in the security zone, southern Lebanon and northern Israel.

The Oslo Accords

Rabin recognized that the situation could not continue. Earlier in the year he had approved informal contacts with the PLO. Several highly secret meetings between PLO officials and the dovish Israeli deputy foreign minister, Yossi Beilin, were held in Oslo, Norway. Prompted by Palestinian spokeswoman, Hanan Ashrawi, agreement was reached in late August 1993 on a Declaration of Principles. The Israel-PLO peace accord, as the Declaration of Principles was called, consisted of two sections: in the first the PLO and Israel agreed on mutual recognition, and the second set an agenda and timetable for negotiations.

On 1 September, after a five-hour debate, sixteen of the eighteen members of the Israeli cabinet voted in favour of the draft declaration. Israel's chief negotiator with the Palestinians said that the accord enshrined fundamental changes in Israel's position to date, including a readiness to discuss the return to the territories of refugees from the 1967 war. The opposition Likud leader, Netanyahu, blasted the accord and said: 'It is not just autonomy and it is not just a Palestinian State in the territories but the start of the destruction of Israel in line with the PLO plan.'[12] Thousands of Jewish settlers and their supporters chanted 'traitor' as they battled police outside Rabin's office. Despite opposition from rejectionist leaders, Arafat secured the backing of the Fatah central committee, in a vote of ten in favour and four against. Disgusted, Hamas leaders labelled Arafat a traitor.

Although the Jordanians and Syrians had not been consulted, King Hussein supported the agreement in the expectation that Jordan, Syria and Lebanon would eventually hammer out their differences and at least sign a statement of principles. For months, Israel and Jordan had had an agenda containing the framework of a peace agreement, and Peres, appearing on American television, commented that the differences with Syria were paper thin. On 9 and 10 September 1993 Arafat and Rabin exchanged letters of mutual recognition. In his letter to Rabin, Arafat renounced violence and pledged support for repeal of clauses objectionable to Israel in the PLO charter. Rabin's brief reply recognized the PLO as the representative of the Palestinian people and accepted the PLO as a negotiating partner.

Although the US had played no part in the negotiations, the Declaration of Principles on Interim Self-Government for the Palestinians (henceforth referred to as the Israel–PLO peace accord) was signed at a ceremony on the White House lawn on 13 September 1993 by foreign minister Peres and PLO representative Mahmoud Abbas, with Warren Christopher and Russian foreign minister Andrei Kozyrev adding their signatures as witnesses, while President Clinton, Arafat and Rabin looked on. Clinton remarked: 'A peace of the brave is within our reach.' In an historic gesture the two men hesitantly shook hands.

The agenda promised to end Israeli rule over the two million Palestinians in the West Bank and Gaza. The timetable stipulated that before 13 December 1993 the parties would sign an agreement on the withdrawal of Israel military forces from the Gaza Strip and Jericho, to be completed within another four months (13 April 1994). The Israeli forces would be replaced by

Palestinian police and 'authorized Palestinians' would take over education, health, social welfare, direct taxation and tourism. Elections for a Palestinian council would be held in the West Bank and Gaza no later than 13 July 1994. Negotiation on the final status of the territories was to begin within two years (13 December 1995), the permanent settlement to become effective at the end of five years (December 1998). The nature of that permanent settlement was not defined.

The Declaration of Principles did not deal with the question of the borders of the Palestinian 'entity', or indeed just what that entity was to consist of. Rabin did not envisage an independent Palestinian state; Arafat was committed to that outcome. Both had vague notions of a Jordan-Palestine confederation at the back of their minds. The status of East Jerusalem, the right of return of the 1948 refugees and the future of the Jewish settlements were also not addressed. Furthermore, Israel retained control of the border crossings from Gaza to Egypt and the Allenby Bridge crossing between the West Bank and Jordan.

The Israel–PLO peace accord has been described as a major historic event in the history of the Arab–Israeli conflict. Certainly, many were swept up in a wave of optimism. Things seemed to augur well. After years of denial, mutual rejection had been replaced by mutual recognition. Arafat and the PLO had accepted the principle of partition, and the PLO had finally achieved independence from Arab states. Rabin and Israel saw negotiations with the PLO as a way to further negotiations with neighbouring Arab states. Within days, Israel and Jordan signed an agenda for peace negotiations, and in December the Vatican announced it would establish diplomatic relations with Israel. In 1994 several Arab states began talking to Israeli officials about lifting the Arab economic boycott and exchanging low-level representatives.

The accords were deeply flawed, however, and the initial goodwill and enthusiasm so carefully built up did not last much beyond a year. The Oslo pact did not recognize the Palestinians as a nation with legitimate claims to the land, nor their national right of self-determination. The major questions – Jerusalem, Palestinian refugees and Jewish settlements – had been postponed and were made conditional upon the successful implementation of interim steps. The agreement was conditional upon reciprocity, and the adjudicator in determining whether the terms were met by both sides was Israel, in particular the Israeli military, who would measure their effects upon Israel's security – essentially an Israeli veto.[13] Israeli negotiators had 1967 in mind when drawing up the declaration of principles, while the Palestinian negotiators had 1947 in mind.

Despite these shortcomings, Palestinian negotiator Ahmed Qurei later said of Oslo that it transformed patterns of thought on both sides and that the spirit of Oslo carried within it the promise of a new relationship between Israel and Palestine. The Oslo covenant, he wrote, could still provide a peaceful substitute for the existing state of confrontation, suffering and bloodshed.[14] Facts on the ground soon negated the promise of the agreements. Extremists on both sides soon began asserting their control over events. If anything, Arafat was more successful in controlling his extremists than Rabin. Despite the accords' provision that nothing should be done to alter the status of the West Bank and Gaza Strip over the next four years, Israel's Labor government oversaw a massive increase in land confiscation, and permitted (if not encouraged) a dramatic increase in settler population in both occupied areas. The construction of border fences, highways and bypass roads, tunnels and military barriers went ahead at an unprecedented rate – far greater than under Likud predecessors. By 1996 the settler population was 144,000, up by 48 per cent in the West Bank and 62 per cent in the Gaza Strip.

One immediate result of the signing of the Israeli–PLO peace accords was the ending of the intifada. Israel was almost universally condemned for its harsh responses to the intifada. On 3 November 1993 the UN General Assembly, by a vote of 130 to 2, condemned Israeli oppression in the occupied territories and the violations of Palestinian human rights (only Israel and the US voted against it). During the uprising almost 1,100 Palestinian civilians had been killed by Israeli forces, and 75 by Israeli civilians, mostly settlers. This total included 237 children under the age of sixteen. On the other side, 101 Israeli civilians had been killed by Palestinians (53 within Israel), and 59 Israeli security force personnel were killed. Tens of thousands of Palestinians and hundreds of Israelis were injured. Around 15,000 Palestinian houses were demolished. Many participants in the intifada were deported: Rabin illegally deported more than 400 Hamas and Islamic Jihad activists to southern Lebanon in December 1992.

Israeli historians and commentators all agree that the intifada came as a shock to almost all Israelis who had been living a life of fantasy in which Palestinians were invisible or did not exist. Israelis came to the realization that there is no such thing as a 'benevolent' occupation, if that is, indeed, what they thought they were doing. They encountered what all occupiers come to experience, popular resistance that renders the most sophisticated weapons virtually powerless. For almost five years they endured relentless punishment from a united and determined opposition, despite inflicting extraordinary levels of injury and death with their overwhelming superiority in weapons. Divisions emerged within Israeli society – among Jews and between Jews and the 700,000 Arab Israelis who made up around 17 per cent of the population – and within the IDF itself. The Arab Israelis, surprisingly to many Jewish Israelis, supported the intifada through strikes and rallies, and with medical and food aid. On 23 January 1988 between 80,000 and 100,000 Israelis demonstrated in Tel Aviv denouncing Israeli settlement policy in the occupied territories. Also, as was the case in the Lebanon war, a small but significant number of IDF reservists refused to serve in the territories or to carry out orders to beat Palestinians.

Israel's leaders learned little from the intifada. The intifada reordered Israel's tactics in that the Palestinian question was brought to the diplomatic forefront of the conflict, but the strategic goal of preventing the emergence of a Palestinian state did not change. The uprising deepened the bitterness and resentment of both sides, making it even more difficult for them to overlook the often-justified resentment of past wrongs. During a second intifada, which began in September 2000, Israel reverted to the methods of the first. The government utilized a wide range of collective punishments. The force used against the second uprising was more lethal than that used in the first but no more successful as a deterrent. Today, placing their faith in high-technology precision weapons, helicopter gunships and modern tanks, Israel's leaders believe they can inflict casualties, often indiscriminate, without suffering losses to the IDF or the civilian population of Israel. Israel still seeks to divide and rule the Palestinian leadership, and through its intransigence and hard-line policies creates conditions that harden the resolve of those with whom, at some time in the future, they will have to negotiate.

Talks to implement the Oslo Accords began in October 1993 but the first target date, 13 December, for the beginning of Israeli withdrawal from Gaza and Jericho passed without any steps being taken by Israel. On 25 February 1994 Baruch Goldstein, an American-born Jewish settler and member of the extremist Kach party, massacred 29 Palestinians praying in the Ibrahimi

Mosque in Hebron. Israel's leaders described him as a lone crazed gunman, but within months he had become something of a national hero to hard-line Israelis. Rabin refused to remove the 400 settlers from Hebron or to dismantle any settlements during the interim period. Members of Hamas carried out reprisal bombings within Israel, killing fifteen civilians.

The Gaza Strip and Jericho were eventually handed over to the PLO and Palestinian policemen amid celebrations on 13 May 1994, ending 27 years of Israeli rule over the almost two million residents of the Gaza Strip. Arafat arrived in Gaza on 1 July, and members of the Palestine National Authority were sworn in on 5 July in Jericho. Negotiations begun in late July ended with the signing by Rabin and King Hussein, on the border between Jordan and Israel in the Negev, of a formal peace treaty between the two states on 26 October 1994, with, once again, Clinton and other heads of state as witnesses.

Negotiations between Jordan and Israel were far more successful than those between Syria and Israel, in part because of the long association and mutual respect felt between the Israeli establishment and King Hussein, and partly because security issues for both states were less prominent. Rabin, to Arafat's frustration, recognized the Hashemite king's claim to have a special role to protect the Muslim holy sites in Jerusalem, and promised additional irrigation water flows down the River Jordan. Hussein, for his part, promised not to allow foreign troops into Jordan that might threaten Israel's security. This treaty effectively put an end to the Likud dream that 'Jordan is Palestine'. Arafat, Peres and Rabin received the Nobel peace prize in December 1994.

Hamas extremists and Israeli settlers continued their acts of violence throughout 1995 in an effort to slow down or prevent the implementation of the 1993 Oslo Accords. Despite their respective domestic oppositions, Arafat and Rabin reached a further agreement at Taba, on the Red Sea, on 24 September 1995. Four days later, in Washington, in the presence of Egyptian President Hosni Mubarak, King Hussein and US President Clinton, they signed the Israeli–Palestinian Interim Agreement of the West Bank and Gaza Strip, popularly known as Oslo II (or the Taba Accord), to implement the 1993 agreements.

This agreement set out provisions for the promised Palestinian Council elections and divided the West Bank into three areas, A, B and C, designating the security arrangements to be implemented in each area. Area A, to be placed under exclusive Palestinian control, consisted of Palestinian towns and urban areas. Area B, where Palestinian police would be responsible for civilian authority but Israeli forces for overall security, consisted of Palestinian villages and less populated areas, and Area C, to be placed under exclusive Israeli control, consisted of land confiscated by Israel for settlement and roads. Areas A and B respectively represented 7.6 per cent and 21.4 per cent of the West Bank and Gaza and covered more than 90 per cent of the local Palestinian population. Area C comprised 71 per cent of the Palestinian territories. In real terms, Israel relinquished approximately 30 per cent of the West Bank to the full or partial control of the Palestinian Authority, and around 65 per cent of the Gaza Strip. Rabin saw Oslo II as a cautious step in the right direction of accommodating Palestinian aspirations, but to Arafat it fell far short of creating the conditions necessary for Palestinian statehood. On the other hand, it was interpreted as a signal to both Palestinians and Israelis that Rabin was putting an end to the dream of an undivided Greater Israel embracing all the former British Mandate west of the River Jordan.

Barely six weeks after Oslo II (and two years after the first Oslo Accords), on 4 November 1995, the 73-year-old Yitzhak Rabin was assassinated by a young Jewish messianic extremist, Yigal Amir. Rabin had just addressed a huge peace rally of 150,000 in Tel Aviv. 'I was a soldier for 27 years', he had told the cheering crowd, 'I fought so long as there was no prospect of peace. I believe that there is now a chance for peace, a great chance, which must be seized.'[15] Israelis were stunned. More than a million filed past his coffin, and his funeral was attended by leaders from over 80 countries. Several Arab states sent representatives. Arafat paid his personal respects to Rabin's widow: 'I have lost a friend', he told her. Leah Rabin, rightly, blamed right-wing elements within Israel for creating the atmosphere of hatred that led Amir to his murderous act.

Looking back, it could be argued that the prospects for peace died with Rabin. Had he lived events might very well have unfolded differently, but within eighteen months of his death, Israel's newly elected Likud leadership set out to diminish and marginalize Rabin's partner in peace, Arafat, with unforeseen and tragic consequences for all concerned. Rabin's death was a turning-point in the Arab–Israeli conflict at least as significant as the accord signed with Arafat two years earlier.

Rabin's successor as prime minister and defence minister was Shimon Peres, who promised to continue the policies of Rabin. The first test of his

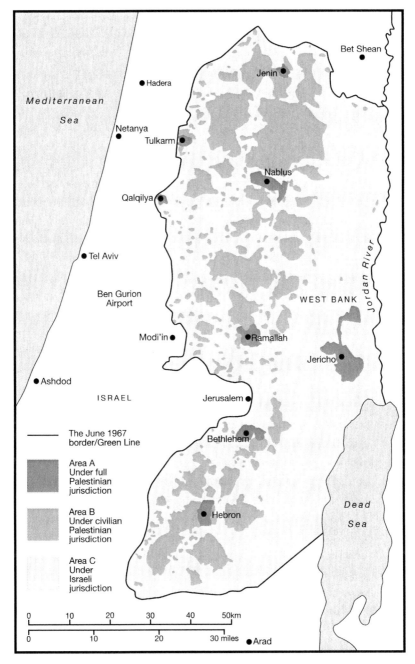

Oslo II Accords, September 1995.

rhetoric came immediately. A week after Rabin's death, Yossi Beilin presented to Peres a 'permanent status' plan, worked out between Israeli and Palestinian negotiators in Stockholm, that had been finalized just a few days before Rabin's assassination. The Beilin plan, worked out with senior PLO figure Mahmoud Abbas, postulated a Palestinian state (demilitarized) in 93 per cent of the West Bank. Israel would annex 6 per cent, where most of the settlements were, and the settlers in the Palestinian state could remain under Palestinian sovereignty or receive compensation. The capital of the Palestinian state would be located at Abu Dis, just outside the municipal boundary of Jerusalem as defined by Israel, but the Palestinians would recognize only West Jerusalem as the Israeli capital. The Muslim holy sites in East Jerusalem would be given extra-territorial status. Peres faltered. Beilin could not persuade him to accept the plan. But in December, the prime minister did speed up Israel's redeployment from the remaining major Arab towns in the West Bank, enabling elections for the 88-seat Palestinian Legislative Council to take place in late January 1996. On the same day, in elections in which around 80 per cent of those eligible to vote turned out, Arafat was elected president of the Palestine National Authority.

Peres made a further serious blunder in January 1996 when he approved the assassination of Yahya Ayyah, the Hamas mastermind of a number of suicide bombings that had killed around 50 Israelis in response to the Hebron massacre of Palestinians by Baruch Goldstein. The murder of Ayyash by Israel's security service, Shabak, in Gaza on 5 January 1996 unleashed a retaliatory series of devastating suicide bombings in Ashkelon, Jerusalem and Tel Aviv in February and March, killing more than 60 civilians. Peres declared war on Hamas and Islamic Jihad. He closed the Gaza Strip to Palestinian workers, and suspended talks with both the Palestinian Authority and Syria.

Initial negotiations with Syria had begun in 1992 with US encouragement and participation, and they had continued until suspended, deadlocked, in mid-1995. The issues were fairly straightforward. Israel wanted a peace treaty, Syria wanted the return of the Golan Heights to the border of 4 June 1967 (not the border drawn up by Britain and France in 1923, which was further east). Neither leader fully trusted the other, however, and there were strong domestic pressures on both not to reach an agreement. Rabin wanted a long period (five years) in which to withdraw, Assad a short one (six months), and neither could agree on precise security arrangements to be put in place. Rabin used the pretext of Israel's security to insist upon arrangements it knew were quite unacceptable to Assad. Peres had resumed negotiations in December 1995. But now Israel alarmed Syria, and other members of the Arab League, by signing a military cooperation agreement with Turkey allowing the Israeli air force use of Turkish bases and air space in February 1996. To many Arabs, Peres did not seem very different from previous Likud governments; like Israeli leaders before him, he went along with right-wing domestic pressure.

On 11 April 1996, just after Passover, Israel launched yet another air and artillery attack on Lebanon, 'Operation Grapes of Wrath', lasting sixteen days. Following a similar (unsuccessful) strategy used against Palestinian guerrillas in Jordan in the 1960s and '70s, Israel believed that military bombardments of Beirut and the Bekaa valley would force the Lebanese government to crack down on Hezbollah groups and thereby stop rocket attacks on northern Israeli outposts. If that was, in fact, the thinking, it was never going to work. Once more, between 300,000 and 500,000 civilians fled their homes. Israel launched more than 2,000 air attacks in an attempt to eliminate Hezbollah's 300 full-time fighters. Washington, in an effort to rescue Israel from the consequences of its intemperate military action, brokered another ceasefire agreement, which came into effect on 27 April. The agreement barred cross-border attacks on civilian targets, as well as using civilian villages to launch attacks. A monitoring committee was set up, comprising representatives from the US, France, Syria, Israel and Lebanon. Between 150 and 170 Lebanese were killed, including more than 106 civilians who died in the Israeli shelling of a UN post at Qana. Some 350 civilians were wounded. Major bridges and power stations were destroyed; according to Human Rights Watch, 2,018 houses and buildings in south Lebanon were either completely destroyed or severely bombarded. Lebanon's total economic damage was estimated at US$500 million. Within Israel 62 civilians were wounded and the damage to Israeli civilian property was estimated at about US$7 million.

The attack on Lebanon produced unintended consequences that far outweighed any benefits Israel may have hoped for. Israel's reputation was damaged; the state was widely condemned, even by friends, for the civilian deaths and infrastructure damage it inflicted. Assad strengthened his political and military hold in Lebanon and Israel's northern region was made no more secure. It may be that Israel was less interested in the security of the northern Israeli localities than it was in ensuring its control over the free passage of trade between Israel and Lebanon with open borders and open markets, and the diversion of water from the Litani River into Israel. Israeli merchandise entered Lebanon encouraged by the Israeli government, without paying custom duties, and it was then re-exported to other countries. Israel did not want to lose control of this profitable source of revenue to Hezbollah. Peres lost all credibility at home and abroad, and the Labor Alignment was defeated by the Likud coalition in general elections held in May 1996. The victory of 46-year-old Revisionist Zionist Benjamin Netanyahu over 73-year-old Peres, in the first elections in which the prime minster was directly elected, ended whatever slim hope there may have been of Israel reaching an accommodation with the Palestinian Authority, or of finding a way to live with peace and security in the region for the next decade at least. The next chapter will examine the impact of Netanyahu's election on the course of the conflict.

CHAPTER 8

Darkness Returns

By the mid-1990s the ambition of most Arab states and Palestinian leaders was no longer to eliminate Israel, but to have it withdraw from occupied Arab territory – in Syria and Lebanon as well as the whole of the West Bank and Gaza. Oslo had been a first step, but there was a long way to go. Benjamin Netanyahu came to office in mid-1996 intending to freeze the Oslo process. He harboured an enduring and unshakeable hostility toward Arabs, especially the PLO. Believing that Israel's military superiority gave him a free hand, he arrogantly, foolishly and wrongly believed that he could force the PLO to give up the goal of a Palestinian state. During the 1996 Israel election campaign Netanyahu had rejected the idea of Palestinian statehood, accused Arafat of aiding and abetting terrorism, insisted that Jerusalem would remain the undivided capital of Israel, and asserted that all the Golan Heights was essential for Israel's security and would not be returned to Syria. This chapter explores the conflict in the decade following Netanyahu's election as Israeli prime minister.

One of Netanyahu's first acts as prime minister was to bring former general Ariel Sharon into the cabinet, creating for him a new infrastructure ministry, responsible for roads, railways, ports, water and land allocation, energy and other related matters. In August Netanyahu lifted the four-year freeze on the expansion of land settlements in the West Bank and work began on paving around 300 miles of roads to link the settlements. Yasser Arafat faced not only a hostile and intransigent Israeli government unwilling to talk to him, but growing discontent within his own ranks. Militant Islamists saw him, at best, as ineffective in keeping Israel to the terms of the Oslo Accords and furthering the cause of a Palestinian state, and, at worst, even as a pawn of Israel. Members of the Palestinian legislative and national councils, also frustrated by the lack of progress, saw him as overseeing a corrupt administration. To add to his woes, thirteen members of the Arab League at a summit meeting in Cairo on 22 June, despite their hostility to the new regime, could not agree on a unified strategy in dealing with Israel.

Netanyahu and Arafat finally met on 4 September 1996 at the Erez checkpoint near Gaza, but nothing came of the meeting but mutual recriminations. On 24 September, as had occurred so often in the past, and would again in the near future, an incident in Jerusalem sparked violence. Without prior notification to senior Muslim clerics, Israel provocatively opened an exit to completed excavations of the ancient Hasmonean tunnel that ran alongside the perimeter of Jerusalem's Temple Mount compound. Deadly riots erupted for several days between Palestinians and Israeli police that threatened to spread. US President Bill Clinton hastily arranged a summit between Netanyahu and Arafat in Washington that ended the violence. Israel delayed its withdrawal from Hebron, largely because of the presence there of around 500 Jewish settlers in the centre of the city surrounded by approximately 160,000 Palestinians, and this became a volatile point of contention. Israel withdrew in mid-January 1997, leaving about 1,000 Israeli soldiers to guard the settlers, and on 19 January Arafat returned to the city he had not entered for thirty years.

In his election campaign, Netanyahu had promised a new path to end the confrontations, but instead he made a U-turn and subverted Oslo. In March 1999 the cabinet agreed to a further small withdrawal (9 per cent) from the West Bank, but to compensate for this, and the redeployment from Hebron, the prime minister announced that 6,500 units housing 30,000 Israelis would be built on expropriated Arab land at Jabal Abu Ghneim (Har Homa), a hill just north of Bethlehem and overlooking East Jerusalem. Once built, the settlement would complete the chain of Jewish settlements around Jerusalem and cut off contacts between Arabs in Jerusalem and those in the West Bank. Almost half the Jewish settlers lived in these settlements encircling Jerusalem, which enclosed 10 per cent of the West Bank. The encirclement was yet another example of creating facts on the ground to pre-empt negotiations. Shocked Palestinians called a general strike. Once again widespread rioting broke out. At an emergency special meeting of the UN General Assembly, all but three members – the US, Micronesia and Israel – called upon Israel to halt work and end all settlement activities in the occupied territories. A Hamas suicide bomber killed himself and three Israeli women at a café in Tel Aviv.

Religious extremists played an increasingly prominent role throughout 1997 and 1998. Netanyahu's Likud coalition was dependent upon Israel's religious parties.[1] Consequently, the prime minister refused further redeployments, as specified by Oslo, and planned more settlements, while Arafat sought to co-opt Hamas and Islamic Jihad. The Clinton administration discovered the limits of US influence with both leaders unwilling to shift, despite persistent appeals from Secretary of State Madeleine Albright who, echoing her boss, over-enthusiastically described the US as 'the indispensable nation'. Eventually Arafat and Netanyahu agreed to meet at the Wye River Plantation in Maryland on 15 October 1998.

Both leaders were under domestic and international pressure to produce some positive outcome at the Wye River meeting. King Hussein, undergoing treatment for cancer at the Chicago Mayo Clinic, visited twice to keep negotiations going. On 23 October, in a White House ceremony, an agreement (known as the Wye River agreement) was signed. The two sides agreed upon a new Israeli redeployment and a security cooperation plan. Under the arrangements, Israel retained full military and civilian control of 60 per cent of the West Bank (designated in the Oslo II or Taba agreement as Area C). The Palestinians increased the area of full control from their previous 3 per cent to about 18.2 per cent (Area A) and shared with Israel control of 21.8 per cent (Area B). The PNC also agreed to eliminate articles in the Palestine Charter calling for Israel's destruction, and Israel agreed to release 750 non-Hamas Palestinian prisoners.

Netanyahu, faced with right-wing and religious opposition, immediately reneged on implementing the agreement. As was the case with the Oslo II accord, Israel once again appointed itself the sole arbiter of Palestinian compliance, and the cabinet and Knesset found reasons to delay. In mid-November housing minister Ariel Sharon urged settlers 'to grab as many hilltops as possible'.[2] Arafat also faced internal problems. Rejectionist religious elements within the PLO, and in Syria, were unhappy as Palestinian police began rounding up Hamas followers, as required in the agreement. Partial Israeli deployments began in late November, and on 24 November a Palestinian international airport was opened in Gaza. Despite a decision by the

PNC, made in the presence of President Clinton in Gaza in mid-December, to remove the offensive provisions of its charter, Israel refused to meet the next deadline for redeployment. Rather than act, the Knesset voted to dissolve the government and elections were slated for May 1999. The dream of a Greater Israel may have been fading, but so were the prospects for peace.

King Hussein, a symbol of stability and moderation in a region of unpredictable leaders, died in February 1999, leaving his inexperienced and untried oldest son, Abdullah (King Abdullah II), to govern Jordan. Ehud Barak, a former chief of staff, and the most highly decorated soldier in Israel's history, led the Labor party to victory in general elections held in May 1999. He had replaced Peres as leader of the party in 1997 and, at its annual convention in May that year, the party had repealed its long-standing opposition to the establishment of a Palestinian state. Barak became leader of a new Labor Alignment known as 'One Israel' in March 1999, and campaigned on the basis that he was committed to the Oslo process.

Barak met with several heads of state, including Arafat, in early July, but took no action. Arafat was forced to accept yet another postponement. At a meeting held at the Egyptian Red Sea resort of Sharm el-Sheikh in early September 2000, six years after Oslo, 'final status' talks began. The issues remained unchanged. Palestinian negotiators wanted a state in all the West Bank and the Gaza Strip, the removal of Israeli settlements unwilling to accept Palestinian jurisdiction, the repatriation of all refugees and sovereignty over East Jerusalem, which would be the capital. Israeli negotiators were not prepared to give up all the occupied territories, to relinquish authority over any of Jerusalem, or allow the return of refugees other than a small number of special cases. The talks went nowhere. In fact, Barak approved 2,600 new housing units in existing settlements in the West Bank, although he did remove 12 of 42 small outposts the Israeli Judge Advocate deemed illegal under the terms of the Wye Agreement, leaving 145 intact.

Putting the Palestinians on hold, Barak turned to Syria. Assad had been seeking a 'full peace for a full withdrawal' with Israel since 1993, but Israel had broken off talks in February 1996. Clinton succeeded in restarting negotiations between the two countries in late December 1999, and again at Shepherdstown, West Virginia, in January 2000. Assad sought the return of the Golan to the 4 June 1967 border between the two countries. Former Prime Minister Yitzhak Rabin had promised the Americans that he would accept this condition providing it was part of a normalization process with Syria. Barak insisted that Syria rein in Hezbollah in Lebanon and sign a permanent peace treaty as the price of Israel withdrawing, not to the pre-June 1967 war boundary, but to the international border drawn up by Britain and France in 1923. This line would ensure Israel's access to all the Sea of Galilee, together with a narrow strip along the eastern shoreline. Despite Washington's efforts, talks faltered, with each side blaming the other. Recent revelations by Martyn Indyk, the former US ambassador to Israel and observer to the negotiations, suggest that it was Barak who reneged, causing the Syrians to break off talks.[3]

Hezbollah attacks between 1995 and 1999 had killed more than 120 Israeli soldiers in Israel's 'security zone' in southern Lebanon. The year 2000 opened with the deaths by ambush of seven soldiers. Barak – and even Sharon – realized that it was time to withdraw. When Lebanese president Emile Lahoud, a Maronite Catholic and former army chief of staff, agreed to the deployment of UN forces in the buffer zone in April, the stage was set for Israel to leave Lebanon. Chaos ensued in May as the Israeli army tried to hand over its military posts and villages to the South Lebanon Army. Instead their place was taken by Hezbollah militia. Hezbollah's leader Sheikh Nazrollah declared Israel's departure a victory for Lebanon, although Israel and Lebanon technically still remained at war. During its eighteen years of occupation Israel had virtually incorporated southern Lebanon, and its population of around 120,000 people, into Israel, providing social services and infrastructure. Hezbollah moved rapidly to replace Israel.

Camp David, Taba and the Return to Violence

Washington had not succeeded in moving Israel-Palestinian negotiations forward in 1999. Barak postponed promised transfers of territory. To-ing and fro-ing continued over what areas would and would not be transferred, and whether or not the Arab village/suburb of Abu Dis was a part of Jerusalem or the West Bank. By the end of March 2000, as a result of land transfers, the Palestinian Authority (PA) was in control of around 40 per cent of the West Bank. Nevertheless, some progress was being made, evidenced by the visit at this juncture of Pope John Paul II, who had extended Vatican recognition to Israel in 1993; on this, the first visit by a Pope to Israel, he extended recognition to the PLO as a representative of the PA. The Pope reiterated the Vatican's position that Jerusalem should be given a special international status guaranteeing Christian, Jews and Muslims free access to the city's holy sites.

Israelis debated how much they should hand over while Palestinians waited for what had already been agreed upon. For a brief time informal discussions were held in Stockholm, Sweden. In June 2000, President Assad of Syria died suddenly and was replaced by his 34-year-old son Bashar, a British-trained eye doctor. Assad's death put the Syrian track on hold for the time being. In June and July, driven by domestic political imperatives, Barak and Clinton both pressed Arafat to meet in a three-way summit. Clinton, in a bid to salvage his presidential reputation, issued an invitation to Barak and Arafat to meet at Camp David in July. Barak readily accepted, although his coalition began to fall apart. Arafat knew he would be asked to accept less than he could, but the future looked even more unpredictable and bleak.

The Camp David summit, which took place between 11 and 25 July 2000, ended with no agreement. Israel offered to withdraw from over 90 per cent of the West Bank, excluding Jerusalem and its environs, but wanted to annex those parts of the territory with major Jewish settlements closest to Israel proper and to retain part of the Jordan Valley. The Palestinians insisted on Israel withdrawing from all the territory captured in the 1967 War. Israel agreed to turn over Abu Dis and other suburbs of East Jerusalem to the Palestinians for the capital of a Palestinian state, and proposed Palestinian municipal autonomy in parts of the Old City, as well as the right to fly the Palestinian flag over the Muslim and Christian holy places. But Barak would not surrender sovereignty of East Jerusalem, as Arafat demanded, and on which he would not yield. On the question of refugees, the Palestinians demanded the right of return of all the refugees, and their descendants, displaced by the creation of Israel in 1948 and an admission by Israel of responsibility for their plight. Israel refused to accept moral or legal responsibility for the refugee problem and wanted it solved not by repatriation but by compensation through international aid.

Barak and Clinton blamed Arafat for the failure to reach agreement and felt bitterly let down after what they both asserted was a 'generous offer' from Israel. Arafat felt equally bitter that Israel had refused to offer the essentials of a Palestinian state. Because of their respective precarious domestic political circumstances, Barak could offer no more and Arafat could not accept what was offered. Neither was prepared to show bold leadership. Both Arafat and Barak had upset the extremist elements within their own ranks, and had apparently gained nothing in return. Arafat threatened to declare a Palestinian state unilaterally on 13 September, but it was a hollow threat. The PNA had all the trappings of state as it was, and there was no way it could force Israel to provide water, electricity, international transport or other essentials of a state. Furthermore, it might cause Israel to unilaterally annex all of the West Bank.

There seemed nowhere to go but backwards. At this critical juncture Sharon, now leader of the Likud party, ignited the violence we have come to know as the second, or al-Aqsa, intifada. On 28 September 2000 Sharon visited the Jerusalem's Temple Mount/Haram al-Sharif (the Noble Sanctuary), accompanied by a phalanx of around 1,000 Israeli police. Although he did not enter the al-Aqsa Mosque or the Dome of the Rock, the Muslim sacred sites built on the Mount, the purpose of his half-hour visit was to indicate that Israel would never give up sovereignty over the Mount, sacred to Jews and Muslims. There were limited disturbances during Sharon's visit, mostly involving stone-throwing at the police. The following day, after Friday prayers, violence occurred in which Palestinian demonstrators were fired on by Israeli soldiers using rubber-coated metal bullets and live ammunition, killing four persons and injuring about 200. Fourteen Israeli policemen were injured. The deaths of several young Palestinians set off a cycle of violence that resulted in the deaths of close to 500 people and the wounding of more than 8,000, most of them Palestinians, within six months. This new wave of violence resembled all-out warfare more than the 'shaking off' of the original intifada.

Many Israelis viewed Sharon's visit as an internal political move against Prime Minister Barak. Palestinians saw it as highly provocative. A report commissioned by President Bill Clinton and published on 20 May 2001 concluded that Sharon's visit did not cause the al-Aqsa intifada, but the visit was poorly timed and the provocative effect should have been foreseen; indeed it was foreseen by those Palestinian and US officials who urged that the visit be prohibited. More significant in escalating the violence was the decision of the Israeli police on 29 September to use lethal means against the Palestinian demonstrators, and the subsequent failure of either party to exercise restraint.

In the next few days, rock-throwing youths were joined by armed Palestinian police against Israeli soldiers. Two widely publicized events early in the intifada symbolized the intensity and hatred driving each side. In Gaza, a twelve-year-old Palestinian boy was caught in the crossfire and appeared to be killed by Israeli soldiers, and in Ramallah, where two Israeli reservists were murdered at a Palestinian police outpost, one was thrown out of a window and his body beaten and trampled upon by the crowd.

By mid-October the intifada was taking on the characteristics of a fully fledged war. The Fatah paramilitary organization, Tanzim, which had branches throughout the West Bank and Gaza, cooperated with Hamas and Islamic Jihad in a loose group called the Nationalist and Islamic Movement. The result was sniper attacks and the planting of roadside and car bombs that blew up Israeli buses and shops, killing or injuring Israeli civilians. Israel responded using US-supplied Black Hawk and Cobra helicopter gunships firing missiles. President Clinton and Egyptian president Mubarak, desperately seeking to end, or at least contain, the upheaval, convened a summit at Sharm el-Sheikh at which the two sides issued public statements calling for an end to violence.

The Sharm el-Sheikh summit was attended by UN Secretary General Kofi Annan, as well as by Jordan's King Abdullah II and the European Union's Javier Solana. The situation was out of control, however, and the ceasefire agreement was never implemented as clashes continued and became even more deadly. The conference did agree to a US-led fact-finding mission to investigate the causes of the intifada. Clinton appointed George J. Mitchell, a former US senator who had mediated in the Northern Ireland conflict as chair of the international commission on disarmament in Northern Ireland. Mitchell's report, published in May 2001, stated that fear, hate, anger and frustration had increased on both sides since the failure of the Camp David summit. The report identified the grievances of each party in the following terms.

Mitchell pointed out that to the Palestinians, 'Madrid' and 'Oslo' had heralded the prospect of a state, and guaranteed an end to Israeli occupation and a resolution of outstanding matters within an agreed time-frame. They were angry at the continued growth of settlements and at their daily experiences of humiliation and disruption as a result of Israel's presence in the Palestinian territories. Palestinians saw settlers and settlements in their midst not only as violating the spirit of the Oslo process, but also as an application of overwhelming force that sustained and protected the settlements. The PLO alleged that Israeli political leaders had 'made no secret of the fact that the Israeli interpretation of Oslo was designed to segregate the Palestinians in non-contiguous enclaves, surrounded by Israeli military-controlled borders, with settlements and settlement roads violating the territories' integrity.' The report stated that, according to the PLO: 'In the seven years since the [Declaration of Principles], the settler population in the West Bank, excluding East Jerusalem and the Gaza Strip, has doubled to 200,000, and the settler population in East Jerusalem has risen to 170,000.' Israel had constructed approximately 30 new settlements, and expanded a number of existing ones to house these new settlers. The PLO also claimed that the Israeli government had failed to comply with other commitments, such as further withdrawals from the West Bank.[4]

Mitchell's committee explained that Israeli leaders argued that the expansion of settlement activity, and the measures taken to facilitate the convenience and safety of settlers, did not prejudice the outcome of permanent-status negotiations. To Israel, security was the key concern. The Israelis, the report continued, maintained that the PLO had breached its solemn commitments by continuing the use of violence in the pursuit of its political objectives. The report noted: 'Security is not something on which Israel will bargain or compromise. The failure of the Palestinian side to comply with both the letter and spirit of the security provisions in the various agreements has long been a source of disturbance in Israel.' According to Israeli leaders, the Palestinian failure took several forms: institutionalized anti-Israel and anti-Jewish incitement; the release from detention of terrorists; the failure to control illegal weapons; and the conduct of violent operations, ranging from the insertion of riflemen into demonstrations to terrorist attacks on Israeli civilians.

The result of these two opposing views, the Mitchell Report concluded, was stalemate and the resort to violence. The committee's principal recommendation was that the parties re-commit themselves to the Sharm el-Sheikh spirit, and that they implement the decisions made there in 1999 and 2000.[5] Peres met Arafat in early November and the two agreed to carry out the steps decided upon at Sharm el-Sheikh to end the fighting. However, a lethal bomb explosion in Jerusalem that killed two Israelis in Mahane Yehuda market sabotaged the proposed ceasefire. Shortly after, Clinton met with Arafat and then Barak in Washington. In mid-November a powerful roadside bomb ripped apart an armoured settlers' schoolbus in Gush Katif near the Gaza Strip, killing two adults and wounding eleven children. Israel retaliated with a massive attack on the Gaza Strip, imposed border closures and road blockades, halted imports and exports, and cut telephone and electricity lines, completely disrupting the Palestinian economy.

Israeli leaders also resorted to a method they had used in the past: political assassination, or, as the Israeli military called it, 'targeted killing'. In November and December a number of Fatah and Hamas activists were murdered, but there seemed little let-up in the number of bombing attacks in Israeli towns and cities. As the Palestinian death-toll mounted as a result of IDF attacks, Israel suffered a series of diplomatic setbacks. The UN condemned Israel's use of excessive force, an Arab summit in Cairo also condemned Israel, and Arab countries with ties to Israel cut those links. Egypt eventually recalled its ambassador, and the new Jordanian ambassador to Israel delayed presenting his credentials. Arafat was unsuccessful, however, in gaining Security Council authorization for an international force to keep the peace.

Meanwhile, political instability in Israel created added uncertainty. Barak could not keep his National-Unity government together and resigned in early December. Elections for a new prime minister were scheduled for 6 February 2001. The Likud leader to face Barak was Ariel Sharon, the Israeli figure most loathed by the Palestinians. Also, in the United States, where the November 2000 presidential election had produced no clear winner for weeks, the newly declared president, George W. Bush, indicated that the US would not directly involve itself in the Israeli–Palestinian situation.

Barak realized that his only hope of re-election depended upon ending the intifada and reaching agreement with Arafat. He explored the possibility of an agreement on the basis of Israeli concessions on Jerusalem in exchange for Palestinian flexibility regarding refugee resettlement. Barak also stated publicly for the first time that he would be willing to recognize a Palestinian state. These propositions became the basis for a final, desperate effort to reach a settlement before the Israeli elections. Barak and Arafat and their negotiating teams met at Taba for six days in late January 2001 and reportedly came very close to an agreement, but the talks ultimately foundered.

Considerable controversy surrounds the breakdown of the 2001 Taba talks. Barak blamed Arafat for turning down his 'generous' offer, which, he claimed, gave the Palestinians everything they wanted, but Arafat refused to sign an agreement. Israelis have pointed to Arafat's unwillingness to sign as yet another in a long line of Palestinian rejections of a two-state solution. Some accounts by observers suggest, however, that it was Barak who walked away from the negotiating table and point out that, although the two teams were close to agreement, Barak's proposals fell far short of the essential minimum for peace. Uri Avnery, the Israeli journalist, Gush Shalom peace-activist and former member of the Knesset, argues that Barak's walk-out was consistent with his inability to finalize an acceptable agreement with Syria in January 2000, and his backing away at Camp David.[6]

Since 2001 there has been little alteration in the negotiating positions of both sides. The unwillingness or inability of Barak and Arafat to reach agreement at Camp David and Taba was another major – and tragic – turning-point in the Arab–Israeli conflict. It gave the green light to extremists. Barak and Arafat were swept aside by those who mistakenly and lamentably believed that a reversion to military arms was the way forward. Barak was replaced by Sharon, and Arafat was marginalized by, first, Palestinian militant factions and then by Israel, supported by the United States.

Israelis punished Barak for his failure to achieve peace. They believed he had been too dovish, and that this had encouraged the Palestinians to demand more and resort to terrorist methods. In the election for prime minister held on 6 February 2001, Ariel Sharon, who promised Israelis security, won decisively receiving 62.5 per cent of the votes to 34.7 per cent for Barak. Only 59 per cent of the electorate turned out, as most Israeli Arabs (20 per cent of the population) and many Israeli Jews sat out the election. Israeli Arabs, who had voted overwhelmingly for Barak in 1999, were protesting the deaths of thirteen of their community during the early stage of the intifada. In a situation reminiscent of Netanyahu's election in 1996, Israeli Jews, deeply pessimistic that peace with the Palestinians was possible and doubtful that Arafat was a true partner for peace, voted for security. The collapse of the centre in Israel left the way open for the hawks to take control.

Palestinians saw Sharon's victory as proof that Israel was not serious about peace, since the hard-line former general was on record as saying that he would never share Jerusalem, or give up more territory to the Palestinians. He was also adamantly opposed to any 'right of return' of Palestinian refugees. Palestinian groups such as Hamas and Islamic Jihad, and others opposed to negotiations with the Jewish state on ideological as well as pragmatic grounds, were encouraged by this turn of events. Although Arafat said that he would continue to extend his hand in peace, his own position as leader was in danger of being challenged by younger and more radical elements within the Palestinian population.

Sharon formed an eight-party National-Unity government that included the more dovish Labor party, the right-wing religious Shas party and the far-right National Union party. It was unstable and untried. Labor party leader Peres was appointed foreign minister. It was not clear how Sharon would provide the security he had promised. However, on 22 May 2001, two days after the release of the Mitchell report, he declared a unilateral ceasefire, leaving Arafat little choice but to follow suit on 2 June. Faced with Sharon's decision, Arafat could scarcely depict himself as someone willing to negotiate if attacks continued. Unilateral action was to become Sharon's preferred approach to the Palestinians as it eliminated bilateral negotiations. It was a way of killing the peace process. Later in the month, President George W. Bush sent George Tenet, Director of Central Intelligence for the CIA, to the Middle East to see if he could come up with a comprehensive ceasefire plan to end the intifada and restore normal political negotiations between the two parties. Both sides accepted a plan worked out by Tenet, but it was quickly made redundant as bitter fighting resumed.

July and August 2001 were particularly violent. The Israeli army besieged Palestinian towns and villages, and killed a number of 'leading' Hamas operatives in the West Bank. Despite these actions, suicide bombings continued: one in a Jerusalem pizzeria killed fifteen and wounded 130. Sharon closed PLO offices in East Jerusalem and sent the army with tanks into the Arab West Bank town of Jenin. Washington made only half-hearted efforts to restrain Sharon. When Hamas politician Sheikh Jamal Mansour was assassinated in early August, marking a deliberate escalation of the conflict, US Vice President Dick Cheney stated that he thought there was 'some justification' in the Israelis trying to protect themselves by the pre-emptive targeted strike on the suspected terrorist. The PA and Arafat were losing control of events to more radical and militant factions within the Palestinian movement, and this process was being accelerated by the fact that Sharon and Bush were determined to ignore Arafat. The Israeli prime minister was acting as if determined to destroy the ability of the PA to act as a government. While demanding that the Palestinian Authority clamp down on activists and meet Israel's rigorous security requirements, Sharon used US-supplied F-15 and F-16 planes as well as tanks to destroy PA police stations, institutions and infrastructure.

The attacks of 11 September 2001 on New York and Washington by members of the little-known al-Qaeda organization caught stunned Americans, Israelis and Palestinians completely by surprise. The Bush administration was galvanized into action, and Afghanistan and Iraq quickly became the focus of Washington's declared 'War on Terrorism'. Gaining the support of moderate Arab states was regarded as vital if the US was to be successful in achieving regime change and a stable democratic replacement in Iraq. Containing the intifada therefore became an urgent priority. Efforts to bring about a ceasefire failed, however, and there was little let-up in violence.

Washington had long regarded Hamas, Islamic Jihad and Hezbollah as terrorist organizations, and Israel's actions suddenly seemed to be part of the broader struggle against terrorism. Given the new tough attitude in Washington, the Palestinian Authority – and Yasser Arafat in particular – were not doing enough to curb terrorist activities. The Bush administration defended what they described as Israel's firm, 'legitimate', military actions of 'self defense' against the Palestinian terrorist threat, thereby reassuring Sharon and Israeli hardliners. On the other hand, in order to gain support from the Arab countries, the US needed to be seen doing something to defuse the situation in the Middle East. On 2 October 2001 Bush told congressional leaders that he affirmed the idea of a Palestinian state, provided it acknowledged Israel's right to exist. At the United Nations in mid-November, President Bush reiterated his support for a Palestinian state, although he refused to meet with Arafat. This was the first time that an American president had used 'Palestine' as the name of the state he endorsed.

When members of the Popular Front for the Liberation of Palestine (PFLP) assassinated Rehavem Ze'evi, a hard-line, right-wing member of the Israeli cabinet, in Jerusalem in October, Sharon demanded Arafat hand over the perpetrators. When Arafat did not, either because he was unwilling or unable to do so, Sharon launched a massive land and air invasion and occupation of the major West Bank cities and towns, causing extensive damage. Bush called on Israel 'to leave these territories and never return to there'.[7] In the course of the military operation, almost one hundred Palestinians were arrested, hundreds were injured and 85 were killed – fifteen by assassination. After several more suicide incidents in mid-December, including a Hamas bombing of a bus in the West Bank, Sharon announced that Israel would have no more contact with Arafat, a decision that strengthened the extremist factions on both sides. Sharon had chosen the path of confrontation as the best means of quelling the Palestinian uprising. He hoped that Israeli's strength would justify a permanent military takeover of the autonomous Palestinian areas. He had never accepted the 'land for peace' formula outlined in the Oslo Accords of 1993.

The continuing turbulence challenged Sharon's claim that only Israeli force and pre-emption could prevent terror attacks. Hamas was demonstrating that it could strike in the heart of Jerusalem or Haifa or anywhere, despite Israeli closures, checkpoints, targeted assassinations and arrests. Nevertheless, the us supported Israel's actions and virtually gave Sharon carte blanche to retaliate. Palestinian militia attacks continued through January 2002, with bombings in Jerusalem and in Tel Aviv, forcing Sharon to hold his first meeting with senior Palestinian leaders, including Ahmed Qurei (Abu Alaa) and Mahmoud Abbas.

In March, 250 Palestinians and 124 Israelis died in an ever-worsening situation. During the first part of the month, there were suicide bombings within Israel. Israeli forces killed many Palestinians, including civilians, in the territories. At the end of March, a suicide blast in Netanya killed at least 29 Israelis as they sat down to a Passover Seder. On the heels of that incident, Sharon launched 'Operation Defensive Shield', in which Israeli troops reoccupied all the major Palestinian population centres. Arafat was confined to his almost completely ruined compound, the Muqata, in Ramallah. Israeli tanks, armoured bulldozers and helicopters tore up roads, destroyed electricity and telephone infrastructure, smashed various Palestinian Authority ministries, and arrested more than 1,000 Palestinians. President Bush sent mixed messages. At first he supported the Israeli assault – 'I fully understand Israel's need to defend herself', he stated – but then urged Israel to withdraw and sent Secretary of State Colin Powell to the area. Powell met with Arafat in his besieged compound, a symbolic victory for Arafat, since for months the us had been backing his isolation. Arafat insisted there could be no ceasefire until Israel ended its military operations and withdrew from occupied Palestinian cities and towns. Both sides were conscious of the parallels between the siege of Arafat in Ramallah and the siege of the Palestinian leader in Beirut twenty years earlier in 1982, also led by Sharon.

In early April Crown Prince Abdullah of Saudi Arabia met with President Bush at the president's ranch in Crawford, Texas, and presented an eight-point 'Saudi Plan' to end the Arab–Israeli conflict. The Saudi plan was basically an updated 'land for peace' proposal. The Saudis proposed that the Arab countries might normalize relations with the Jewish state if Israel returned to the pre-June 1967 borders. Nothing came of the idea at the time.

On 17 June 2002 Israel began to build what it called a 'security fence', a wall or barrier mainly constructed in concrete and eight metres high, surrounded by an exclusion area roughly 60 metres wide. Initially it ran roughly along the Green Line that marked the pre-June 1967 borders of the West Bank. The astonishing incongruity of a Jewish state building such a fence/wall deserves note. The idea of separation came from the realization within Israel's political, military and intelligence communities that if Israel did not withdraw from almost all of the territories, the Palestinians might very well demand a 'one-state solution' – a single bi-national state based on the principle of one-person, one-vote – rather than insisting upon a state of their own. This would result in Israelis having to choose between living in a Jewish state, or living in a democratic state. To some that would mean losing everything. The wall was regarded as a means of detaching Israel politically and economically from the growing and impoverished Palestinian population; indeed, one Israeli geographer, Arnon Soffer, who has studied the political implications of Palestinian population growth, has described the fence as 'a last desperate attempt to save the state of Israel'. Sharon amended the route so that the barrier would encompass major Israeli settlements within the West Bank.[8] The length approved by the Knesset was approximately 436 miles (703 km). In July 2007 the *Jerusalem Post* reported it would not be fully constructed until 2010.

Palestinians were outraged at what they saw as another attempt by Israel to create facts on the ground, and a pretext for seizing Palestinian land and extending its territory. In addition to the security fence proposal, Sharon began to advocate unilateral Israeli disengagement from the Gaza Strip settlements and from some in the West Bank. The Knesset initially balked at this proposal but began the approval process in late 2004. Nevertheless, Sharon's efforts at disengagement spurred Abbas to enter negotiations to try to cut the best deal possible. Palestinians realized that the Palestinian Authority needed reform; even members of the majority Fatah party criticized its corruption and ineffectiveness. Palestinian legislators challenged Arafat, and in early September he accepted the resignation of his cabinet. Elections were scheduled for 20 January 2003. Hamas and Islamic Jihad continued to carry out suicide missions in Israel.

A Roadmap to ?

In a speech on 24 June 2002, US President George W. Bush outlined a three-year, three-stage 'Roadmap' to achieve peace and establish a Palestinian state next to Israel by the year 2005. The plan had been developed by the US, UN, Russia and the EU, quickly dubbed the 'Quartet'. Bush stated: 'The Roadmap represents a starting point toward achieving the vision of two states, a secure State of Israel and a viable, peaceful, democratic Palestine. It is the framework for progress towards lasting peace and security in the Middle East.'[9] He did not release details of the plan at that time, however.

The Roadmap required the Palestinian Authority to make democratic reforms and abandon the use of terrorism. Israel was required to accept the reformed Palestinian government and end settlement activity in the Gaza Strip and West Bank as the Palestinian 'terrorist threat' was removed. The PA welcomed the concept, focusing on the promise of an independent Palestinian state and an end to Israeli occupation. Israel, on the other hand, expressed reservations. Sharon focused on the provisions for calling for a cessation of Palestinian violence and those guaranteeing Israel's security; he was not interested in furthering the Palestinian cause. The plan was flawed as its implementation depended upon mutually agreed, performance-based, reciprocal steps, and the referee for compliance was Israel. The Quartet's Roadmap also shared one of the flaws of the Oslo Accords, namely an 'interim period', which would enable extremists on both sides to torpedo the plan.

In late October 2002 the Palestinian Legislative Council approved a new nineteen- member cabinet. Israelis overwhelmingly re-elected Sharon on 28 January 2003. The Likud party won 40 Knesset seats, up from nineteen in the previous election. Sharon assembled a right-wing coalition.[10] Netanyahu was appointed finance minister. While still demolishing homes of West Bank and Gaza families of militants and approving more settlements, Sharon resumed direct contact with senior Palestinian officials about the possibility of a ceasefire. As the US-led coalition unleashed the highly destructive war in Iraq in March 2003, Arafat signed legislation to create the post of prime minister. Following the approval of his cabinet by the PLA, Mahmoud Abbas was sworn in as the first Palestinian prime minister on 30 April 2003.

Meanwhile, on 5 March 2003, the World Bank published a report assessing the state of the Palestinian economy. The bank reported a 53 per cent unemployment rate, a two-year, 40 per cent drop in gross national income, a 25 to 30 per cent decline in per capita food consumption over the previous two years, with child malnutrition rates climbing, and 60 per cent of the population living on less than US$2 a day. The Israeli economy was also said to be in steep decline, and for the first time the bank said that political progress was indispensable to a resumption of economic and social development in both Israel and the Palestinian areas. As of that date, 2,287 Palestinians and 763 Israelis had been killed. More than 5,000 Palestinians were in Israeli prisons. The army had moved in and out of Palestinian cities and towns in the West Bank, carried out targeted assassinations of suspected – always 'senior' – terrorists and demolished homes. These actions had some success and many attacks were averted, but the indiscriminate and general punitive measures seemed only to have provoked and emboldened the militants, while imposing crushing burdens on the Palestinian population.[11]

On 17 May 2003 Sharon and Abbas met for the highest level talks in two years. Sharon offered to withdraw the army from the centres of most Palestinian cities in the West Bank and from the northern Gaza Strip, in exchange for a commitment to crack down on terrorism from those areas; but Abbas insisted that Sharon formally accept the Roadmap in its entirety first, so the talks ended inconclusively. The two sides were talking past each other.

Desperate to gain results, Washington assured Israel that it would 'recognize' a written list of fourteen Israeli reservations about the Roadmap; essentially removing the provisions required of Israel. The Israeli cabinet then reluctantly voted to accept it. The cabinet's vote marked the first time an Israeli government formally accepted the principle of a Palestinian state. In defending himself the next day, 26 May, the veteran hawk, Sharon, told a stunned Likud Knesset caucus:

> I think the idea that it is possible to continue keeping 3.5 million Palestinians under occupation – yes, it is occupation; you might not like the word, but what is happening is occupation, is bad for Israel, and bad for the Palestinians, and bad for the Israeli economy. Controlling 3.5 million Palestinians cannot go on forever. You want to remain in Jenin, Nablus, Ramallah and Bethlehem?[12]

Sharon continued: 'I want to say clearly that I have come to the conclusion that we have to reach a [peace] agreement.' The next day, however, under intense party criticism, he backtracked, re-defining the term occupation as occupation over the people, not the territory, and declared: 'We are not occupiers, this is the birthplace of the Jewish people, and in diplomatic terms these are territories in dispute between two peoples.'[13] In any event, the Palestinians did not believe Sharon had altered his position.

President Bush pressed ahead with a summit between Abbas and Sharon, hosted by King Abdullah II, on 4 June at the Jordanian port city of Aqaba. In advance of the president's visit, Sharon and Abbas met again on 29 May. Some progress appeared to be made, but Sharon made it clear that any Israeli cooperation was dependent upon his favorable assessment of the PA's success in preventing violence. Prior to the meeting a senior Hamas spokesman in Gaza, Abdel Aziz Rantisi, stated Hamas was willing to declare a ceasefire, declaring: 'The Hamas movement is prepared to stop terror against Israeli civilians if Israel stops killing Palestinian civilians.'[14] Sharon rejected the Hamas offer. It was not enough, he said: the PA had to use forceful means to ensure an end to terrorism. Sharon was, in effect, insisting upon a civil war among Palestinians.

On 3 June President Bush met with the Arab leaders President Mubarak, King Abdullah II, Crown Prince Abdullah of Saudi Arabia, King Hamad of Bahrain and Mahmoud Abbas in Sharm el-Sheikh. The Arab leaders endorsed the Roadmap, condemned terror and violence and called upon Israel to 're-build trust and restore normal Palestinian life'. The following day Bush met with Abbas and Sharon in Aqaba, and all three also committed themselves to the plan. Within days of Bush's departure, however, violence resumed. Accusing Abbas of being too conciliatory toward Israel, Hamas vowed to continue the intifada. The Palestinian prime minister, caught between the demands of the militant groups, the Israelis and the Americans, was powerless to stop the militants. On 10 June, Abdul Aziz Rantisi – a pragmatic Hamas leader prepared to talk to Israel – escaped an assassination attempt by the Israeli army using two helicopter gunships.[15] Within days the Islamist group retaliated. A suicide bomber blew up a bus in central Jerusalem, killing sixteen and injuring more than a hundred. Israel then launched helicopter gunship attacks in Gaza City, killing some Hamas officials along with several civilians, and injuring scores more. In one week alone, the combined Israeli–Palestinian death toll climbed past fifty.

On 29 June the Al-Aqsa Brigades, Hamas and Islamic Jihad agreed to a three-month ceasefire. Israel was deeply suspicious that the militants would regroup and rearm. On 1 July 2003 Sharon and Abbas held a ceremonial open-ing to peace talks in Jerusalem, televised live in both Arabic and Hebrew. Both leaders said the violence had gone on too long and that they were com-mitted to the US-led Roadmap. The next day Israeli troops pulled out of Bethlehem and transferred control to Palestinian security forces. The plan required Palestinian police to take over from withdrawing Israeli forces and stop any anti-Israeli militant attacks. Sharon also said that some roadblocks in the West Bank would be removed, and that more 'unauthorized' outposts would be dismantled. On the other hand, there was no sign of a let-up in building activity in other settlements, and the majority of roadblocks and checkpoints remained. At the same time, Washington announced a US$30 million aid package to the Palestinian Authority to help rebuild infrastruc-ture destroyed by Israeli incursions.

The summer of 2003 was relatively calm – until 19 August, when a terrible bus bombing in Jerusalem claimed the lives of twenty-two Israelis, including six children. Israel immediately froze security talks and the planned withdrawal from any additional West Bank cities, and closed off the West Bank and Gaza. Israel also killed a political leader of Hamas in Gaza, Ismail Abu Shanab. On 21 August Hamas and Islamic Jihad announced that the truce was over.

Abbas resigned in early September. Arafat's nomination to replace him was an ally, Ahmed Qurei, Speaker of the Palestinian parliament, who had helped put together the Oslo Accords in 1993. A few days later President Bush declared that Arafat had 'failed as a leader'. On 11 September the Israeli secu-rity cabinet declared that the Palestinian leader was a 'complete obstacle to any reconciliation between Israel and the Palestinians', and said the gov-ernment would work to 'remove' this obstacle 'in a manner and time of its choosing'. Ehud Olmert, then deputy prime minister, even called for Arafat to be assassinated. There were huge demonstrations in Ramallah and throughout the Palestinian territories supporting Arafat, and the cabinet announcement served only to enhance his stature and restore him once again to centre stage. Meanwhile, the Israeli government in early October approved the extension of its security fence or barrier, which at some points would now jut into the West Bank for ten miles or more, and announced that it would build more than 600 new homes in Jewish settlements.

On 12 November the PLA approved Qurei's new government. A week later the UN Security Council endorsed the Roadmap on 19 November (UNSC Res.

1515). By the end of 2003, despite a decline in the level of disorder, the Palestinian Authority had not halted Palestinian attacks, and Israel had neither withdrawn from Palestinian areas occupied since 28 September 2000 nor frozen settlement expansion. The Roadmap had stalled.

Prime Minister Ariel Sharon surprised everyone in December 2003 when he proposed a unilateral withdrawal of all 21 Jewish settlements and the evacuation of the 8,000 settlers from the 137 square-mile Gaza Strip. Israeli settlers, right-wing and religious nationalists, opposed to any territorial withdrawals anywhere, were shocked; they saw it as the first step to further territorial concessions. Members of the Labor party were unhappy that Israel was acting unilaterally, jeopardizing future bilateral negotiations with the Palestinians. Some suspected, as did the Palestinians, that it was an indication that Sharon intended to hold on to all the West Bank and the Jewish settlements there. To Sharon, the Gaza disengagement was essentially a way of reducing the cost of Israel's security. Israel retained control the coastline, airspace and the borders of Gaza, leaving the questions of how the PA would administer the area, and how Palestinians – and their goods – would transit between the Gaza and West Bank (and Egypt), unanswered.

In fact, the PA was losing control of the Gaza to Hamas and Islamic Jihad. Israel's assassination of Hamas's founder, Ahmad Yassin, on 21 March and, on 17 April, his successor and Hamas co-founder, Abdul Aziz Rantisi, just days after President Bush had endorsed Sharon's disengagement plan, added to Gaza's instability. Bush not only endorsed the Gaza withdrawal, calling it historic and courageous, he also enraged the Arab and Muslim world by going much further than previous US policy. In an exchange of letters with Sharon, Bush stated that the US would not object to Israel retaining some West Bank settlements, adding that it was unrealistic to expect that a Palestinian state would lead to a full and complete return to the 1949 armistice boundaries, or that Palestinian refugees could return to Israel. To demonstrate he was tough on terrorism, in May, ahead of the 6 June cabinet decision to withdraw from Gaza, Sharon ordered the Israeli army into the Egyptian-Gaza town of Rafah to destroy tunnels used for smuggling arms to Palestinian militants who were firing rockets into the southern Israeli town of Sderot. More than 1,000 Palestinians were made homeless as 1,000 troops destroyed dwellings. Palestinian militants defiantly continued firing their home-made rockets, leading Israeli troops to occupy northern Gaza as well.

In November 2004 the 75-year-old Yasser Arafat died in a Paris hospital. Twenty thousand mourners attended his burial in Ramallah. Although he did not achieve statehood for his people, Arafat made a separate Palestinian identity a reality and created a liberation movement that received worldwide recognition. Many observers thought that new opportunities for peace would arise following his death. In January 2005 Mahmoud Abbas was elected president of the PA, and in February he met with Sharon, heading a newly formed National-Unity government, at Sharm el-Sheikh. The meeting was hosted by Egyptian president Mubarak and attended by King Abdullah II; no Americans were present. Both sides announced an end to the violence.

The Israeli parliament approved the disengagement plan during the same month and also gave approval for the route of the security barrier in the West Bank. The wall incorporated Ma'ale Adumim, Ariel and Gush Etzion and a large majority of the 240,000 settlers in the West Bank as well as the 200,000 Israelis living in eastern Jerusalem annexed by Israel after 1967. It was estimated that 99.5 per cent of Palestinians would live outside the barrier in 92 per cent of the West Bank, while 74 per cent of Israeli settlers would live inside it. Fewer than 10,000 Palestinians would live inside the fence. In March 2005 Palestinian militant groups agreed to a lull in the fighting. While not a full truce, this was considered major progress and some have argued that it marked the end of the al-Aqsa intifada.

Between September 2000 and February 2005 approximately 3,000 to 3,300 Palestinians and 950 to 1,010 Israelis had been killed in the intifada fighting. B'Tselem, the Israeli human rights group, estimated that Israel had destroyed about 675 Palestinian dwellings since September 2000. The UNRWA estimated that about 17,000 Palestinians had lost their homes. Hundreds of hectares of agricultural land had been bulldozed. Before the uprising around 30,000 of the 1.4 million Palestinians in Gaza had worked in Israel, but by 2005 that number had been reduced to a few thousand. The average daily wage in Gaza was US$12.00, and unemployment had reached about 60 per cent. The 1.8 million Palestinians living in the West Bank faced about 160 checkpoints as well as the security wall. Sharon defended IDF policies of targeted assassinations and incursions into Palestinian neighbourhoods on the grounds that they deterred attacks by suicide bombers, but Israel was probably less, rather than more, secure as a result of these policies.

In August 2005 all settlers were evacuated from the Gaza Strip (and four settlements in the West Bank), ending thirty years of Jewish presence. Israel kept control over all the entries into the Strip by land, sea and air. A small Egyptian security force took up positions along the Gaza-Egyptian border. Israel, no doubt, hoped that Egypt would take some responsibility for the area, but there was no way Egypt wanted to get involved. It had been there before. The PA celebrated what it called a great and historic victory, but Hamas claimed credit for the Israeli withdrawal and vowed to continue the armed struggle. In local elections held in 42 towns in the West Bank on 15 December, the militant group won a number of towns.

On 17 November Sharon announced a general election to be held early in 2005. A few days later (21 November) he resigned as leader of the Likud party – a party he had helped found in 1973. He stated he intended to form a new centrist party, Kadima (Forward). Fourteen members of the Likud immediately joined him, including Finance Minister Olmert. On 30 November Peres said he would also join Kadima. In mid-December, the Likud elected Netanyahu as leader. Sharon, 77 years old, suffered a massive stroke in January 2006 and leadership of the Israeli government fell to Olmert, a 60-year-old hawk and former mayor of Jerusalem.

Olmert and the Kadima party were committed to the unilateral approach followed by Sharon. The first goal the new prime minster set about was to isolate and bring down the Hamas government. Hamas refused to accept, and resisted, Israel's agenda of dictating the boundaries in which a Palestinian state would be permitted. Israeli politics, like those of the West, had moved so far to the right that there was no 'left' any more. The catchphrase 'Greater Israel' may have been abandoned, but the claims made by Olmert on the West Bank restricted the Palestinians to small enclaves not even Abbas could accept.

Surprising many, Hamas won a convincing victory in elections for the Palestinian Legislative Council held in January 2006, winning 74 of the 132 seats. Fatah was unwilling to accept this verdict, as were Israel and the US. Although Hamas had observed a self-declared ceasefire for the previous eighteen months, Israel, backed by Washington, stated that it would not negotiate with a Palestinian administration that included members of the radical group, which it regarded as a terrorist organization. This was a foolish decision if Israel wanted any acceptable agreement with the PA. Although Abbas was a moderate who had opposed the second intifada, given Hamas's victory Abbas could not reach any agreement with Israel without its participation and support. And Hamas was not going to allow itself to be marginalized.

Israel argued that it would not, and could not be expected to, deal with a government led by a party whose charter called for its destruction, as did the 1988 founding charter of Hamas. The Islamist party argued in reply that it accepted the existence of the state of Israel, but would not officially recognize it until the establishment of a Palestinian state in the West Bank and Gaza. The Hamas leader in Damascus, Khaled Meshal, stated that the party did not seek the destruction of Israel as written in its charter. Israel is a 'reality, there will remain a state called Israel – this is a matter of fact', he stated, adding, 'The problem is not that there is an entity called Israel. The problem is that the Palestinian state is non-existent.'[16] Several Hamas leaders have stated they would halt their armed struggle if 'the Israelis are willing to fully withdraw from the 1967 occupied territories and present a timetable for doing so.'[17] Hamas, in some ways, became a victim of George W. Bush's war on terrorism. Bush, quite erroneously, saw the Islamic party as part of the 'axis of evil', dedicated to the establishment of a global caliphate. In reality, the party is completely at odds with Al-Qaeda, which does not believe in national liberation movements like Hamas.

Hamas's Gaza leader, Ismail Haniyeh, formed a government in mid-February. Olmert's Kadima party retained power in Israeli elections in March 2006. On 25 May 2006, following a meeting with Israel's Foreign Affairs Minister Tzipi Livni at the World Economic Forum held at Sharm el-Sheikh, Palestinian President Abbas issued an ultimatum to Hamas leaders to recognize Israel or face a national referendum. On 27 June it was reported that the two parties had reached an agreement in which Hamas gave implicit recognition to a two-state solution to the Israel–Palestine conflict, although Hamas reserved the right to continue resistance in the occupied territories. A collision course between Hamas and Fatah was set in motion.

In early June 2006 Israeli shelling of northern Gaza killed a Palestinian family of seven. Olmert apologized for the tragedy, but on 10/11 June Palestinian militants retaliated with rockets attacks into the southern Israeli border town of Sderot. The period of calm in place since March 2005 had come to an end. On 22 June Olmert met with Abbas in Petra, Jordan, as guests of King Abdullah II. Hamas continued to launch rockets from the Gaza Strip. On 25 June 2006 an Israeli soldier, Corporal Gilad Shalit, was taken prisoner and two others were killed in a raid into Israel by militants as revenge, it was claimed, for the Israeli assassination of Jamal Abu Samhadana, a leader of the Popular Resistance Committee, in Rafah earlier in the month. Israel responded with heavy air and artillery bombardments of the Gaza Strip and the detention of 64 Hamas leaders, including 38 members of the Palestinian Legislative Council and eight cabinet members.

Lebanon Once Again

Events in July and August 2006 reminded observers that the Arab—Israeli conflict is not restricted to confrontations between Israelis and Palestinians. On 12 July 2006, Lebanese-based Shia Hezbollah militants killed three Israeli soldiers patrolling the Israeli side of the border fence in the north of Israel and captured two others. The Hezbollah leader Hassan Nasrallah, a 46-year-old cleric, stated that the reason for the attack was that Israel had broken a previous deal to release Hezbollah prisoners, and he recklessly and disingenuously claimed that, since diplomacy had failed, violence was the only remaining option. Israeli prime minister Ehud Olmert described the seizure of the soldiers as an 'act of war' by the sovereign country of Lebanon. Lebanese prime minister Fouad Siniora denied any knowledge of the raid and stated that he did not condone it.

Israel responded with massive airstrikes and artillery fire on targets in Lebanon including Beirut's International Airport (which Israel alleged Hezbollah used to import weapons and supplies), an air and naval blockade, and a ground invasion of southern Lebanon. Hezbollah then launched more rockets into northern Israel and engaged the IDF in guerrilla warfare from hardened positions.

This unexpected outbreak of war engendered worldwide concerns over infrastructure damage to Lebanon and the risks of escalation of the crisis. Hezbollah and Israel both received mixed support and criticism. President Bush declared the conflict to be part of the War on Terrorism. On 20 July 2006 Congress voted overwhelmingly to support Israel's right to defend itself and authorized Israel's request for expedited shipment of precision-guided bombs, but did not announce the decision publicly. Among neighbouring Middle Eastern nations, Iran, Syria and Yemen voiced strong support for Hezbollah, while the Arab League, Egypt and Jordan issued statements criticizing the organization's actions, and declared support for the Lebanese government.

The war against Lebanon continued until a United Nations-brokered ceasefire went into effect in the morning on 14 August. It formally ended on 8 September, when Israel lifted its naval blockade of Lebanon. Many Lebanese accused Washington of stalling the Security Council ceasefire resolution until it became clear that Hezbollah would not be easily defeated. US representative to the UN, John Bolton, confirmed that the US and UK, with support from several Arab leaders, had in fact delayed the process. The Lebanese and Israeli governments accepted the UN resolution, which called for disarmament of Hezbollah, for Israeli withdrawal from Lebanon, and for the deployment of Lebanese soldiers and an enlarged United Nations Interim Force in Lebanon (UNIFIL) in southern Lebanon. The Lebanese army began deploying in southern Lebanon on 17 August; by 1 October most Israeli troops had withdrawn across the border. The Lebanese government, Syria and Hezbollah later agreed that the military group would not be disarmed.

Iran and Syria proclaimed a victory for Hezbollah while the Israeli and United States administrations declared that the group had lost the conflict. On 22 September, some eight hundred thousand Hezbollah supporters gathered in Beirut for a 'victory rally'. Nasrallah then said that Hezbollah should celebrate the 'divine and strategic victory'. The majority of Israelis believed that no one won. Olmert admitted to the Knesset that there were mistakes in the war. In response to media and public disquiet over Israel's handling of what was now called the Second Lebanese War, and the conduct of the armed forces, military and political enquiries were set up in mid-August. By 25 August, 63 per cent of Israelis polled wanted Olmert to resign due to his handling of the war. The total cost of the war to Israel was estimated at around US$3.3 billion. In the wake of the war two Israeli senior military commanders resigned, and on 17 January 2007 the head of Israel's armed forces, Lt Gen. Dan Halutz, quit after internal investigations pointed to his responsibility for Israel's conduct during the invasion.

Some estimated that Hezbollah had 13,000 missiles at the beginning of the conflict, supplied by Syria, Iran, Russia and China. During the campaign Israel's air force flew more than 12,000 combat missions, its navy fired 2,500 shells, and its army fired over 100,000 shells. Large parts of the Lebanese civilian infrastructure were destroyed, including 400 miles (640 km) of roads, 73 bridges and 31 other targets, such as Beirut's international airport, ports, water and sewage treatment plants, electrical facilities, 25 fuel stations, 900 commercial structures, up to 350 schools and two hospitals, and 15,000 homes. Some 130,000 more homes were damaged. The hostilities killed more than a thousand people, mostly Lebanese civilians, and displaced approximately one million Lebanese and around 300,000 Israelis. After the ceasefire, some parts of Southern Lebanon remained uninhabitable due to unexploded cluster bomblets.[18]

Following its attack on Lebanon, Israel withdrew its forces from Gaza on 25 July 2006, although air and artillery attacks continued. During July 150 Palestinians (the majority civilians) were killed, including 26 children. Palestinians (mostly Sunni Muslims) rallied in support of the Shi'ite Hezbollah in Lebanon. Israeli attacks on Gaza Strip targets continued in August. In the following month Prime Minister Olmert authorized the construction of 600 houses in the West Bank. Tension rose between Hamas and Fatah. Because Hamas refused to recognize Israel, the PA was unable to pay its employees; Israel and the international community had demanded that Hamas recognize Israel as a prerequisite to passing on tax revenues and providing international funding. PA employees went on strike in early September.

On 11 September senior Hamas and Fatah leaders announced they had reached a tentative agreement to form a national-unity government. Addressing the UN General Assembly in New York on 21 September, President Abbas stated that the new unity government would recognize Israel. The following day, however, Hamas Prime Minister Ismail Haniyeh stated that his party would agree to less than full recognition. Tension over the PA's strike action broke into fighting between Hamas forces and Fatah protestors in the Gaza Strip on 1 October, bringing an end to talks on a unity government. At least eight people were killed and more than fifty wounded in the civil unrest. The UN World Food Programme announced that 70 per cent of the Gaza population could not meet their family's food needs.

In the first week of November 2006 Israel launched a major assault around Beit Hanoun in the northern Gaza Strip, killing at least 30 Palestinians. Thirteen members of one family were killed because of a 'technical failure', according to Israel, and an investigation was ordered into the incident. In mid-November Arab states promised economic aid to the PA. Abbas negotiated a ceasefire at the end of November and Israeli troops withdrew. On 29 December an Israeli human rights group reported that Israeli occupation forces had killed 660 Palestinians in 2006 – three times higher than the number killed in 2005.

Between December 2006 and February 2007, rival factions Fatah and Hamas continued fierce street gun-fighting in Gaza, agreeing and breaking temporary truces in what closely resembled a civil war. Israel and the US made no secret of which side they were on, and the Americans armed Fatah's security forces and financed their training and equipment. On 23 December President George W. Bush signed a law blocking US aid to the Hamas-led Palestinian government and banning contact with the ruling party. The Israeli government handed over US$100 million in frozen tax funds to the PA on 19 January 2007 as part of Israel's bid to boost President Abbas in his power struggle with Hamas.

In late February 2007 Israeli forces entered Nablus and imposed a curfew in the centre of the city in what the army said was an open-ended operation aimed at searching for weapons caches and arresting Palestinian resistance fighters responsible for carrying out attacks against Israeli targets. More than 50,000 Palestinian residents remained confined to their homes as the Israeli army pressed on with one of its biggest military campaigns in the West Bank.

In early March, Prime Minister Olmert admitted before the Winograd Commission, the government inquiry investigating the 30-day war against Hezbollah in Lebanon, that the strategy adopted in Israel's military offensive was drawn up months in advance of the capture of two Israeli soldiers. Olmert's testimony contradicted claims that the military campaign on 12 July 2006 was launched by Israel in response to Hezbollah's action. One newspaper opinion poll suggested that the prime minister was trusted by only 2 per cent of the Israeli public. At the end of April the commission released an interim report highly critical of Olmert; however, he resisted pressure to resign.

In mid-March 2007, Hamas Prime Minister Ismail Haniyeh unveiled a new national-unity cabinet after months of negotiations between his ruling Hamas party and the Fatah movement of President Abbas. Under the terms of the deal, Hamas was allocated twelve cabinet posts and Fatah six, with the rest going to either independents or small parties. On 8 February Fatah and Hamas had signed a historic unity deal, 'The Declaration of Mecca', at a ceremony hosted by Saudi King Abdullah to end their bitter power struggle. The Hamas cabinet resigned on 15 February to allow the formation of the new national-unity government. Nevertheless tension remained high between the two factions, and a number of civilians were killed and injured in gunfights in May as Fatah sought to take over security for the Gaza Strip.

Jerusalem's city council took advantage of the factional fighting among Palestinians to announce in May that it intended to build 20,000 new apartments around Jerusalem to link with existing settlements in the West Bank. On 21 May the first Israeli in six months to die owing to a rocket fired from the Gaza Strip was killed in Sderot. Israel assisted Fatah with a number of air strikes on Hamas targets and by arresting 33 Hamas politicians and detaining Hamas legislators across the West Bank on 24 May.

In mid-June 2007, after fierce and bitter fighting against Fatah soldiers in which more than 55 people were killed, Hamas took control of the Gaza Strip. President Abbas dissolved the Hamas-led national-unity government and declared a state of emergency. After summarily suspending clauses in the basic law that called for legislative approval for the new government, he swore in a new emergency government. The president also outlawed the militias of Hamas. Israel and the US quickly endorsed Abbas's actions; Israel released frozen taxes, and the US and EU ended their economic embargos of the PA. There were now, in effect, two Palestinian territories, each with its own government. Almost all border crossings into the Gaza Strip were closed. On 27 June Israel launched attacks in the Gaza Strip killing twelve people. In an effort to play a role in breaking the cycle of violence, the EU announced it had appointed Tony Blair, the recently resigned British prime minister, as its representative to work for peace in the Arab–Israeli conflict.

In mid-August the US and Israel signed a US$30 billion military aid package. The aid deal signed in a ceremony in Jerusalem represented a 25 per cent rise in US military aid to Israel, from a current US$2.4 billion each year to US$3 billion a year over ten years. Abbas continued his meetings with Olmert throughout the autumn, and Israel released more than 300 Palestinian West Bank prisoners. In late October 2007 Israel tightened its blockade of the Gaza Strip, announcing it would restrict the flow of food, medical and fuel supplies into the area. The Middle East peace conference first suggested by President Bush in July was held at Annapolis, Maryland, on 27 November, attended by the leaders of Israel, the PA, the US, the EU, the UN, Syria, the Arab League and the G8 countries. A 'joint-understanding' was reached whereby Olmert and Abbas agreed to negotiate a peace agreement by the end of 2008. In a joint statement read by President Bush at the end of the conference, both leaders expressed their support for a two-state solution. Both agreed that: 'The final peace settlement will establish Palestine as a homeland for the Palestinian people just as Israel is the homeland for Jewish people.' However, extremists on both sides voiced their dissent.

Seeking to maintain – or, more accurately, create – some momentum in the 'peace process', in early January 2008 George Bush arrived in Israel at the start of a nine-day tour of the Middle East. The US president said there was a 'new opportunity' for peace between Israelis and Palestinians, whose would-be state he also visited. He went on to Kuwait, Bahrain, the United Arab Emirates, Saudi Arabia and Egypt. Despite international calls for a freeze on settlement activity, in mid-April 2008 the Israeli housing ministry invited tenders for the construction of 100 new homes at the settlements of Ariel and El Kana in the northern-occupied West Bank. The Israeli group 'Peace Now' reported that between November 2007 and April 2008 tenders had been issued for 750 homes in the East Jerusalem settlements. Meanwhile, destruction of Palestinian homes in the West Bank, especially those in the vicinity of the West Bank barrier, continued. Despite all the negotiations, promises and bloodshed, little seemed to have changed.

CHAPTER 9

Unfinished Business

The US and Israel

No discussion of the Arab–Israeli conflict in the contemporary world would
be complete without some comment on the role played by the United States.
Over the past thirty-five years, since the 1973 war, furthering the Arab–Israeli
'peace process' has become a central issue in US domestic politics and foreign
policy. Every president since Richard M. Nixon has devoted considerable
energy to ending the ongoing violence. The task has taken on added urgency
since 11 September 2001. Washington's support for Israel has become a focal
point inciting hostility toward the US as Arabs and Muslims see themselves as
a primary target in America's war on terrorism. Peace in the Arab–Israeli
conflict would remove this source of threat.

In the immediate aftermath of World War II, the future of Palestine was
not a high-level priority for the US; it was just one of several nations involved
in the international deliberations that led to the foundation of Israel. Driven by
the paranoia of the Cold War and the need to ensure unrestricted access to the
region's oil, the US for many years stood aloof from the ensuing wars between
Israel and the adjacent Arab states, and sought primarily to limit the influence
of the Soviet Union in the Middle East. Today, Israel regards the US as its principal supporter and ally, and the US regards Israel as a vital regional partner in
the war against terrorism. Israel's enemies are America's enemies, and vice
versa. How and why did the US become the champion of the Jewish state, and
what impact has this close relationship had on the long-running hostilities?

The Arab–Israeli conflict, and the US-Israel relationship in particular, occupy a central place in US domestic politics. However, we should not confuse the high level of domestic political activity with America's ability to influence Israel, or the Arabs. The United States has quite limited power to shape the course of the confrontation. If peace, reconciliation and harmony in the Arab–Israeli conflict were the goals of US policy, it has surely failed. If achieving a two-state solution based on the formula first proposed by the United Nations General Assembly in 1947 was an American ambition, it has failed. If the key to peace is to pressure Israel into making the 'land for peace' concessions that Washington itself proposed in UN Resolution 242 of 1967, and which are necessary for the formation of a viable Palestinian state, then again the US has failed. If the creation of a stable, peaceful and US-friendly Middle East was America's goal, it has also failed. The gap between the aspirations and outcomes of US actions reveals the huge gulf that exists between military power and diplomatic success.

For all its military and economic might, US influence over Israel and the Arabs in shaping the course of the Arab–Israeli conflict is far less than most Americans think. Americans have an inflated view of their importance in dealing with the parties to this conflict. Israelis, Palestinians and the adjacent states, with the possible exception of Egypt, see the issues dividing them as existential. The United States has no sense of such concerns; its territorial integrity has never been threatened. The US is surrounded by benign, less powerful neighbours; participants in the Arab–Israeli conflict believe they are surrounded by powerful enemies. The US is big, they are small. There is a huge contrast in perceptions of threat and security between Americans and those fighting in the Arab–Israeli struggle. It is difficult to see how Americans can bridge that difference to imagine how life must be for Arabs and Israelis. To them, the goals and policies of the great powers, including those of the US, are less important than local considerations. Proximity is the key element in the factors influencing the course of the Arab–Israeli conflict. Despite the inducements offered or threats uttered to Arabs and Israelis, events at home matter far more than events in Washington, London, Moscow or Strasbourg.

Despite the ineffectiveness of US policy, it suits everyone to argue that the US holds the key to peace in the Arab–Israeli conflict. It suits the US government, and the American people, to give the impression that the US can – and does – project its power in the Middle East, and over the discord. It reinforces those who want to be seen as shapers of powerful US foreign policies, and those who oppose such activities. It flatters legislators who wish to be seen responding to the requests of those constituents urging US intervention. It reassures Israel to have the Arabs, especially the Palestinians, think that they can rely upon the US to carry out its wishes. And it suits the Arabs, and Palestinians, to be able to blame the US for their own diplomatic and military failures to achieve their goals.

Most who hold the view that the US is a key player in the dispute believe that the US has failed to apply the pressure at its disposal to force Israel to make the concessions necessary to reach a peaceful solution. There are two schools of thought as to why the US has not done so. The first asserts that Washington uses a well-armed and powerful Israel as a proxy to create and further US hegemonic control over the region. Thus it is argued, for example, that in the 1980s and '90s the US attempted to use Israel and the Christian militias of Lebanon to loosen Syria's hold over Lebanon, and again, in 2006, to weaken Hezbollah and its ally, Iran. Given the convergence of these goals emerging from Washington and Jerusalem, the argument goes, it is unlikely that the US would strenuously oppose Israeli policies in relation to the West Bank, the Golan Heights, Jerusalem or any other important issue.[1]

The second school of thought holds that US policy is controlled by a powerful Jewish, or Israel, lobby within the United States that prevents the US from implementing any genuine opposition to Israeli policy – whether or not that policy is in America's best interests. To this group, it has become an article of faith that since the birth of the Jewish state the United States has been the mainstay of Israel, and that American support has been due to the presence of a Jewish/Israel lobby. Volumes have been written on the pervasive role and influence – generally seen to be pernicious – of the Israel lobby on US Middle East policy.[2] This is not the place to rehash the pros and cons of that argument, but in my view the influence of the lobby in shaping policy has been considerably overstated. Proponents of the Israel lobby as a key factor in driving US Middle East policy, while they document the public actions of the lobby, do not, and indeed cannot, demonstrate the causal link between those actions and policy outcomes. Vociferous oral testimony notwith-standing, the archival material needed to evaluate the influence of the Israel lobby on executive branch decision-making is simply not available. Often policy emanating from Washington coincides with the wishes of lobby members, but that is not proof of causation.

But what of United States military and economic aid to Israel? Does that give Washington power to control Israeli policy, or is it a reflection of Israeli influence over the US? The United States is the largest supplier of military equipment and economic assistance to Israel. And Israel has received more US aid than any other country, and the highest amount received per capita by any population. At first glance, the sums Israel has received seem enormous. In 2007 the United States increased the military aid promised to Israel to an average of US\$3 billion per year for the next ten-year period. At the same time, the US\$1.2 billion a year in economic support funds Israel had been receiving was to end. Surely, it might be supposed, with that leverage the US could influence Israeli policy in the direction of a peaceful solution. Arabs and Palestinians point out that US assistance has been used by Israel to maintain its occupation of the West Bank and the Golan Heights, to expand settlements, and to employ high-technology weapons against them.

However, it is quite mistaken to think that Washington can require Israel to act against what it sees at its national self-interest as a result of the military and economic assistance it receives from the US. In the first place, the financial arrangements, military and non-military, are extremely complex and have changed many times over the past sixty years. Until the 1980s most assistance was in the form of loans or tied grants to be repaid – admittedly at preferential interest rates. Since the 1980s the balance has shifted to direct grants and loan guarantees. But in the case of military assistance, Israel is required to spend most of it on American military equipment and supplies. Only 26 per cent of US military aid can be spent on services and materiel manufactured within Israel. Obviously, if the US did not sell aircraft, tanks, missiles and anti-missile systems to Israel, it would purchase them elsewhere. And there are plenty of alternatives. For the first twenty years of its existence Israel did not receive significant military assistance from the US. Israel purchased its aircraft from France. And France was the country that did most to assist Israel develop its nuclear industry, enabling it to build its nuclear weapons during the 1950s and '60s. US arms manufacturers are probably more dependent upon Israeli sales than the other way round. Arms sales to Israel, like all arms sales to overseas buyers, represent a hidden subsidy to the US arms industry by the federal government, although they are never discussed as such. The Americans were certainly anxious to put a stop to Israel's attempts to manufacture a new fighter airplane, the Lavi, in the 1980s.

Much the same can be said of US economic aid. Most economic assistance to Israel was tied, in that moneys were provided for specific projects, or were to be spent on goods or services provided by American suppliers. The US economy received a great infusion of capital from the 'aid' provided to Israel, just as it had from the Marshall Plan to reconstruct Europe after World War II. In 1985 the US and Israel signed a Free Trade Agreement, the result of which was that the US became Israel's leading export market. Israel has developed an advanced industrial economy that, according to the World Bank, places it among the top 50 richest nations in terms of per capita income. Israel is currently ranked second in the world (after Silicon Valley in California) in the number of information technology start-up companies created annually. There are lots of alternatives available to Israeli entrepreneurs should the US foolishly give up its privileged position. In 1998 Israel proposed gradually eliminating the US$1.2 billion economic aid it was receiving from the US, and it was scheduled to end in 2008. In short, Israel is not dependent upon US economic aid, however enticing such a view may be to some.

While the US and Israel may see eye to eye on many issues relating to the Middle East, it is fanciful to think that the US is capable of controlling Israeli actions, especially when it comes to questions relating to Israeli security. There is no way Israel's leaders will allow their policies to be dictated to – or shaped – by any outside party, including the United States. Nor does Israel, or the Israel lobby, direct US Middle East policy. The strategic focus of the US policy has always been, and remains, the Persian Gulf. During the 1950s and '60s Washington somewhat heavy-handedly attempted to persuade the Arab states to join the Western camp in the Cold War. These efforts failed, in part, because of a growing Arab fear and distrust of the West, and because of the perception that the US aided and abetted Israel. This, in turn, strengthened America's belief that Israel would be a valuable strategic ally against the few radical Arab states who wished to increase Soviet influence at the expense of that of the US.

Despite their rhetoric to the contrary, the Persian Gulf oil-producing sheikhdoms, including Saudi Arabia, did not allow Washington's pro-Israeli orientation to weaken their economic, and increasingly military, ties with America. They were more concerned about the threat to their regimes of communism and radical Islam than they were with the state of play in the dispute with Israel, and they welcomed a US presence in the region. In the 1970s and '80s Washington took upon itself the role of actively managing what it called the 'peace process' in the Arab–Israeli conflict, and at first appeared to produce positive outcomes. Agreements were signed and a number of summits and international conferences promised progress towards peace. In the mid-1990s the Palestinian national movement, no longer regarded by the international community as a radical, marginal militant group bent on the destruction of Israel, assumed the character of a genuine nascent state willing to live side by side with the Jewish state. Israel, of course, did not agree that a change of attitude had taken place among Palestinian leaders. Neither did a majority of Americans, especially those belonging to the politically active Christian 'moral majority', who remained deeply suspicious of all things Islamic.

Arab leaders became alarmed about what they saw as US identification with Israel's progressively more belligerent and expansionist policies, especially in the years following September 2001. It appeared to many of them that Israel was not only unwilling to withdraw from the West Bank territories it occupied in 1967 to meet the basic territorial requirements of a Palestinian state, but also that, in not so doing, Israel had the unqualified support of the US. This view was confirmed when George W. Bush publicly acknowledged Israel's right to retain the settlements around Jerusalem, and supported Israel's invasion of Lebanon and military reprisals launched on the Palestinians in 2006. Many in the region also believe that the US has weakened the chances of a negotiated settlement by its hostility toward Hamas and Hezbollah, and in its calls for a military strike against Iran. Participants in the conflict wonder anxiously what the next US administration will do.

Economic Union?

Of the three elements that must be addressed to achieve permanent success in any Israel–Palestinian rapprochement – the security of Israel, the end of Israeli occupation of the West Bank, and joint economic growth and development of the eventual two states – most observers believe that economics is the key. From this viewpoint, the core issue in the conflict is not borders, but economics. The discrepancy between the standards of living of Israelis and

Palestinians is one of the major obstacles to peace. Israelis enjoy one of the highest living standards in the world, while Palestinians languish in subsistence conditions. In this respect, the Palestinian Nakba could be described as an ongoing, rather than as an historic, event.

Israelis blame the Palestinians for their terrible predicament. They say the unrelenting hostility of, and use of armed force by, Hamas, and extremist militant groups before them, leave Israel with little choice but to unilaterally separate themselves from and impose restrictions and controls upon the Palestinian population. They assert that military incursions into the Gaza Strip and West Bank are necessary to defend the state against terrifying rocket attacks and the infiltration of suicide bombers. The PA and Hamas, on the other hand, see the curfews and closures, the targeted assassinations and military incursions into the Palestinian territories, and the frantic expansion of Israeli settlements as deliberate attempts by Israel to prevent the emergence of a viable, stable Palestinian state with a sustainable economy. From each side's own perspective, both are right. But given the disproportionality of power and casualties inflicted – even the amount of extreme rhetoric used – favouring Israel, it is difficult to escape the conclusion that the weight of evidence supports the Palestinian assessment of the evolving situation.

In the first decade of the twenty-first century, the transformations in land, labour, economy and demography in Israel and the Occupied Territories have been stunning. Palestinians have suffered losses not seen since the beginning of Israeli occupation in 1967 and even, arguably, since the losses of 1948. The current economic context has many dimensions but is defined primarily by Israel's continued occupation of Palestinian lands, perhaps most vividly expressed in the widespread expansion of Israeli settlements, the isolation of the West Bank and Gaza, the internal cantonization of the West Bank and the bureaucratization of Israeli control. The contemporary catastrophic situation is also defined by rapid socio-economic decline, the total fragmentation of the geographical base of the Palestinian economy, the reduction of the Palestinian people to dependence upon international humanitarian aid, and the destruction of political life.[3]

In addition to dividing Palestine into two separate states, the UN partition resolution of November 1947 added the rider that the two entities should be bound in an economic union. Members of the General Assembly believed that economic cooperation would create jobs and wealth and achieve mutual prosperity, and go a long way toward alleviating hostility and friction between the two groups. Whether or not they were correct in this view will never be known, because for many years there was very little economic cooperation or union. The 1948–9 war saw to that, and the 1967 war and subsequent Israeli occupation of the West Bank and Gaza made economic cooperation, let alone union, an impossibility. Between 1967 and the end of the 1980s Israel integrated some of the Palestinian West Bank working population into its economy, but it was far from a voluntary arrangement entered into by two equal parties.

The 1993 Oslo Declaration of Principles offered some promise by providing for joint economic committees, free-trade zones, and cooperation on energy, water and electricity. Palestinian and Israeli representatives immediately began discussions of some of these issues. In November 1993 the working group on regional economic development adopted what became known as the 'Copenhagen Action Plan', comprising 35 projects in various fields including highway construction, electricity grids, energy, tourism, agriculture, financial markets and investment opportunities. It transpired that the economic dynamics created by Oslo between 1993 and 2000 maintained and strengthened Israel's occupation, rather than assisted the emergence of a Palestinian state. Nor did the establishment of the Palestinian Authority in 1994, pursuant to the Oslo Accords, bring about an alleviation of the situation in the Gaza Strip, or in the West Bank. Israel's system of blockades, first developed during the first intifada in December 1987, became a permanent closure of the West Bank and Gaza in March 1993, when Israel instituted a system of 'entry permits' to control the flow of people across the Green Line. Palestinians without a permit were, and continue to be, refused entry into Jerusalem and Israel.

The demographic separation of Palestinians that resulted from the division of the West Bank into Areas A, B and C, set out in the Taba Accord of September 1995, prevented Palestinians from developing a self-sustaining economy and made it easier for Israel's army to prevent the movement of Palestinian residents in the West Bank. The fragmentation, basically cantonization, of the West Bank and Gaza Strip meant that it was not possible for the Palestinian population to develop an economic infrastructure upon which a stable political structure could be built. Isolation of towns led to the de-urbanization of the West Bank, as movement between towns and cities was restricted. In recent years, Israel has increased the bureaucratization of its occupation of the West Bank, essentially 'normalizing' it. Centres like

Ramallah have become something akin to disconnected 'city-states'. Jerusalem has been progressively de-Arabized. The outcome of all this was massive economic loss, a second intifada and internal political division among Palestinians. The status quo of separation and the fragmentation and isolation of Palestinian enclaves in the West Bank is now widely viewed internationally as 'acceptable'. Today it is the Palestinians who are regarded as the 'intruders' into Israeli sovereignty.

The heightened level of violence, loss of life and strikes that have resulted from the second intifada, the rise of Hamas, and Israeli hard-line policies of curfews, closures, withholding of tax money, and denying entry to labourers have exacted a heavy price on both sides. The Palestinian economy has been destroyed and the Palestinians reduced to living on international humanitarian aid. Israel has also suffered economically from the ongoing hostilities. By early 2009 the Israeli economy had lost as much as US$11 billion in the previous two years of conflict with the Palestinians. The security wall is costing billions and the money spent on security checkpoints could well be spent on productive projects to improve lives rather than diminish them.

Today, the economic linkages proposed during the 1990s have ceased. As noted in previous chapters, Palestinians are poor and growing poorer. Israel's unilateral redeployment from the Gaza Strip and the building of the security/ separation fence has proven disastrous for Palestinian farmers. Since June 2007, and the ascendancy of Hamas in the Gaza Strip, conditions have worsened because of the cycle of rocket attacks and reprisals, and Israeli closures that have sealed the borders and prevented Palestinians from reaching their jobs in Israel or selling their produce. The international community, led by the US, has supported Israel's blockade of the Hamas-ruled Gaza Strip. Israel has succeed in having international donors regard the Palestinians as perpetrators of violence – not as negotiating partners or a national group with a workable economy. What Palestinians regard as resistance to occupation is now seen by the wider world as illegitimate, to be punished. Palestinians are regarded merely as a humanitarian crisis in need of such things as food, fuel and electricity. In addition, the economic circumstances in which Gazans live has been made worse by mismanagement, instability and uncertainty that have prevented more than a trickle of funds from donor countries being disbursed to the population. Palestinian political leadership is caught up in a civil war that has stultified economic activity.

Regardless of where the borders of the two states are ultimately drawn, the question today is how could the inhabitants of a Palestinian state make a living? One answer is by trading with, and labouring for, wealthy Israel. If some form of economic cooperation or union were to be established, then the border between the two states would become less relevant. It becomes merely a line on the map – admittedly an important symbolic one – but one easily and frequently crossed by people and goods. This would require mutual and simultaneous steps to enable freedom of movement within the West Bank, and between the West Bank and Gaza, joint economic ventures, trade and currency arrangements, and the provision of deep-water port facilities in Gaza.[4] Properly devised, these measures would bring benefits to both Palestinians and Israelis. Peace would attract international investment, both private and governmental, into the area and be beneficial to all the countries of the region.

Water Resources

Closely related to economic questions, and hidden by the political and religious rhetoric of the Arab–Israeli conflict, is the need to control the region's water sources. One historian has noted that during the negotiations between 1919 and 1924, when the boundaries of the Jewish homeland were under discussion between the British government and the World Zionist Organization, the Zionist negotiators based their conceptions of borders more on engineering considerations than of ancient history.[5] Agreement on sharing the region's water resources is, as it always has been, essential if peace is to have a chance. Because of the arid nature of much of Israel/Palestine and the surrounding region, water is a highly prized and valuable resource, and much of the conflict has been focused on that scarce vital commodity. The issue, however, is not so much one of insufficient supply, as of uneven and inequitable distribution. Allocation of the existing available water is the problem. In any future peace agreement with the Palestinians, Israel will likely have to give up some of its current 74 per cent of the mountain aquifer that straddles the border between Israel and the West Bank.

There are two natural sources of water in the immediate area: rivers and aquifers. The major rivers are the Jordan and the Yarmouk, which with their tributaries make up what is known as the Jordan drainage basin. The headwaters of the River Jordan are located in northern Israel, the Golan Heights and southern Lebanon, and feed Lake Tiberias/Kinneret (the Sea of Galilee). Below Lake Tiberias the River Jordan is fed by the Yarmouk and other rivers that rise in Syria and Jordan, as well as by springs in the West Bank and Israel. Aquifers that store large quantities of water are found under much of Israel, the West Bank and Jordan. These aquifers flow west from the heights of the West Bank towards the Mediterranean Sea.

Although Israeli territory contributes only minimally to the Jordan basin waters, Israel controls and utilizes the majority of the water resources. Because of its occupation of the Golan Heights, it is in command of most of the head-waters of the River Jordan. And through its occupation of the West Bank, and restrictions on Palestinian access to their water resources, Israel manages the use of the aquifer waters. Israel has imposed rigorous quotas on the Pales-tinians and since 1967 has refused the vast majority of requests to dig new wells. Palestinians are required to pay considerably more for their water, both for domestic and agricultural use.

Israelis use four to five times more water per day than either Palestinians or Jordanians. Israelis consume on average 160 litres per person per day, while Palestinians in the West Bank consume around 60 litres per person per day; this is 40 litres per day less that the World Health Organization minimal global standard. (Germans, by contrast, use around 126 litres per person per day.) A total of 26 per cent of Palestinian households are not connected to piped water. This means that when Israelis block entrances to Palestinian towns and villages with tanks and soldiers, it is difficult and dangerous for villagers to go to nearby wells and for water tankers to get into villages. Within Israel itself, Arabs constitute 20 per cent of the population, yet only 2 per cent of Israel's water supplies is utilized in Arab villages.

The water problem has been further exacerbated by population growth. Before 1948 the population of Gaza was approximately 50,000. It is now one of the most densely populated regions in the world with a population of around 1.5 million. The population of the West Bank is close to 2.6 million. This Palestinian population increase has created tremendous demands upon water resources. The crisis in the Gaza Strip, where the ground water level is decreasing and the water increasingly saline, has reached catastrophic pro-portions. Israel has impounded the only upstream waters, the Wadi Gaza, and has sunk wells on the outskirts of Gaza while preventing the Palestinians from sinking wells of their own.

Israel and Jordan provide an example of how water and peace go together. In the late 1970s and early 1980s, the two states held a series of secret meetings that resulted in cooperative management of the Yarmouk. From 1979 the two states cooperated on a series of day-to-day decisions made by the local water authorities, approved by Jerusalem and Amman, about water allocations to accommodate each other's seasonal agricultural needs. In 1984 Israeli prime minister Peres hoped that the cooperation on the Yarmouk would help in progress toward a peace settlement with Jordan. This led to several secret meetings under the nominal supervision of the UN and observed by US representatives, which resulted in the joint dredging of the Yarmouk in October 1985 to improve water flow. By 1987 both countries had come to an understanding that limited water-related conflicts along the Jordan Valley, and encouraged economic development along the river, primarily in Jordan. These secret meetings assisted in building confidence between the two countries and helped lay the foundations for future negotiations, leading eventually to a peace treaty in 1994.

The October 1991 Madrid conference and 1993 Oslo Accords set up multilateral talks on water but little real progress was made. Syria and Lebanon boycotted the talks and Israel did not want water rights as an agenda item. Likud governments continued Israel's traditional unilateral water policy, arguing that its security needs required that it not be dependent for water upon any neighbouring state. The Netanyahu government opposed Palestinian self-rule over West Bank aquifers, arguing that Palestinian control over the water would constitute a threat to Israeli security because they would pollute the water either deliberately or accidentally. Labor governments tended to favour regional cooperation, recognized Palestinian water rights and assisted in the formation of the Palestinian Water Authority. In this context it is interesting to note that in the agreement signed in May 1994, which provided for the withdrawal of Israeli forces from the West Bank town of Jericho, the area allocated to the Palestine Authority in Jericho was defined in such a way that it excluded all but one of the standing springs, which stayed under Israeli control. Well water from the Jericho area is too saline for domestic use. The PA is obliged to buy additional water from Mekoroth, the Israeli State Water Company.

In May 1998 Syria and Jordan announced plans to build a hydroelectric dam on the upper reaches of the Yarmouk River on their common border, near the old Maqarin Dam site. An agreement to build this dam, the Unity or al-Wahdah Dam, was first signed in 1987. Syria hoped to utilize the waters of the Yarmouk to develop agricultural villages in the southern Syrian Yarmouk basin, thereby reducing overpopulation in Damascus, providing employment for army veterans and making Syria less dependent upon Jordanian agricultural produce. Jordan hoped the dam would increase its available water supply, and enable it to increase its cultivated land in the Jordan Valley from 865,000 acres to 1.24 million acres. Work on the dam finally got under way in 2004 and Jordan announced its completion in 2006, but the dam is a solution for only a small part of the problem of allocating water in the region.

Any comprehensive solution to the water issue is going to have to be based on the principles of the mutuality of interests. Each party arguing its individual legitimate national interest will not work. International law on riparian waters is ambiguous and complex; questions such as existing or prior usage, economic and social need, and national security, will simply aggravate the situation. All the parties need water to build towns, industries and agriculture, to build modern nation states. No party can claim primacy in this issue. Resolution of the water issue will occur only when the emphasis passes from water rights to enhancing the water supply and responsible water management.

The process should start with confidence-building measures by Israel, such as providing the Gaza Strip with some much needed water through its national water carrier, reducing the cost of water allocations to the Palestinians, and increasing water allocations to the West Bank. Israel will require some incentive to make such concessions. Some link should be established between development and equity in the water matter; World Bank loans for water projects, for example, could be made dependent upon progress in the water discussions.

Even if the issue of water resources is solved, however, it is clear from the above discussion that there are many fundamental economic questions to be addressed before a solution to the Arab–Israeli conflict is to be reached. The steps to be taken to achieve peace – and the shape of the peace – are acknowledged and known by all concerned. What is lacking is the ability or capacity or courage of the leaders on both sides to carry them out.

Conclusion

The core element of the Arab–Israeli conflict has been two groups, Jews and Arabs, seeking national self-fulfilment in the same place, while at the same time each has sought to prevent the other from realizing its aspirations. Two peoples believe they have been promised the same land (often!). This is to state the obvious and does not advance the search for a solution very far. Israel as a modern state has existed since 1948 and no amount of rage, rocket launching or suicide bombing by Palestinians and Arabs will alter that reality. Palestinians also have recognized legitimate national rights, and no amount of obfuscation, fence building or targeted assassinations by Israel will alter that reality. The past cannot be altered or undone; it is always present and it cannot be overlooked or ignored, but new paths will have to be found, new perceptions created, if peace is to be achieved.

The past is not another country; it creates obligations and responsibilities. As the American novelist William Faulkner brooded, 'The past is not dead. In fact, it's not even past.' While proudly recognizing their own admirable achievements, and while perhaps not taking direct personal responsibility for the predicament of the Palestinians, it is essential that Israelis recognize and acknowledge one other over-arching truth: that the Palestinians have experienced an overwhelming tragedy. Israelis must recognize that their process of state-building involved, among other things, the murder, dispossession, domination and exclusion of thousands of, admittedly hostile, Palestinians, and that Israel has played a role in creating the present shocking condition of the Palestinians as a people.

Equally, it is essential that the Palestinians accept that, although they have suffered a tragedy, their unwillingness to recognize the changes taking place in their region and their armed resistance to Jewish migration and the establishment of a Jewish state led not only to loss of life and terror among Israelis, but also contributed to much of the suffering that Palestinians have experienced. Nonetheless, as Israel is the militarily and economically dominant power, the future relationship between Israel and neighbouring Arabs lies to a large degree in Israeli hands, and a peaceful resolution depends as much on Israeli actions as it does on the conduct of the Palestinians.

The problems facing the participants in the Arab–Israeli conflict today remain those posed in 1947 and 1948 when the fledgling UN General Assembly met to determine the future of the British Mandate: namely, how can western Palestine be shared between Jews and Arabs? Where are the boundaries to be drawn between the areas of their jurisdictions, and what is to be the relationship between the two entities – and their neighbours? As previous chapters have shown, these issues centre around identity and links to the land. All parties have failed to resolve the particular manifestations of these issues over the past sixty years. Questions such as to whom the area formerly known as Palestine belongs; the location of the boundaries of the land in question; ownership and access to various sites regarded as sacred by both parties; and, perhaps most vexatious of all, the ongoing use of force to resolve disputes, remain unanswered.

Translated into concrete problems faced today, these issues come down to differences over the formation, nature and boundaries of a Palestinian state (and by implication the boundaries and nature of the Jewish state), the future status of Jerusalem, Hebron and other holy places, Israeli withdrawal in the territories occupied since 1967, and the future of Jewish settlers and settlements in the Israeli-occupied West Bank, and the demand by Palestinians that refugees be permitted to return to their former localities. Relations between the two groups will have to be 'normalized' with the two living in peace and security and some form of economic union, including the allocation and development of the scarce water resources.

The issue for Israel, the Palestinians and the Arab states of the region today is their relationship in the near future. The choices are largely Israel's, and they remain those the Jewish state has faced since 1967. Israel can attempt to integrate the Palestinian Arabs into a 'Greater Israel' – or force their removal;

it can try to maintain the existing Palestinian enclaves or South African-like 'Bantustans'; or it can negotiate peaceful coexistence with a Palestinian state within mutually agreed borders. The challenge for Israel is to work through these issues without destroying its domestic fabric. The reciprocal challenge for the Palestinians is to accept Israel and eschew violence – against Israel and between themselves – and create a democratic structure and the economic infrastructure that will support a state prepared to live with Israel as a neighbour.

As detailed in previous chapters, the conflict between these two groups has also involved other nations to a quite extraordinary degree. And it continues to do so as the first decade of this century draws to a close. To mention just one current example: Iran has been developing a nuclear power programme since the 1950s, it claims for electrical power generation. In recent years it has begun enriching uranium. There is considerable international opposition to Iran's enrichment programme as it is feared that Tehran's goal is to build nuclear weapons. Israel, in particular, has stated that such an eventuality is totally unacceptable and has not only vowed to prevent it, but in June 2008 carried out air force exercises widely believed to be a rehearsal for a strike on Iran's nuclear facilities. It is to be hoped that common sense and restraint will prevail in resolving the international stand-off over Iran's nuclear programme, and that negotiations rather than the use of military force will resolve the issue.

When considering the Arab–Israeli conflict it is all too easy to accept the arguments of one side or the other concerning the justness of their cause and, more importantly, the wisdom of their more often than not military actions. Why should Israel tolerate terrifying daily rocket or mortar attacks by Palestinian militants on the town of Sderot just north of Gaza, for example? What better way to stop these attacks than with military force? Equally, why should Palestinians, or Lebanese, not resist the massive Israeli air and tank incursions over and into their towns and cities? What better way to deter these murderous attacks than by encouraging suicide martyrs to enter Israel or by firing rockets? And so on. While shocking and tragic, the actions of those involved in the Arab–Israeliconflict do not seem so very different from the actions of other nations engaged in war today – nations like the United States and its allies and their Iraqi or Afghani enemies, or the Russians and

Chechens. All claim moral certainty and rectitude, and argue they fight for the preservation of universal human rights.

Repeated exposure to TV images of the mutilated and dead bodies and destroyed buildings resulting from missile strikes and bombings, followed by reassuring and seemingly sympathetic statements from officials regretting the unintended but unavoidable 'collateral damage', has conditioned us to accept unacceptable brutality and destructive violence against civilians that a generation ago would have shocked us to the core and caused outrage. We have become desensitized to death and violence. In the Arab—Israeli conflict politics has become war. It all seems so straightforward, so normal.

The state of conflict does seem normal until you hear the words of someone who questions the paradigms that support the war and looks at the realities behind the soothing words spoken to us by the perpetrators of violence. Someone like Daniel Barenboim, for example. Famed conductor and pianist, Argentinean-born Daniel Barenboim is the sole Israeli citizen to bear a Palestinian passport. He is also conductor of the West-Eastern Divan Orchestra, an Arab—Israeli youth orchestra he formed with noted American-based Palestinian scholar Edward Said. Barenboim states that he is 'living evidence' that only a two-state solution can bring peace to the Middle East.

In 2004 Barenboim was awarded the prestigious Israeli Wolf Prize for artistic merit. In his acceptance speech before an audience of members of the Wolf Foundation, Barenboim related that the Israeli Declaration of Independence was, to him, a source of inspiration. He read aloud the following passage from that document:

The State of Israel will dedicate itself to the development of this country to the benefit of all its people. It will be founded on the principles of liberty, justice and the welfare of all its people guided by the visions of the prophets of Israel. Regardless of the differences of faith, race or sex, it will guarantee all its citizens equal social and political rights. It pledges the assurance of freedom of religion, opinion, language, education and culture. On behalf of all, the signatories of the declaration of independence vow their allegiance to: 'Peace and Good Neighbourly Relations with all bordering states and their peoples.'

Barenboim then went on to ask:

> Does the occupation of another state and rule over its people accord with the declaration of independence? Is there any sense in the independence of one country at the expense of the fundamental rights of another? Can the Jewish people, whose history is one of persistent suffering and persecution, allow itself to be indifferent to the basic rights and the sufferings of a neighbouring state? Can the state of Israel permit itself to indulge in the unrealistic dream of an ideological end to the conflict, instead of striving for a pragmatic, humanitarian solution based on social justice?[1]

His answer was simple and powerful: 'I have always believed that there can be no military solution to the conflict, neither on moral nor on strategic grounds.' Barenboim declared that he would donate the prize money to his Arab–Israeli youth orchestra. Tzipi Livni, at the time minister for education, culture and sport, was unable to accept such a radical point of view. She was furious and publicly chastised one of Israel's greatest goodwill ambassadors for using the podium to 'attack the state of Israel', by daring to question Israel's use of armed force.

In May 2008 Barenboim returned to this antiwar theme. In an article published in the British newspaper *The Guardian,* he wrote:

> For decades we have seen headlines about exploding violence; one war and terrorist act follows another. This has cemented the situation in people's minds. Today, in the time of Iraq and Iran, one hardly reads anything more about it, which is even worse. Many Israelis dream that when they wake up, the Palestinians will be gone, and the Palestinians dream that when they wake up, the Israelis will be gone. Both sides can no longer differentiate between dream and reality, and this is the psychological core of the problem.[2]

The Israeli icon wrote that while Jews had a right to their own state, it was all too easy to forget that there was a moderate Zionism. Austrian-born Israeli philosopher Martin Buber, for example, had maintained from the beginning that the right to a Jewish state must be made acceptable to the existing population, the non-Jews. Unfortunately, militant Zionists had not explored these possibilities. Barenboim believes many still espouse the lie that the land settled by the Jews was empty.

Today, Barenboim continued, many Israelis have no idea what it must feel like to be Palestinian – how it is to live in a city such as Nablus, a prison for 180,000 people where there are no restaurants, no cafes, no cinemas. Why, he asked, does Israel continue to feed the hate in the Gaza Strip? As Barenboim sees it, there will never be a military solution. Two peoples are fighting over one and the same land. No matter how strong Israel becomes, its people will always be insecure and fearful. The conflict is eating away at the Jewish soul, and it has been allowed to do so. Israelis wanted to own land that had never belonged to Jews and to build settlements there. He reminded his readers, especially his Israeli readers, that the Palestinians see this as imperialistic provocation, and rightly so. 'Their resistance is absolutely understandable – not the means they use to this end, not the violence nor the wanton inhumanity – but their "no"', he concluded.[3]

The artist is right. Sixty-one years of violence have demonstrated that military force will not end the Arab–Israeli conflict. Barenboim appeals to Israelis to finally find the courage to not react to this violence, to find 'the courage to stand by our history'. To Barenboim the tragedy is that the two parties are no further today than they were in 1947, when the UN voted to divide Palestine. Worse, in 1947 one could still imagine a bi-national state; sixty years later this seems unthinkable. The only solution in his view is for each side to recognize the dignity and value of the other, because 'before a Beethoven symphony, Mozart's *Don Giovanni* or Wagner's *Tristan and Isolde*, all human beings are equal.'[4]

It is only when we hear and reflect upon such obvious but profound truths that we realize that what we are hearing and seeing from the politicians on a daily basis in the Arab–Israeli conflict is not normal, it is normality gone awry, hijacked by the disciples of Mars. It is insanity.

References

Preface

1 Amos Elon, 'Israelis and Palestinians, What Went Wrong,' *New York Review of Books*, 19 December 2002.

Introduction

1 Bishop Joseph Butler (1692–1752), sermon VII, 'On the Character of Balaam', 1726.
2 Barry Rubin, 'The Great Game', www.gloriacenter.org, 6 June, 2008. Cited by Australian/Israel Jewish Affairs Council, 'Israel's Strength as a Society', 13 June 2008, 06/08, # 04.
3 Jeffrey Goldberg, 'Unforgiven', *Atlantic Monthly* (May 2008).
4 David Hazony, 'Is Israel Like Any Other Country?', *New Republic*, 11 June 2008.
5 Goldberg, 'Unforgiven'.
6 Avi Shlaim, 'Israel at Sixty, The "Iron Wall" Revisited', www.opendemocracy.net, 8 May 2008.
7 Ian J. Bickerton, 'President Truman's Recognition of Israel', *American Jewish Historical Quarterly*, LVIII/2 (1968), pp. 173–240.
8 See also Ian J. Bickerton and Carla Klausner, *A History of the Arab Israeli Conflict*, 5th edn (Upper Saddle River, NJ, 2006).
9 The 'new' – sometimes called revisionist – Israeli historians are a disparate group of scholars, journalists and activists, and a short list of the better known would include (alphabetically) Jeff Halper, Benny Morris, Ilan Pappe, Tom Sejev, and Avi Shlaim.
10 Robert Frost, 'The White Tailed Hornet', *Selected Poems* (New York, 1971), pp. 167–9.

11 Percy Bysshe Shelley, 'Ozymandias', *Selected Poetry* (New York, 1966).
12 Theodore Herzl, *The Jewish State* (London, 1936), p. 19.

1 The Unfolding Situation, 2008–9

 1 See Israel Ministry of Foreign Affairs, 'The Annapolis Conference', 27 November 2007.
 2 Israel Ministry of Foreign Affairs, Press Release, 21 August 2008.
 3 David Barak, 'Olmert: Peace Talks are a National Obligation', *Ha'aretz*, 22 May 2008.
 4 Aluf Benn, 'PA Rejects Olmert's Offer to Withdraw from 93% of West Bank', *Ha'aretz*, 12 August 2008.
 5 Aluf Benn, Barak Ravid and Avi Issacharoff, 'Olmert to Press Abbas to Accept Framework for Two-state Solution', *Ha'aretz*, 31 August 2008.
 6 Aluf Benn, 'PA Rejects Olmert's Offer'.
 7 Ibid.
 8 United Nations Office of Coordination of Humanitarian Affairs, 'The Humanitarian Impact on Palestinians of Israeli Settlements and Other Infrastructure in the West Bank', published July 2007.
 9 Settlement Watch Team, 'Report: Israel is Now Eliminating the Green Line, and Continuing to Build in the Isolated Settlements', *Peace Now*, August 2008, available at www.peacenow.org.il.
10 In *Unintended Consequences: The United States at War* (London, 2007), US naval historian Ken Hagan and the author explored this gap, and exposed its dangers, in the case of the wars fought by the United States.
11 Yonatan Mendel, 'Diary', *London Review of Books*, 6 March 2008. See also Israeli TV journalist Shlomi Eldar, *Azzar kemavet* [Eyeless in Gaza] (Tel Aviv, 2005), and David Grossman, *The Yellow Wind* (New York, 1998), who detail examples of the new language used by Israeli journalists reporting on the conflict.
12 Ziv Hellman, 'Preparing for the Morning After', *Jerusalem Report*, 1 September 2008.
13 Galia Golan, 'A Time for Peace', *Jerusalem Report*, 12 May 2008.
14 Indeed, Israel is sending mixed messages in relation to the battle taking place between the PA and Hamas in the West Bank. While actively engaged in arresting Hamas members and closing down Hamas institutions in the West Bank, Israel has freed a number of Hamas prisoners in negotiations for the release of soldier Gilad Shalit, despite warnings from Abbas that if Israel releases Hamas members of the Palestinian parliament he will dismantle the Palestinian Authority.
15 Gideon Levy, 'The Neighbourhood Bully Strikes Again', *Ha'aretz*, 28 December 2008.
16 Amira Hass, 'Gaza Strike is not against Hamas, it's against all Palestinians', *Ha'aretz*, 29 December 2008.

17 Daniel Barenboim, 'The Illusion of Victory', *The Guardian*, 1 January 2009.
18 Chris McGreal, 'Why Israel Went to War in Gaza', *The Observer*, 4 January 2009.

2 Prelude: The British Mandate

1 Britain recognized Transjordan as a state on 15 May 1923, and gradually limited its oversight to financial, military and foreign policy matters. In March 1946, under the Treaty of London, Transjordan became a kingdom and on 25 May 1946 the parliament of Transjordan proclaimed the emir king, and formally changed the name of the country from the Emirate of Transjordan to the Hashemite Kingdom of Transjordan. In April 1949 after capturing the 'West Bank' area during the 1948–9 war with Israel, Abdullah took the title King of Jordan, and he officially changed the country's name to the Hashemite King-dom of Jordan.
2 'Mandate of Palestine', available at http://avalon.law.yale.edu/20th_century/palmanda.asp.
3 Bernard Lewis, *Semites and Anti-Semites, an Enquiry in Conflict and Prejudice* (New York, 1986), pp. 121–2.
4 Nabi Musa is an annual pilgrimage made by Muslims from Jerusalem to the tomb of Moses, believed to be near the city of Jericho.
5 'British White Paper of June 1922', available at http://avalon.law.yale.edu/20th_century/brwh1922.asp.
6 Tom Segev, *One Palestine Complete: Jews and Arabs under the British Mandate* (New York, 2001), pp. 191–6.
7 By the late 1930s the Jewish population of Tel Aviv was double that of Jerusalem; around 177,000 Jews lived in Tel Aviv, while 82,000 lived in Jerusalem.
8 Segev, *One Palestine Complete*, pp. 295–313.
9 Statement by David Ben-Gurion, cited in Ian J. Bickerton and Carla L. Klausner, *A History of the Arab–Israeli Conflict*, 5th edn (Upper Saddle River, NJ, 2007), p. 54.

3 The First Arab–Israeli War

1 Meron Benvenisti, *Sacred Landscape: The Buried History of the Holy Land since 1948* (Berkeley, CA, 2000), p. 3
2 'Anglo-American Committee of Inquiry, Report to the United States Govern-ment and His Majesty's Government in the United Kingdom, Lausanne, Switzerland, April 20, 1946,' Washington, 1946, available at http://avalon.law.yale.edu/20th_century/angcov.asp.
3 Ibid.
4 Ibid.

5 *Sydney Morning Herald*, 1 December 1947.
6 Ibid., 2 and 3 December 1947.
7 Ibid., 1 December 1947.
8 'The Declaration of the Establishment of the State of Israel', published in the *Official Gazette*, No. 1 of the 5th, Iyar, 5708 (14 May 1948).
9 I have drawn upon the following three books in my account of the war. Avi Shlaim, *The Iron Wall: Israel and the Arab World* (London, 2000); Ahron Bregman, *Israel's Wars: A History since 1947* (London, 2000) and Benny Morris, *Righteous Victims: A History of the Zionist–Arab Conflict, 1881–1999* (London, 1999).
10 Yoav Gelber, *Palestine 1948: War, Escape and the Emergence of the Palestinian Refugee Problem* (Brighton, 2006). See Chapter 8.
11 See endnote 9 of Introduction.

4 The 1956 War

1 Mark Tessler, *A History of the Israel-Palestinian Conflict* (Bloomington, IN, 1994), pp. 338–9.
2 Yossi Beilin, 'EU Should Absorb Palestinian Refugees', *Jerusalem Post*, 17 July 2008.
3 Walid Khalidi, *All that Remains* (Washington, DC, 1992), pp. xv–xvi, and Ilan Pappe, *The Ethnic Cleansing of Palestine* (Oxford, 2007), p. xiii.
4 Benny Morris, *Righteous Victims: A History of the Zionist-Arab Conflict, 1881–1999* (London, 1999), p. 276.
5 Peter L. Hahn, *Caught in the Middle East, U.S. Policy toward the Arab–Israeli Conflict, 1945–1961* (Chapel Hill, NC, 2004). See especially Parts II and IV for a detailed analysis of the US and the Suez War.
6 Avi Shlaim, *The Iron Wall: Israel and the Arab World* (London, 2000). See especially Chapters three and four. See also Chapter two of Ahron Bregman, *Israel's Wars: A History since 1947* (London 2000).
7 Yoav Stern, '50 Years After the Massacre, Kafr Qasem Wants Answers', *Ha'aretz*, 20 October 2006.
8 Special Report of the Director of UNRWA, November 1956–December 1956 (New York, 1957).

5 Altered States: The Wars of 1967 and 1973

1 Avi Shlaim, *The Iron Wall: Israel and the Arab World* (London, 2000), p. 254.
2 Amos Elon, 'Israelis and Palestinians, What Went Wrong,' *New York Review of Books*, 19 December 2002. See also Gershom Gorenberg, *Occupied Territory: The Untold Story of Israel's Settlements* (London, 2007), Chapter two. See also Idith Zertal and Akiva Eldar, *Lords of the Land: The War over Israel's Settlements in the Occupied Territories, 1967–2007* (New York, 2007).

3 Henry Siegman, 'Grab More Hills, Expand the Territory', *London Review of Books*, 10 April 2008.

4 This view was made explicit by Ariel Sharon in an op-ed essay published on the front page of the *New York Times* on 9 June 2002.

5 CIA Cable to White House Situation room, 25 May 1967, National Security File, 'History of the Middle East Crisis, 15 May–10 June, 1967', Lyndon Baines Johnson Presidential Library, Austin, TX.

6 Walt Rostow, 'Memo to President', 25 May 1967. Also, Lyndon Baines Johnson message to Abba Eban, 26 May 1967, National Security File, 'History of the Middle East Crisis, 15 May–10 June, 1967', Lyndon Baines Johnson Presidential Library, Austin, TX.

7 Michael B. Oren, *Six Days of War: June 1967 and the Making of the Modern Middle East* (Oxford, 2002), pp. 34–5.

8 Ahron Bregman, *Israel's Wars: A History since 1948* (London, 2000), pp. 84–5.

9 Shlaim, *The Iron Wall*, p. 254.

10 Elon, 'Israelis and Palestinians, What Went Wrong'; Akiva Aldar, 'Border Control: The Peace that Could have Been in '67', *Ha'aretz*, 5 June 2007.

11 Ibid.

12 Ibid.

13 Ilan Pappe, *A History of Modern Palestine*, 2nd edn (Cambridge, 2006), pp. 186–7.

14 Elon, 'Israelis and Palestinians'.

15 'The Jarring Initiative and the Response, 8 February 1971', *Israel's Foreign Relations, Selected Documents, 1947–1974*, vols. 1–2 (Tel Aviv).

16 Bregman, *Israel's Wars: A History since 1948*, pp. 102–23.

17 Abraham Rabinovich, *The Yom Kippur War: The Epic Encounter that Transformed the Middle East* (Princeton, NJ, 2003), p. 39.

18 Ibid., p. 57.

19 Ibid., p. 89.

20 Howard M. Sachar, *A History of Israel from the Rise of Zionism to Our Time* (New York, 1982), p. 755.

21 Bregman, *Israel's Wars: A History since 1948*, p. 131.

22 Rabinovich, *The Yom Kippur War*, p. 304.

23 Ibid., p. 487.

24 Ibid., p. 498.

6 Peace Gained, Peace Lost

1 Avi Shlaim, *The Iron Wall: Israel and the Arab World* (London, 2000), p. 320.

2 Ibid., p. 313.

3 Ibid., pp. 330–31.

4 Charles D. Smith, *Palestine and the Arab–Israeli Conflict*, 4th edn (Boston, 2001),

p. 356, and *Newsweek*, 27 March 1978; *Time*, 3 April 1978; cited in Noam Chomsky, *Towards a New Cold War* (New York, 2003), p. 485.

5 Abu Nidal's Fatah Revolutionary Council targeted anyone identified with Israel or the West and was reportedly responsible for the death or wounding of 900 people in twenty countries after breaking away from Arafat in 1974.

6 Ze'ev Schiff and Ehud Ya'ari, *Israel's Lebanon War* (New York, 1984), p. 301.

7 The First Intifada, and the Oslo Accords

1 Don Peretz, *Intifada: The Palestinian Uprising* (Boulder, CO, 1990), p. 39.

2 Ahron Bregman, *Israel's Wars: A History since 1947* (London, 2003), p. 190.

3 Ibid., pp. 191–2.

4 Ilan Pappe, *History of Modern Palestine*, 2nd edn (Cambridge, 2006), p. 233.

5 Peretz, *Intifada*, pp. 185–6.

6 'Palestine National Council, Palestinian Declaration of Independence', Algiers, 15 November 1988, official translation available at http://www.al-bab.com/arab/docs/pal/pal3.htm.

7 'Palestine National Council, Political Communiqué', Algiers, 15 November 1988, official translation available at http://www.al-bab.com/arab/docs/pal/pal4.htm.

8 'Arafat Clarifies Statement to Satisfy U.S. Conditions for Dialogue', 14 December 1988, available at http://www.jewishvirtuallibrary.org/jsource/Terrorism/plotstate1.html.

9 Avi Shlaim, *The Iron Wall: Israel and the Arab World* (London, 2000), p. 466.

10 Ibid., pp. 498–500.

11 Ibid., p. 507.

12 Cited in Ian J. Bickerton and Carla L. Klausner, *A History of the Arab–Israeli Conflict*, 5th edn (Upper Saddle River, NJ, 2005), p. 255.

13 Pappe, *A History of Modern Palestine*, pp. 242–3. See also Jeff Halper, *An Israeli in Palestine: Resisting Dispossession, Redeeming Israel* (London, 2008), pp. 175–6. Ghada Karmi, *Married to Another Man: Israel's Dilemma in Palestine* (London, 2007), pp. 133–55 gives a Palestinian perspective on the Oslo Accords.

14 Ahmed Qurie, *From Oslo to Jerusalem: The Palestinian Story of the Secret Negotiations* (London, 2006), p. 297.

15 Shlaim, *The Iron Wall*, p. 547.

8 Darkness Returns

1 The religious parties that joined Netanyahu's coalition were the National Religious Party, the United Torah Party, the Sephardic Orthodox Party (Shas), the Third Way, and Israel Be'aliya.

2 *Agence France Presse*, 15 November 1988. See also Gerson Gorenberg, *Occupied Territories: The Untold Story of Israel's Settlements* (London, 2006), pp. 271–2.

3   Cited in Leslie Susser, 'Did Barak Blow a Deal with Syria', *Jerusalem Report*,
    29 September 2008, p. 20. See also Martin Indyk, *Innocent Abroad: An Intimate
    Account of American Peace Diplomacy in the Middle East* (New York, 2001),
    pp. 365–72.

4   The Mitchell Report of the Sharm el-Sheikh Fact-Finding Committee, 20 May
    2001, www.mideastweb.org.mitchell_report.

5   Ibid.

6   Uri Avnery, 'Politicus Interruptus', 23 February 2002, www.gush-shalom.org/
    archives/article.183html.

7   Ahron Bregman, *Israel's Wars: A History since 1947* (London, 2003), p. 234.

8   Benjamin Shwartz, 'Will Israel Live to 100?', *Atlantic Monthly* (May 2005).
    Shwartz draws upon a study by right-wing Haifa University professor Arnon
    Soffer, 'Demography of Eretz Israel'.

9   'Roadmap for Peace in the Middle East', Israeli/Palestinian Reciprocal Action,
    Quartet Support. US Department of State, Bureau of Public Affairs, 16 July
    2003.

10 Sharon's coalition consisted of Likud, the secular Shinui party, the National
    Union party, which was virulently opposed to the creation of a Palestinian
    state and prepared to expel Arafat, and the fervently pro-settlement National
    Religious party.

11 The World Bank, 'Two Years of Intifada, Closures and Palestinian Economic
    Crisis: An Assessment', 5 March 2003, available at
    http://go.worldbank.org/UNMWT94BO0.

12 Cited in Joe Conason, 'Ever so Slowly, Progress in Mideast', *New York Observer*,
    1 June 2003.

13 Gideon Alon, 'Sharon Redefines Occupation', *Ha'aretz*, 28 May 2003.

14 Arnon Regular, 'Hamas: Ceasefire is a Viable Option', *Ha'aretz*, 25 May 2003.

15 The Israelis succeeded in killing Rantisi on 17 April 2004.

16 Cited by Conal Urquhart, 'Hamas Leader Acknowledges "Reality" of Israel',
    The Guardian, 11 January 2007.

17 Matthew Gutman, Nina Gilbert and Herb Keinon, 'Hamas Official Has a
    Vision of Living Next to Israel', *Jerusalem Post*, 25 June 2003. Cited in Henry
    Siegman, 'Hamas, the Last Chance for Peace?', *New York Review of Books*, LIII/7,
    27 April 2006.

18 Frank Gardner, 'Hezbollah Missile Threat Assessed', BBC News, 3 August
    2006. David Fickling, 'Amnesty Report Accuses Israel of War Crimes', *The
    Guardian*, 23 August 2006. On Wednesday 16 July 2008, Hezbollah transferred
    the coffins of captured Israeli soldiers Ehud Goldwasser and Eldad Regev in
    exchange for notorious Lebanese prisoner Samir Qantar and four Hezbollah
    militants captured by Israel during the war, in addition to the bodies of 199
    Palestinian and Lebanese fighters killed in clashes in recent years. The return

strengthened Hezbollah and unified the fractured country. The Lebanese Prime Minister, Fouad Siniora, who had cracked down on Hezbollah, almost causing a civil war, was present to greet the released men.

9 Unfinished Business

1 Noam Chomsky, *Hegemony or Survival: America's Quest for Global Dominance* (Sydney, 2004) and Edward W. Said, *From Oslo to Iraq and the Road Map* (New York, 2004) are among the many who have written on this subject.
2 The most recent study is that of John J. Meirsheimer and Stephen M. Walt, *The Israel Lobby and US Foreign Policy* (London, 2006). This book has an extensive bibliography. For an Arab perspective on US policy in the conflict, see Rashid Khalidi, *Resurrecting Empire: Western Footprints and America's Perilous Path in the Middle East* (Boston, 2004), chapter 4.
3 Sara Roy, *Failing Peace: Gaza and the Palestinian-Israeli Conflict* (London, 2007) explores the economic circumstances of the Palestinians in great detail.
4 Shlomo Maital, 'Who Needs Lines on a Map?', *Jerusalem Report*, 29 September 2008.
5 I have drawn upon Miriam Lowi, *Water and Power: The Politics of a Scarce Resource in the Jordan River Basin* (Cambridge, 1993), for an analysis of the water resources issue.

Conclusion

1 Daniel Barenboim, speech, available at http://youtube.com/watch?v=cTpf_jUXHYI.
2 Daniel Barenboim, 'My Hope for Peace in the Middle East', *The Guardian*, 14 May 2008.
3 Ibid.
4 Daniel Barenboim, speech, available at http://youtube.com/watch?v=CTpf_jUXHyI.

Select Bibliography

The number of books on the Arab–Israeli Conflict is endless. This list is highly selective and contains only items that have been found particularly useful in the writing of this volume.

Ball, George W., and Douglas B. Ball, *The Passionate Attachment: American Involvement with Israel, 1947 to the Present* (New York, 1992)

Barenboim, Daniel, and Edward Said, *Parallels and Paradoxes: Explorations in Music and Society* (London, 2003)

Beilin, Yossi, *Israel: A Concise Political History* (London, 1992)

Benvenisti, Meron, *Sacred Landscape: The Buried History of the Holy Land since 1948* (Berkeley, 2000)

Bickerton, Ian J., and Carla L. Klausner, *A History of the Arab–Israeli Conflict*, 5th edn (Upper Saddle River, NJ, 2007)

Bregman, Ahron, *Israel's Wars: A History since 1947*, 2nd edn (London, 2002)

Carter, Jimmy, *Palestine: Peace not Apartheid* (New York, 2006)

Chomsky, Noam, *Hegemony or Survival: America's Quest for Global Dominance* (Sydney, 2004)

—, *Towards a New Cold War* (New York, 2003)

Christison, Kathleen, *Perceptions of Palestine: Their Influence on us Middle East Policy* (Berkeley, 1999)

Elon, Amos, *The Israelis, Founder and Sons* (Tel Aviv, 1981)

Fisk, Robert, *The Great War for Civilization: The Conquest of the Middle East* (London, 2005)

—, *Pity the Nation: Lebanon at War* (Oxford, 1992)

Friedman, Thomas, *From Beirut to Jerusalem* (London, 1993)

Gelber, Yoav, *Palestine 1948: War, Escape, and the Emergence of the Palestinian Refugee Problem* (Brighton, 2006)

Gilbert, Martin, *Israel, A History* (London, 1998)

Goldschmidt, Arthur, Jr, *A Concise History of the Middle East*, 4th edn (Boulder, CO, 1991)

Gorenberg, Gershom, *Occupied Territories: The Untold Story of Israel's Settlements* (London, 2006)

Hahn, Peter L., *Caught in the Middle East: US Policy toward the Arab–Israeli Conflict, 1945–61* (Chapel Hill, NC, 2004)

Halper, Jeff, *An Israeli in Palestine: Resisting Dispossession, Redeeming Israel* (London, 2008)

Hobsbawm, Eric, *On History* (London, 1997)

Karmi, Ghada, *Married to Another Man: Israel's Dilemma in Palestine* (London, 2007)

Khalidi, Rashid, *Resurrecting Empire, Western Footprints and America's Perilous Path in the Middle East* (Boston, 2004)

Kimmerling, Baruch, *Politicide: Ariel Sharon's War against the Palestinians* (London, 2003)

—, and Joel S. Migdal, *Palestinians, the Making of a People* (New York, 1993)

Lewis, Bernard, *From Babel to Dragomans: Interpreting the Middle East* (New York, 2004)

—, *Semites and Anti-Semites: An Enquiry in Conflict and Prejudice* (New York, 1986)

Little, Douglas, *American Orientalism, The United States and the Middle East since 1945* (Chapel Hill, NC, 2002)

Louis, Wm Douglas, *The British Empire in the Middle East, 1945–1951* (Oxford, 1984)

Lowenthal, David, *The Past is a Foreign Country* (Cambridge, 1985)

Lowi, Miriam, *Water and Power: The Politics of a Scarce Resource in the Jordan River Basin* (Cambridge, 1993)

Margalit, Avishai, *Views in Review, Politics and Culture in the State of the Jews* (New York, 1998)

Masala, Nur, *Imperial Israel and the Palestinians: The Politics of Expansion* (London, 2000)

Masalha, Nur, *Politics of Denial: Israel and the Palestinian Refugee Problem* (London, 2003)

Mearsheimer, John J., and Stephen Walt, *The Israel Lobby and US Foreign Policy* (London, 2007)

Miller, Aaron David, *The Much Too Promised Land: America's Elusive Search for Arab–Israeli Peace* (New York, 2008)

Morris, Benny, *Righteous Victims: A History of the Zionist–Arab Conflict, 1881–1999* (London, 2000)

Neff, Donald, *Warriors at Suez: Eisenhower Takes America into the Middle East* (New York, 1981)

Oren, Michael, *Power Faith and Fantasy: America in the Middle East, 1776 to the Present* (New York, 2007)

—, *Six Days of War: June 1967 and the Making of the Modern Middle East* (New York, 2002)

Pappe, Ilan, *A History of Modern Palestine*, 2nd edn (Cambridge, 2006)

—, *The Ethnic Cleansing of Palestine* (Oxford, 2006)

Peretz, Don, *Intifada: The Palestinian Uprising* (Boulder, CO, 1990)

Qurie, Ahmed ['Abu Ala'], *From Oslo to Jerusalem: The Palestinian Story of the Secret Negotiations* (London 2006)

Rabinovich, Abraham, *Waging Peace: Israel and the Arabs, 1948–2003* (Princeton, NJ, 2003)

Rabinovich, Itamar, *The War for Lebanon, 1970–1983* (New York, 1984)

Rogan, Eugene L., and Avi Shlaim, eds, *The War for Palestine: Rewriting the History of 1948*, 2nd edn (Cambridge, 2007)

Ross, Dennis, *The Missing Peace: The Inside Story of the Fight for Middle East Peace* (New York, 2004)

Roy, Sara, *Failing Peace: Gaza and the Palestinian-Israel Conflict* (London, 2007)

Sachar, Howard M., *A History of Israel from the Rise of Zionism to Our Time* (New York, 1982)

Said, Edward W., *From Oslo to Iraq and the Road Map* (New York, 2004)

—, *Orientalism* (London, 1995)

Schiff, Zeev, and Ehud Ya'ari, *Israel's Lebanon War* (New York, 1984)

Segev, Tom, *One Palestine Complete: Jews and Arabs under the British Mandate* (New York, 2000)

Shipler, David, *Arab and Jew: Wounded Spirits in a Promised Land* (New York, 1987)

Shlaim, Avi, *The Iron Wall: Israel and the Arab World* (London, 2000)

—, *The Politics of Partition: King Abdullah, the Zionists and Palestine, 1921–1951* (Oxford, 1988)

Smith, Charles D., *Palestine and the Arab–Israeli Conflict*, 4th edn (Boston, 2001)

Spiegel, Steven L., *The Other Arab–Israeli Conflict: Making America's Middle East Policy from Truman to Reagan* (Chicago, 1985)

Tessler, Mark, *A History of the Israeli-Palestinian Conflict* (Bloomington, IN, 1993)

Wasserstein, Bernard, *Divided Jerusalem: The Struggle for the Holy City* (New Haven, CT, 2001)

Acknowledgements

A book is never the product of just one person. On this occasion, many – students, colleagues and mentors – who have generously shared their views on the Arab–Israeli conflict over a number of years may not wish to be named here! However, I value their assistance and trust they recognize their contribution, even if they do not agree with all my conclusions. I would like to acknowledge Bruce Clunies-Ross, Dominic Kelly, Jim Levy and Bunty Turner, who listened to my ramblings and offered constructive advice. No one could have been more helpful than my colleague and previous co-author, Kenneth Hagan, who did all he could to save me from many errors of substance and style. I should also like to thank Judy Echin for her skill in the preparation of the maps. However, no one but myself should be held responsible for any shortcomings the reader may find in the work.

At Reaktion, Ian Blenkinsop and Martha Jay were unfailingly helpful in the preparation of the manuscript for publication, and I thank publisher Michael Leaman and series editor Jeremy Black for placing their faith in me on such a perilous venture as writing about the Arab–Israeli wars.

Finally, I thank Jenny, upon whom I depend for so much, who has cheerfully given up a great deal of her time and energy to accommodate my demands while writing.

Index